The Ethics of
Numbers

Rabbi Dr. Abba Engelberg

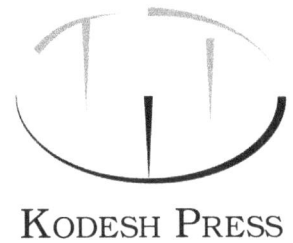

Kodesh Press

The Ethics of Numbers
© Abba Engelberg 2020

ISBN: 978-1-947857-37-7

All rights reserved. Except for brief quotations in printed reviews, no part of this publication may be reproduced, stored in a retrieval system, or transmitted in any form or by any means (printed, written, photocopied, visual electronic, audio, or otherwise) without the prior permissions of the publisher.

The Publisher extends its gratitude to
Michele Scheer for her editing work.

Ver. 1.4

Cover Art: Nicolas Poussin
The Spies with the Grapes of the Promised Land (c. 1664)
(Part of a four-part series known as *The Four Seasons*.)

Published & Distributed by

Kodesh Press L.L.C.
New York, NY
www.KodeshPress.com
kodeshpress@gmail.com

Table of Contents

Introduction 9

Bamidbar 13
   The Tribe of Dan 15
   Modern Application - the Ten Tribes Today 23
   Conclusion 24

Naso 25
   Becoming a Nazirite – Pro and Con 26
   Turning from Evil – a Task for Every Jew 40
   Doing Good 55
   Summary 58

Beha'alotcha 60
   Understanding the Two Most Serious Positive Commands . 61
   Korban Pesach 66
   Miriam's Leprosy 81
   Summary 87

Shlach 88
The Story of the Spies – the Basics 89
What Was the Sin of the Spies? 91
Was It Necessary to Send Spies? 92
Why Did the Spies, and Then the Nation, Sin? 99
The Case of the Sabbath-Desecrating Wood Gatherer, and Moses' Apparent Lapse 100
Summary 107

Korach 109
Participants in the Rebellion of Korah 110
What Was the Sin of Korah? 120
Modern Commentators 128
The Classical Commentaries 133
Summary 141

Chukat 143
Moses and Aaron 144
Moses and Miriam 154
The Triumvirate 159
The Passing of Moses, Aaron, and Miriam 163
Summary 170

Balak 172
Balak's Fears 179
Balaam's Strategy and Philosophy 187
Summary 194

Pinchas 195
Divine Punishment at Baal Peor 198
The Intervention of Phinehas 207
Restrictions on Vigilantism 212

THE REWARD OF PHINEHAS	215
SUMMARY	219

MATOT	221
VOWS AND OATHS	222
ETHICAL CONCLUSIONS	240
SUMMARY	250

MASSEI	252
ALLOCATING THE LAND	254
THE DAUGHTERS OF ZELOPHEHAD	263
SUMMARY	278

APPENDIX I - ZIPPORAH	281
THE FIRST MEETING	282
ZIPPORAH'S PERSONALITY	282
IN THE VIEW OF THE COMMENTATORS	284
MODERN APPLICATION	285
A MODERN EXAMPLE	286
WHY DID MOSES INTERMARRY	288
SUMMARIZING ZIPPORAH'S PERSONALITY	290

APPENDIX II - R. AKIVA'S OPINION REGARDING THE ORAL LAW	294
APPENDIX III – ANGER MANAGEMENT:	
IS IT EVER PERMITTED TO GET ANGRY?	303
APPENDIX IV – LAW ENFORCEMENT IN JUDAISM	318
APPENDIX V – INTIMATE RELATIONS WITH GENTILES	322
APPENDIX VI - AGE OF CULPABILITY	328

SOURCE MATERIAL	338
COMMENTATORS	343

Introduction

The oldest name for the fourth book of the Pentateuch is *Chumash ha-Pikkudim*, the Book of Numberings, since it opens with a census taken at the beginning of the forty years that the Israelites spent in the desert, and closes with a census taken at the end of those forty years (Num. 26). This name appears already in the Mishnah (*Yoma* 7:1, *Menachot* 4:3, and *Sotah* 7:7), and is used frequently in the Tosefta, Talmud, and Midrashic literature. Hence its name in English translations as Numbers.

The common name for the book today is based on its fifth word, *be-midbar* (in the phrase *be-midbar Sinai*, "in the Sinai Desert") or *ba-midbar* (in the wilderness). The name parallels the Hebrew names for the previous books of the Bible, *Bereishit*, *Shemot*, and *Vayikra*, each of which is based on the first or second Hebrew words of that book. Like *Bereishit* (meaning "in the beginning"), the chosen name *Bamidbar* is actually quite descriptive of its contents, all of which took place during the voyage of the Israelites through the desert; to be more exact, during the second and last years of their travels. The break between the early part of the journey and its last segment occurs in ch. 20, in the portion of *Chukat*, where the Torah states: "The entire congregation of the Children of Israel arrived at the desert of Zin in the first month" (Num. 20.1), whereupon Ibn Ezra explains: "[the first month] of the fortieth year, and behold there is not to be found in the Torah any activity or prophecy, only in the first year [in the desert, i.e., the second year after their departure from Egypt] and the fortieth year."

In contrast to *Bereishit*, which is entirely narrative in nature, and *Vayikra*, which is entirely legislative, *Bamidbar*, like *Shemot*, combines both aspects, with the narrational facet predominant. The legislative portions concern temporary rulings with respect to the designated behavior of the Israelites in the desert (chs. 1-4, 7-10), as well as laws of a more permanent nature, many of which were to be implemented soon after their arrival in the Land of Israel. The latter include laws concerning the ordeal of jealousy (ch. 5), Naziritic vows (ch. 6), priestly blessings (ch. 6), the *menorah* (ch. 8), ritual fringes (ch. 15:37-41), duties and emoluments of priests and Levites (ch. 18), the red heifer and ritual impurity (ch. 19), sacrificial laws (chs. 28-29), vows (ch. 30), cities of refuge (ch. 35:9-15), and murder contrasted with manslaughter (ch. 35:16-34).

The narrative portions include the stories of the murmurings and rebellions at Taberah and Kivrot ha-Ta'avah (ch. 11), the appointment of the seventy elders (ch.11:16-17), the slander of Moses (ch. 12), the mission of the spies (chs. 13-14), the rebellion of Korah (chs. 16-17), the sin of Moses and Aaron (ch. 20:7-13), the passing of Miriam and Aaron (chs. 20:1-2, 22-29), the traversing through foreign countries and the eventual conquest of the Amorite lands (chs. 20:14-21:35), Baalam's attempted curses (chs. 22-24), Phinehas and the sin at Baal Peor (ch. 25), the appointment of Joshua to succeed Moses (ch. 27:12-23), and the apportionment of the land and the case of the daughters of Zelophehad (chs. 26:52-57, 27:1-11, 36:1-13).

Some of the questions dealt with in this book are the whereabouts of the ten tribes, the benefits and drawbacks of being a Nazirite (asceticism), the sins of the spies and of Korah, Balaam's strategy and philosophy, and the appropriateness and limitations of vigilantism.

The Ethics of Numbers

The appendices deal with a characterization of the personality of Zipporah (**Appendix I**), differing opinions regarding the written and oral law (**Appendix II**), anger management (**Appendix III**), law enforcement in Judaism (**Appendix IV**), intimate relations with Gentiles (**Appendix V**), and the age at which young boys and girls become responsible for their actions (**Appendix VI**).

The book of Numbers deals with numerous ethical issues, many of which are examined in this book. These include sexual morality within marriage (*Naso*) and on the part of the nation as a whole (*Pinchas*), slander and lack of gratitude on a personal (*Beha'alotcha*, *Korach*, Appendix I) and national (*Shlach*) level, and finally the ethics of proper demeanor (*Korach*, *Matot*, Appendix III) and national law (*Massei*, Appendices II, IV, VI).

In preparing this material, I have based myself on the Talmud and Midrash, as well as the many commentaries which have been written from the Middle Ages until the present. I have availed myself of the Soncino translation of the Talmud, as well as Chabad's translation of the Bible with Rashi and of the *Yad ha-Chazakah* of Rambam, all freely available on the Internet. Citations from the Talmud are preceded by BT or JT, indicating the Babylonian or Jerusalem Talmud, respectively, while Mishnaic citations are referenced only by tractate name, chapter, and number. To give the reader an idea of the scope of the material upon which the book is based, I have included a glossary of sources, followed by a glossary of the authorities quoted. Since the title rabbi appears frequently, I have abbreviated it using the letter "R." I have also used "b." to denote *ben*, meaning "son of." Most of the information which appears in these lists has been culled from the Internet, especially from Wikipedia.

I would like to take this opportunity to thank my loving wife Ruthie, who helped in myriad ways, and in particular did a very thorough job of commenting on and proof-reading the entire

The Ethics of Numbers

book. I fervently wish that this book be of benefit to those who read it.

    Abba Engelberg
    Jerusalem 2020

Bamidbar

The first three portions in the book of Numbers (*Bamidbar*, *Naso*, and *Beha'alotcha*) devote much attention to the twelve tribes and their leaders (called "princes"), the grouping of the tribes into four sets of three tribes each (called *degalim* or "flags"), and the leading tribe within each flag. The present chapter will examine the traits displayed by the various princes which made them worthy of being leaders, and those displayed by the specific tribes which were chosen to be the leaders of their flags. It is important to discuss these traits, since nearly everyone wishes to be a leader, not necessarily of other people, but perhaps in his profession or just in his own household.

In *Bamidbar*, a census is taken and the tribal leaders are chosen to participate in its implementation. The Bible states: "You should number them group by group, you [Moses] and Aaron. And [together] with you, there should be a man from every tribe, every one a head of his father's house" (Num. 1:3-4). Although at a later stage the "man from every tribe" is designated as being a prince (Num. 1:16), initially each one is referred to simply as "a man." The implication is that he empathizes with the common members of his tribe and considers himself to be one of them; he is aware of their struggles, and feels called upon to alleviate them to the greatest possible extent. Empathy may thus be said to be the first important attribute of a leader.

The Ethics of Numbers

In *Beha'alotcha*, the description of the marching order of the various flags opens as follows: "And the flag [led by] the children of Judah travelled first according to their legions; and over the legions was Nachshon the son of Amminadav" (Num. 10:14). The word "legion" is a military term indicating a large force of soldiers. By naming Nachshon in that context, the text may wish to indicate that he possessed important attributes of a military leader, namely the combination of courage and decisiveness, which serves as the second desirable characteristic of a leader.

The first place the title of the leaders as princes is emphasized is in the portion of *Naso*, in connection with their offerings at the dedication of the Tabernacle (Num. 7), where the Torah dedicates 89 verses to their description. The chapter is composed of an eleven-verse introduction, which notes the six wagons jointly donated by each set of two tribes, a six-verse listing of the contribution of each of the twelve tribes (making a total of seventy-two verses), and a six-verse conclusion containing the totals of the gifts of the princes.

The twelve sets of six verses each are identical in content. The Midrash focuses on this point by stating of the silver and golden gifts: "Their length, width, and weight were identical" (*Num. Rabbah* 14:13). It is not surprising that Ramban (Num. 7:12), followed by *Akedat Yitzchak* (Introduction to the book of Numbers) and Abravanel (Num. 7), asks why it would not have sufficed to write the gifts of the first only and follow it by a verse stating that the remaining princes made the same donation. Ramban answers that God wished to bestow an equal degree of honor on each prince. Had the Torah described the gifts of Nachshon b. Amminadav in detail, followed by a verse stating that the other princes brought the same, the latter would in effect be mistreated.

R. Jonathan Sacks[1] has extended this idea to the entire tribe of Levi and the entire nation. With regard to the former, he explains

---

1. Jonathan Sacks, "The Politics of Envy," *Naso* (2014), *Covenant and Conversation*.

that members of the tribe might have felt excluded if they were not members of the family of Aaron. To avoid such feelings, each Levitical clan was assigned a special role in carrying the vessels, furnishings, and framework of the Tabernacle, as described at the end of *Bamidbar* (Num. 4:1-16) and the beginning of *Naso* (Num. 4:21-49). With regard to non-Levites, R. Sacks notes that the possibility of becoming a Nazirite, introduced in the portion of *Naso* (Num. 6:1-21), provides an option for those individuals who aspire to a higher level of holiness.

In short, the Torah wishes to engender self-confidence in each Israelite, and certainly in the nation's leaders. However, if the Torah merely wanted to avoid favoring one of the tribes, it could have described the gifts without mentioning the name of any tribe at all, adding only a short note to the effect that their contributions were identical. Ramban apparently wants to stress another point as well, namely that the reason the gifts were the same was that they formulated them together and even contributed some items in tribal pairs. No prince attempted to outshine the others. The Torah purposely names each one as an award for his positive cooperation and lack of jealousy or competitiveness. As the Midrash concludes: "And not one of them brought more than his colleague" (*Num. Rabbah* 14:13).

In summary, three desirable characteristics of a leader have been presented: empathy, decisiveness/courage, and cooperation with other leaders.

The Tribe of Dan

As previously noted, when the Israelites encamped in the desert, they did so in four groups called *degalim* (flags). Each flag consisted of three tribes. The eastern flag was led by Judah, who was destined for kingship; the southern flag was led by Reuben, the first-born;

the western flag was led by Ephraim, who had been promised greatness by his grandfather Jacob; and the southern flag was led by the tribe of Dan.

The question that arises is: what special leadership qualities were possessed by Dan? Dan was not the son of one of the matriarchs. One would have thought that Issachar, known for its outstanding scholars, or Zebulun, whose members were known as successful merchants, would be more appropriate.

It will be shown that the same leadership qualities displayed by the princes were also associated with the tribe of Dan.

EMPATHY

The tribe of Dan was the second largest both in the first census (62,700), described in the portion of *Bamidbar* (Num. 1:38), and the second (64,400), described in the portion of *Pinchas* (Num. 26:42). It was not only one of the largest tribes, but one of the strongest as well. The marching order of the camp was such that the flag of Judah marched first (Num. 10:14), while that of Dan, referred to as "the rear-most of all the camps" (Num. 10:25), marched last.

Abravanel (Num. 2:1) asks why the census results are initially stated in the first chapter of Numbers, and then repeated when the flag groupings are introduced in the second chapter. He answers that the most vulnerable positions in a caravan are at its beginning and its end, and Judah and Dan were the largest and strongest of the flags. The population of Judah's group was 186,400 (Num. 2:9), while that of Dan's group was 157,600 (Num. 2:31). These tribes were also considered to be the strongest, both having been compared to a lion cub (Gen. 49:9, Deut. 33:22), and of course Samson was a descendant of the tribe of Dan (Judg. 13:2, 24).

Bamidbar

Yigael Yadin[2] asked the following question: if the tribe of Dan was so strong, why was its army unable to conquer the portion that was allocated to it, namely the region called *Gush Dan* (Dan's bloc) in modern times, stretching from today's Tel Aviv area eastward to the Ayalon Valley? In desperation they went north, conquering what is now labeled Tel Dan. The verse which describes the progression of their campaign states: "And they travelled from there, [soldiers] of the family of Dan, from Tzorah and Eshtaol, 600 men equipped with weapons of war" (Judg. 18:11). This verse generates a second question: how is it that they could only muster 600 men when the census indicated that they had over 62,000 able-bodied warriors?

Yadin suggested that apparently a large segment of the tribe absconded. He based this on a verse from the Song of Deborah, where the prophetess prepares a "report card" for each tribe, assigning a grade reflecting how much that tribe contributed to the war effort against Yavin, king of the Canaanites. Concerning the tribe of Dan, Deborah says: "and Dan, why did he gather [in] ships?" (Judg. 5:17), which *Metzudat David* interprets to mean: "Why did he [the tribe of Dan] collect all he has, place it in ships and run away?" In other words, a large portion of the tribe of Dan may have escaped either before or during the rule of Deborah, leaving too few warriors to capture the Ayalon Valley.

Support for this possibility may be found in the works of Diodorus Siculus (Theodore of Sicily, a Greek historian who lived in the first century BCE), who wrote as follows:

> All the foreigners were forthwith expelled from Egypt, and the most valiant and noble among them, under some notable leaders, were brought to Greece and other

---

2. Cited by Heinrich Guggenheimer, *parsha* sheet for the portion of *Bamidbar*.

places, as some relate; the most famous of their leaders were Danaus and Cadmus. But the majority of the people descended into a country not far from Egypt, which is now called Judea and at that time was altogether uninhabited (Book 40).

Note the specification of the tribe of Dan by name. Although Diodorus may have erred in assuming that the tribe of Dan went directly from Egypt to Greece, his observation that there was indeed an ancient group of Jews in Greece is conceivably reliable. Furthermore, 1 Maccabees (ch. 12) speaks of a Jewish delegation to Rome, led by Jonathan (son of Mattathias) the high priest, which stopped in Sparta to bless the Jewish inhabitants on its way back to the Holy Land.

It is also possible that the tribe of Dan travelled to Africa rather than Greece. In the 9th century, a sojourner named Eldad ha-Dani made an appearance in a number of Jewish communities in Babylonia, Spain, and Kairawan in North Africa.[3] He told how the tribe of Dan had left Israel during the reign of King Ahaz, after they lost hope that the Israelite Kingdom would be able to withstand the onslaught of the Assyrian army. In addition, there were battles between the kingdoms of Israel and Judea, and they did not want to be involved in a civil war. The tribe found shelter in Abyssinia where, according to Eldad, they led a very peaceful life until that very day. When the Israelite Kingdom fell, the tribes of Asher, Gad, and Naphtali joined the tribe of Dan, so that all of the tribes which descended from Jacob's concubines (Bilhah and Zilpah) were then located in Africa. Eldad, an adventurous type, set out to see the world together with a partner from Asher. Unfortunately, they were captured by cannibals. Since his

---

3. Max L. Margolis and Alexander Marx, *A History of the Jewish People* (1927), pp. 278-280.

partner was pleasantly plump, he was immediately made into the centerpiece of an elaborate feast. Fortunately for Eldad, he was rather scrawny, and so was placed in prison to be fattened up. The cannibals did not realize that Eldad was an observant Jew, which meant that he would not indulge in most of the food that was offered and therefore did not gain weight. In fact, the process took so long that in the meantime enemies attacked, defeated the cannibals, and took their belongings, including Eldad, who was eventually freed.

Of course, Eldad had no knowledge of the Mishnah or Talmud, as his tribe had left long before they emerged, but he did bring with him a written list of the laws of *shechitah* (ritual slaughter), which are only tangentially mentioned in the Torah, thus indicating awareness of the existence of the oral law, which according to tradition was also transmitted at Mt. Sinai. Interestingly, he attributed these laws to Joshua b. Nun and Othniel b. Kenaz, both of whom lived shortly before Deborah.

The main question has not yet been broached, namely: why did the tribe of Dan run away? To answer that, it may be noted that the name of the son of Dan, as recorded in the book of Genesis, is Hushim (Gen. 46:23). However, in the portion of *Pinchas*, it states: "These are the sons of Dan according to their families: Shuham (an anagram of the name Hushim), the family of the Shuhamites" (Num. 26:42). Eliezer Ben Yehuda[4] found a *Midrash Yelamdenu* which reads: "Do not pronounce the word Shuhamites, but rather Shahumites." The latter comes from the Hebrew word *shachum*, meaning dark-skinned. Ben Yehuda is intimating that Dan and his descendants may have had darker pigmentation than the brothers and the eponymous tribes, and they may have consequently been disdained by the other Israelites. Nevertheless, the Midrashic

---

4. Cited by Heinrich Guggenheimer, *parsha* sheet for the portion of *Bamidbar*.

interpretation of Shuham need not be taken literally. On the other hand, although Jews in general pride themselves on not being racists, the sad plight of the Yemenites in Israel during the 1950s may be recalled. The latter were discriminated against to the point that some of their children were even kidnapped.

People who are the object of discrimination become very sensitive to the feelings of others, and especially the unfortunate and oppressed. The importance of such sensitivity cannot be overemphasized, since the Torah strongly emphasizes that one of the major lessons of (and perhaps justifications for) the Egyptian enslavement was the emergence of the former bondsmen as compassionate, altruistic personae. Consider the following verses:

1. "And you should remember that you were a slave in the land of Egypt, and the Lord your God redeemed you; therefore, I command you this thing today" (Deut. 15:15), said in connection with the command to treat Hebrew slaves mercifully.
2. "You must not pervert the justice due to the stranger or to the fatherless, nor take the widow's raiment to pledge. For you should remember that you were a slave in Egypt, and the Lord your God redeemed you from there" (Deut. 24:17-18).
3. "When you beat your olive tree, you may not go over the boughs again; it should be for the stranger, for the fatherless, and for the widow. When you gather the grapes of your vineyard, you should not glean it after you; it should be for the stranger, for the fatherless, and for the widow. And you should remember that you were a slave in the land of Egypt" (Deut. 24:20-22).

It is thus understandable that the tribe of Dan as a whole might be characterized as being especially compassionate toward the downtrodden, and consequently possessed of the first attribute of leadership—empathy.

Bamidbar

COURAGE AND DECISIVENESS

The second important trait for a leader to possess is the combination of decisiveness and courage, which may also be associated with the tribe of Dan, based on a Midrash (BT *Sotah* 13a). The Midrash describes the arrival of the brothers to bury Jacob at the Cave of Machpelah, where they found Esau blocking their entry and saying that the burial plot belonged to him. When they reminded him that he had sold his birthright, he said: "I sold my double portion, but not my single portion, so I am entitled to at least one-third of the joint plot (i.e., two-thirds of the remaining plot, since Jacob had utilized the first half for Leah). At this stage, the brothers told Esau that their father had told them that he had independently bought out the entire plot from Esau, whereupon the latter said to them: "Prove it," and the brothers answered: "No problem, we have a deed." Esau then asked them to display it, whereupon they answered that they had left it at home in Egypt. Esau made it clear that he would not budge until they produced the deed, so the brothers decided to send Naphtali, who was as swift as a deer, to retrieve it from Egypt. Hushim, the son of Dan, was standing nearby, but did not understand what had happened, since he was hard of hearing and did not follow the details of the conversation. When he was filled in as to what had occurred, he called out saying: "How dare my holy grandfather lay here in disgrace while the entire cortege waits for the return of Naphtali." He then grabbed a club and smote Esau on the head, killing him instantly, and his blood rushed out and spurted all over the feet of the dead Jacob.

One might wonder what kernel of text serves as the basis of this Midrash. It must be remembered that the Rabbis literally had the Bible on their fingertips, and they recalled the verse in Psalms (58:11): "The righteous will rejoice when he sees vengeance; he will wash his feet in the blood of the wicked." Furthermore,

Rebecca had said: "Why should I be bereaved of you both in one day" (Gen. 27:45).

Although Rebecca's statement was conditional (i.e., she feared that both her sons would die on the same day if Jacob did not escape, and in fact he did run away), nevertheless it is a Midrashic belief that when a righteous person makes a prediction, it must be fulfilled—even if the statement was conditional. In the end, they did not both actually die on the same day, but they were buried on the same day.

At any rate, Hushim the son of Dan is seen to be determined to do what is right without hesitation, even if it is not popular, and this is a positive attribute for a leader.

Cooperation with Other Leaders

Of the four flag leaders, Dan was the only one who was not a descendant of either Rachel or Leah (the matriarchs). It will be recalled that according to the Midrash, one of the accusations which Joseph conveyed to his father concerning the sons of Leah was that "they treated the sons of the handmaids with contempt" (Rashi, Gen. 37:2, based on *Gen. Rabbah* 84:7). Dan must have been flattered that he alone among the sons of the concubines was chosen to be a flag leader, and such prominent tribes as Issachar and Zebulun were passed over. It is fair to assume that under these circumstances, Dan would have accepted his position with delight and modesty, and certainly not with conceit, and that he would have been more than glad to cooperate in a positive manner with his more distinguished brothers.

Bamidbar

MODERN APPLICATION: THE TEN TRIBES TODAY

In addition to helping justify the choice of Dan to head one of the flags in the desert, the story of the ten tribes might have relevance to the everyday lives of Orthodox Jews. The Mishnah (BT *Sanhedrin* 110b) cites an argument between R. Akiva and R. Eliezer. The former says: "The ten tribes will not return in the future," i.e., they have assimilated among the Gentiles and are lost to the Jewish nation. The latter, on the other hand, says that when the dead are revived (*techiyat ha-metim*), the ten lost tribes will be included and will also share in the world to come.

There is a seemingly independent difference of opinion between Rabbeinu Tam and Ramban concerning whether the Jubilee year (*yovel*) was celebrated during the time of the Second Temple. Rabbeinu Tam says it was, while Ramban says not only was *yovel* not observed, but even *shemittah* (the sabbatical year) was required only by rabbinical decree.

The *Chatam Sofer* relates these two debates. He notes that *yovel* is observed only if the majority of each tribe resides in Israel. There is a tradition that Jeremiah, toward the end of the First Temple period, toured the diaspora, and returned with a majority of each of the ten lost tribes (BT *Arachin* 33b; BT *Megillah* 14b). Most of them were later exiled at the time of the destruction of the First Temple. The *Chatam Sofer* explains that Rabbeinu Tam accepts the view of R. Akiva that the ten tribes are lost to Judaism. That being the case, the small number of those who remained in Israel from among those whom Jeremiah returned from the diaspora constitute the entirety of each tribe, implying that the majority of each of the tribes was in Israel and *yovel* could be observed. Ramban agrees with R. Eliezer that the bulk of each tribe is yet to return. In the meantime, those who remained from among those returned by Jeremiah constitute a minority of each tribe, and accordingly *yovel* need not be observed.

In recent times there is a modern-day Jeremiah named Michael Freund,[5] who returns people allegedly descended from the ten tribes to the Land of Israel. If he is thorough in his job, then, according to R. Akiva, those who have not identified as being members of one of the tribes are not destined to be part of Israel, and those who do declare themselves to be tribe members thus constitute a majority of the tribe, meaning that once more observance of *yovel* will be required. On the other hand, according to R. Eliezer, there is no doubt that a great number of the exiled are unaware of their connection to the Jewish people and have merged with the surrounding nations, yet at the time of *techiyat ha-metim* they will rejoin the Jewish nation. Until then, only a minority of each tribe dwells in the Land of Israel, and the observance of *yovel* is held in abeyance.

Conclusion

Three important attributes of a good leader have been presented: empathy, decisiveness, and cooperation with other leaders, based on an analysis of Biblical verses from the first three weekly portions in the book of Numbers. The tribe of Dan excelled in these three attributes, justifying its being chosen to lead one of the flags despite Dan's being of slightly less distinguished lineage.

---

5. Sam Sokol, "Michael Freund: 'Our Goal Is to Bring All Bnei Menashe to Israel,'" *Jerusalem Post* (October 20, 2013).

Naso

The portion of *Naso* continues to focus on the tribes, their leaders, and their encampment in the desert. It completes the detailing of the duties of the Levites (Num. 4:21-49), which was commenced at the end of *Bamidbar*; defines accession rules to the various sections of the encampment for the purpose of safeguarding its ceremonial purity (Num. 5:1-4); formulates the blessing to be invoked by the priestly clan of the tribe of Levi (Num. 6:22–27); and describes the donations of the princes at the inauguration of the Tabernacle (Num. 7:1-89). The camp was composed of a rectangular area for the Tabernacle (called the camp of the *Shechinah*, the Divine Presence), which was enclosed by a larger rectangle where the priestly and Levitical families resided (the Levitical camp). This in turn was contained within the Israelite camp, whose perimeter in each direction housed one of the four flag groupings of three tribes each (Num. 1:54-2:34; 3:23, 29, 35, 38). Regarding impurities in the camps, Rashi (Num. 5:2) explains:

> The leper was sent out from all of them [the three camps]; the person suffering from a flux [*zav*] was allowed to stay in the Israelite camp, but was sent out from the two [inner camps]; while a person who had become unclean from a corpse [*tamei meit*] was allowed to stay in the Levitical camp also and was sent out only from that of the

Shechinah. All this have our Rabbis deduced in treatise *Pesachim* (67a) from the verses of our text.

Mei Shiloach (*Naso*, p. 47) looks upon these three types of impure people symbolically, explaining that the leper represents a hot-tempered individual, the *zav* a lustful person, and the *tamei meit* a depressed person. The Talmud (BT *Arachin* 16a) states that Biblical leprosy is caused by various sins, including bloodshed and robbery. *Mei Shiloach* considers these to stem from anger, which he feels is inappropriate for any Israelite (based on *Avot* 2:10; *Hilchot De'ot* 2:3), as indicated by excluding such a person from the Israelite camp. The *zav*, who suffers from a gonorrheal flow, is associated with immoral sexual behavior, which is inappropriate for a scholar. Since the Levites are considered to be learned, a *zav* has no place in their camp. Finally, the *tamei meit* is associated with death and morbidity. Since occasionally even scholars are mildly depressed, they are permitted in the Levite camp, but are prohibited from entering the Divine camp, since the Jew is commanded to "serve the Lord with gladness; come before His Presence with singing" (Ps. 100:2).

BECOMING A NAZIRITE: PRO AND CON

Three subjects in the portion of *Naso* do not naturally fall into the framework of the tribal structure, namely the laws of the Nazirite (Num. 6:1-21), the adulteress woman (*sotah*, Num. 5:11-31), and those concerning restitution for stolen property (Num. 5:5-10).

As previously noted, R. Sacks[6] sees a relationship between self-actualization and the case of the Nazirite, who separates himself by abstaining from drinking wine, cutting his hair, and exposure to a

---

6. Jonathan Sacks, "The Politics of Envy," *Naso* (2014), *Covenant and Conversation*.

Naso

dead body. The majority of the nation cannot be priests, Levites, or princes, but every Jew has the opportunity to achieve holiness by becoming a Nazirite, about which the verse states: "All the days of his Nazirism he is holy unto the Lord" (Num. 6:8), which Sforno interprets as a promise that:

> He will merit enlightenment in the light of life [sacred knowledge], which will enable him to understand and adequately teach the holiest people of his generation [and serve as a spiritual mentor for the nation].

Sforno uses this insight to solve a problem with respect to the prophet Samuel. His mother Hannah, barren for many years, had prayed for a son whom she promised to bring up as a Nazirite and turn over to Eli the priest to spend his life in the service of God (1 Sam. 1:11). After Samuel was born, Hannah's husband Elkanah said "if only God will fulfill His word" (1 Sam. 1:23). What is Elkanah referring to? He cannot be talking about having a child, since Samuel was already born. Sforno says that he is relating to the expectation that as a Nazirite, Samuel would achieve holiness and be worthy of serving as a prophet, guide, and educator for the entire nation.

On the other hand, there is reason to believe that the Torah wishes to discourage such behavior, for it says with regard to the sacrifices brought by a Nazirite who was inadvertently exposed to a dead body, that they "make atonement for him, for he sinned on account of the soul" (Num. 6:11). Did he sin only by breaking his vow not to become impure (*tamei*), or was the initial acceptance of the Naziritic vow itself a sin? Regarding this question the Talmud cites the following Tannaitic argument:

Shmuel said: Whosoever fasts [unnecessarily, for the sake of self-affliction] is called a sinner. He holds like the following Tanna. For it has been taught: Elazar ha-Kappar be-Rabbi [Rashi, BT *Chullin* 56b: the greatest in his generation, i.e., the *gadol ha-dor*] says: What does the verse mean when it says "make atonement for him, for he sinned on account of the soul" (Num. 6:11)? Against which soul did he sin? It must be because he denied himself wine [and thus sinned against his own soul]. We can now use *a fortiori* logic: If this man, who only deprived himself of wine, is called a sinner, how much more so is he who deprives himself of everything.

R. Elazar says: He [who fasts] is called "holy," for it says [regarding one who vows to be a Nazirite]: "He will be holy. He must let the locks of the hair of his head grow wild" (Num. 6:5). If this man who only deprived himself of wine is called "holy," how much more so is he who deprives himself of everything [called "holy"]. According to Shmuel, is he not called "holy"? [He can answer:] That refers to the locks growing wild [Rashi: from his hair; it is forbidden to benefit from them, but he himself is not holy]. And according to R. Elazar, is he not called a sinner? That is because he defiled himself [by contact with the dead]. But did R. Elazar say so? Did he not say: Let a man always consider himself as if there is holiness within him [Rashi: as if his innards are holy, and he must not weaken them... and so it is forbidden to fast]? ... That is no question. Here it speaks of one who is able to bear self-affliction, and there it speaks of one who is not able [to do so] (BT *Ta'anit* 11a).

Compared to R. Elazar's point that the verse terming the Nazirite a sinner was written only with respect to one who defiles himself

Naso

by becoming impure (*tamei meit*), and not with respect to the very act of becoming a Nazirite, the Talmud in *Nedarim* (10a) explains that his disputant, Elazar ha-Kappar, believes that it refers to both cases, just that it was written with respect to the former because there he performed two sins: becoming a Nazirite and breaking his vow. A further point in favor of Elazar ha-Kappar is that both defiled and full-term Nazirites bring a sin offering,[7] implying that in any event some level of trespass was involved.

Regarding fasting, clearly everyone agrees that it is not to be undertaken voluntarily if it seriously weakens one's body. If that is not the case, the Tannaim still argue whether it is desirable, just as they argue with respect to vowing to be a Nazirite. The intrinsic question seems to be whether self-deprivation is a legitimate means of worshipping God, and if for that reason becoming a Nazirite is compared to taking upon oneself a self-imposed fast. In other words, the question is whether abstinence is praiseworthy or sinful, which in turn depends on whether the pleasures of the world distract one from loving and fearing the Lord or help one to appreciate Him more.

The Talmud brings varying opinions, some in support of Elazar ha-Kappar's view that becoming a Nazirite is sinful, and others opposed; for example, the following dispute (BT *Nedarim* 10a) between R. Yehuda (who agrees with R. Elazar) and R. Shimon (who agrees with Elazar ha-Kappar):

> R. Yehuda said: The early *chassidim* were eager to bring a sin offering, because the Holy One, blessed be He, never caused them to inadvertently sin [and a sin offering cannot be brought voluntarily]. What did they do? They arose and made a voluntary vow of *nezirut* to God, so as to be liable to a sin offering to God. R. Shimon said…

---

7. However, a guilt offering is only brought by one who becomes defiled.

The Ethics of Numbers

they did not take *nezirut* upon themselves, so as not to be called sinners, for it says: "And [the priest] will make atonement for him, for he sinned on account of the soul" (Num. 6:11).

Clearly, R. Yehuda sees nothing wrong with making a vow to be a Nazirite, and perhaps even looks upon doing so positively, while R. Shimon considers it to be a sin.

Another Talmudic tale (BT *Nedarim* 9b)[8] is also open to various interpretations:

Shimon ha-Tzaddik [who served as high priest for forty years during the time of the Second Temple] said: "I have never eaten the guilt offering brought by a defiled Nazirite except for one time. On one occasion a Nazirite came from the South, and I saw that he had beautiful eyes, was of handsome appearance, and his hair was arranged in curls. I said to him: 'My son, what [reason] did you see to destroy this beautiful hair of yours?' [At the conclusion of the period, the Nazirite must shave his hair (Num. 6:18).] He said to me: 'I was a shepherd for my father in my town. [Once] I went to draw water from the well, and I gazed upon my reflection in the water, whereupon my evil desires overcame me and sought to drive me from the world. [Rashi: From seeing in the water my handsome reflection, my evil inclination prevailed over me and wished to stimulate me to do bad deeds which would drive me from the world.] But I said to it [my lust]: "Wicked being! Why do you glorify yourself in a world that is not yours, with one who is destined to become worms and dust? [I swear] by the service of the Temple that I will shave you [the

---

8. Also found in BT *Nazir* 4b; Tosefta *Nazir* (4:7).

Naso

beautiful hair] off for the sake of Heaven." I immediately arose and kissed his head, saying: "My son, may there be many Nazirites like you in Israel! Of [people like] you the verse says: 'If a man or woman clearly utters a Nazirite's vow, to set himself apart for the Lord'" (Num. 6:2).

Although it would seem from the passage that Shimon ha-Tzaddik looked askance at any Naziritic sacrifice, the Talmud hints that he might have been willing to partake of the sacrifice of an undefiled Nazirite. In that case, the Nazirite willingly accepts upon himself the length of his vow. However, if he becomes defiled, the initial period is cancelled, and a new period initiated. The unexpectedly long period of abstinence might make him regret his initial vow, thus cancelling the holiness of the sacrifice and causing it, if sacrificed, to be forbidden to be eaten.

However, one may still ask why Shimon ha-Tzaddik had no qualms about partaking of the guilt offering in this case but not in other cases. It must be that the initial vow was on a higher level, and this seems to follow from Me'iri's words:

> Anyone who says, "I will become a Nazirite if I perform this [sinful] act or if I do not perform this [righteous] act," this is not a measure of piety, for it is done in anger, and certainly [this is true of] one who became a Nazirite to atone for his sins; but one who becomes a Nazirite in order to sanctify himself by [prohibiting] what is permitted, and [who wishes] to subjugate his evil inclination, this is a measure of piety (Me'iri, BT *Nedarim* 9b).

In other words, Shimon ha-Tzaddik looked positively upon one accepting the Naziritic vows only in certain well-defined situations.

The Talmud (Me'iri, BT *Nedarim* 10a) equates Shimon ha-Tzaddik with Elazar ha-Kappar, but the Ran explains that their views are not equivalent, since Shimon ha-Tzaddik only denigrates one who breaks his vows and must bring special sacrifices and start over,[9] while Elazar ha-Kappar denigrates all Nazirites. However, according to Me'iri's interpretation, the comparison is understandable, since Elazar ha-Kappar believes that it is never justified to become a Nazirite, while Shimon ha-Tzaddik believes it is rarely justified, as opposed to R. Elazar, who highly praises those who do so.

It has been shown that the Tannaim argue about the advisability of voluntary fasting and taking Naziritic oaths, which the Talmud sees as being equivalent. What do the Amoraim hold concerning this subject? The Talmud (BT *Ta'anit* 11b) brings the following statements:

1. Reish Lakish says: He [Rashi: who fasts] is termed pious, as it is said: "The pious man does good to himself, but he that is cruel [Rashi: who is greatly weakened (by fasting)] harms himself" (Prov. 11:17). In other words, unless physically debilitating, fasting is praiseworthy.
2. R. Sheishet, said: The young scholar who would afflict himself by fasting [Maharsha: and be greatly weakened by it], let a dog devour his meal [Rashi: fasting does not help him any more than if he fasted unwillingly because his food was eaten by a dog].
3. R. Yirmiya b. Abba further said in the name of Reish Lakish: A scholar may not afflict himself by fasting because he lessens thereby his heavenly work [by fasting, his studies suffer].

According to Rashi, these Amoraim take the view that fasting is spiritually beneficial, although the latter two passages imply that

---

9. This lengthens the period of abstention, which might cause him to regret becoming a Nazirite, in which case the sacrifices brought at the end of the period are not valid and contaminate the Holy Temple.

for a scholar it is not appropriate, since it might affect his studies. Since this is not necessarily true concerning a Naziritic vow, Rashi might encourage such behavior even for a scholar. Tosafot [s.v. *gomel*], on the other hand, believes that the one who is termed "pious" in the first passage is he who does not fast, and interprets the other passages as also disdaining the practice of fasting and probably of vowing to be a Nazirite as well.

Rambam (*Hilchot De'ot* 3:1), supported by Rashba (responsum 431), accepts the view of Tosafot, which is also that of Elazar ha-Kappar, as is obvious from the following citation:

> Possibly a person may say: "Since lust and honor-seeking and the like are a bad way [to live] and drive a man out of the world, I will avoid them to the utmost, and distance myself to the extreme," to the point that he will not eat meat, nor drink wine, nor marry, nor dwell in an attractive home, nor wear comely apparel, but rather sackcloth and coarse wool and the like, just as the Edomite priests do. This too is the wrong way, and it is forbidden to follow it. Whoever follows such a path is termed a sinner. Of the Nazirite it is said "He [the priest] must make atonement for him, for the sin that he committed against the soul" (Num. 6:11). The Sages stated: "If the Nazirite who only abstained from wine needs atonement, he who deprives himself of everything [how much more so has he sinned]" (BT *Ta'anit* 11a). The Sages accordingly enjoined that a person should restrain himself only from that which the Torah restrains him, and he should not restrict himself by means of vows and oaths from things that are permitted. So spoke the Sages: "Does it not suffice you that which the Torah prohibits, that you prohibit from yourself additional things?" (JT *Nedarim* 9:1). This includes those

who constantly fast; they are not in a good way, and the Sages (BT *Ta'anit* 11a) prohibited a person to torment himself by fasting. And concerning all of these things and similar ones, Solomon commanded [us] saying: "Do not be over-righteous, nor excessively wise. Why should you be [i.e., make yourself] desolate?" (Ecc. 7:16).

The *Torah Temimah* (Num. 6:84) suggests that Rambam's approach might be acceptable even to R. Elazar, since the latter encourages fasting only for small stints, comparable to the thirty-day Naziritic vow (*Nazir* 1:3), while Rambam only disparages fasting as a way of life. According to this approach, the previously cited Amoraim who denigrated fasting (especially according to Tosafot) would not be in conflict with R. Elazar, since they too must agree that fasting to achieve specific goals may be beneficial, such as on Yom Kippur.

At any rate, the *Torah Temimah* assembles numerous sources which praise the enjoyment of worldly pleasures and criticize deprivation, for example:

1. "He created it [the earth] not to be chaotic, [rather] He formed it to be lived in (Isa. 45:18)." The implication is that man was placed in this world to improve his surroundings and promote scientific developments which ease man's stay on earth and make it more livable. If man weakens his body and drains his energy by fasting, not only is he not enjoying life in this world, but he is too weak to innovate. This approach harmonizes with the previously cited view of R. Yirmiya b. Abba that scholars should not indulge in prolonged fasting.
2. The Jerusalem Talmud states:

    It is forbidden to live in a city where there is no doctor [*Korban ha-Edah* (KE): perhaps one will become ill and

Naso

endanger himself; alternatively, (it refers to) a *mohel*] or no bath-house [KE: which is needed for health reasons], or no court for punishing and imprisonment [KE: if not for fear of punishment, men would swallow each other up alive].... It is forbidden to live in a city where there is no vegetable garden [KE: which is needed for human nourishment].... In the future man will be held accountable for everything [that is kosher] that his eyes saw and he did not eat [KE: for he deprived himself unnecessarily] (JT *Kiddushin* 4:12).

From the above text, it is clear that Judaism is not an ascetic religion but, on the contrary, is in favor of insuring quality of life in terms of health, cleanliness, and overall enjoyment. In fact, from the time of creation God promoted savoring the world's delights when He told Adam: "Of every tree of the garden you may freely eat" (Gen. 2:16).

3. Jehoiakim the son of Josiah was the third to last king of the Judean dynasty. Unlike his father, he was an immoral and wicked king, who oppressed his people and was chastised by Jeremiah in the following verses:

Woe unto him that builds his house by unrighteousness [toward the workers], and his chambers by injustice; who uses his neighbor's service without wages and does not give him his wages; who says: "I will build myself a wide house and spacious chambers," and makes windows and cedar panels painted with vermilion. Should you reign as king just because you strive to excel in cedar? *Did your father not eat and drink, and yet do justice and righteousness?* Then things went well with him. *He judged*

The Ethics of Numbers

[fairly] the cause of the poor and needy; then it was well. "Is not this what knowing Me means?" says the Lord. But your eyes and your heart are only used for covetousness, and for shedding innocent blood, and for oppression, and for doing violence (Jer. 22:13-17).

This passage highlights two important principles of Judaism. First, that knowledge of God implies acting morally. The realization that there is a Supreme Being is the first of the Ten Commandments, the first mitzvah in Rambam's *Yad ha-Chazakah* and *Sefer ha-Mitzvot*. Furthermore, in his *Guide for the Perplexed* (3:17), he states "that the idea of God necessarily implies justice." In other words, anyone who is immoral lacks understanding of the true nature of God.

The second principle is that God does not demand or even desire self-denial. One can and should enjoy the pleasures of life, as did King Josiah, just not at the expense of others, especially not of the needy and unfortunate.

4. *Tanna de-Vei Eliyahu* (*Ish Shalom*, ch. 15) says: "Being disgusted with the good life in this world is a bad sign for anyone that does so [i.e., who denigrates pleasure]." One authority compared such a person to one who commits suicide, thus depriving himself of the felicity which this world has to offer (*Afarkasta de-Anya* 4:370).

It would seem, then, that taking upon oneself a Naziritic vow is not the preferred way for an Israelite to distinguish himself. But this does not mean that there is no other option, as may be understood from the Mishnah: "R. Shimon said: There are three crowns: the crown of Torah [scholarship], and the crown of priesthood, and

Naso

the crown of royalty; and the crown of a good name rises above them all" (*Avot* 4:13).[10]

In this listing of celebrities in the Jewish milieu, the scholar is mentioned before the priest and king. In fact, another Mishnah stresses that in terms of both holiness and pedigree, a scholar who happens to be of illegitimate birth is superior to an ignorant high priest (*Horayot* 3:8).

In addition to becoming a Talmudic scholar, any non-Levite may become a devotee of the religion as if he were a Levite, as may be understood from the following paragraph from *Yad ha-Chazakah* (*Hilchot Shemittah ve-Yovel* 13:13):

> And not the tribe of Levi alone, but any one of the inhabitants of the earth whose soul moves him and whose intellect gives him the understanding [that it is desirable] to separate himself [from worldly pursuits], to stand before God, to serve Him in order to know God and to act properly as God created him to do, and to relieve himself of the various considerations that humans busy themselves with; this person has become the holiest of the holy, and God will be his portion and his inheritance for all eternity. And God will bless him with sufficient means to live on [Radbaz: God will enable him to earn in this world a sufficient amount to support himself, but not that he should cast himself upon the community (to support him, rather that he should live humbly)], just as He does for the priests and Levites. Behold David said, "God is my portion and my sustenance, You support my fate" (Ps. 16:5).

---

10. In some versions, the reference is to *Avot* 4:17. Commentaries point out that while R. Shimon states there are three crowns, the list counts four, although the fourth may be considered to relate to each of the first three.

The Ethics of Numbers

What is involved in becoming a scholar or religious devotee? Note the last verse of the previously cited Mishnah: "the crown of a good name rises above them all." In other words, one is only considered a scholar if, in addition to being proficient in religious matters, he also has a good name, i.e., he is respected as a righteous and moral person. There are two stages involved in achieving morality, as indicated by the twice repeated verse in the book of Psalms: "Turn from evil and do good" (Ps. 34:15, 37:27). First one must "turn from evil" by overcoming his negative traits (BT *Avodah Zarah* 19b). In fact, in order to achieve a true understanding of God, Rambam says that one must "thoroughly refine his moral character and subdue his passions and desires" (*Guide for the Perplexed* 1:5). He goes even further by saying that "all the commandments and exhortations in the Pentateuch aim at conquering the desires of the body" (*Guide for the Perplexed* 3:8). The second stage is to actively seek justice, as did Aaron the priest by pacifying litigants (*Avot de-Rabbi Natan* A:12) and R. Yosi through social contact in the market place (*Avot de-Rabbi Natan* B:24). Regarding this stage, the Talmud (BT *Gittin* 59b) says: "But the whole of the Law is (also) for the purpose of promoting peace, as it is written, 'Her ways are ways of pleasantness and all her paths are peace'" (Prov. 3:17), a maxim which the Rambam adopts verbatim (*Hilchot Megillah ve-Chanukah* 4:14).

Rambam is consistent in his approach. He divides his halachic magnum opus, the *Yad ha-Chazakah*, into fourteen books. In his introduction, he explains that the first, *Sefer ha-Madda*, comprises those precepts which compose fundamental principles. In that book, the section on belief in God (*Hilchot Yesodei ha-Torah*) is followed immediately by the section on individual moral behavior (*Hilchot De'ot*), and only afterwards by the laws associated with learning Torah (*Hilchot Talmud Torah*).

Naso

One may ask, how can the Talmud state in one place that "study is greater than performing *mitzvot*, because study enables one to perform *mitzvot* properly" (BT *Kiddushin* 40b), implying that one may be respected as a scholar even if he is not morally impeccable. Three answers may be given:

1. It is obvious that the text refers only to positive commands that may at times be ignored in favor of Torah study. Certainly, transgression of negative commands connected to moral behavior and personality traits is never considered. In fact, even positive time- or event-oriented commands, such as morning and evening prayers, Sabbath and holiday rituals, and benedictions before and after eating, are not in question. Only non-scheduled passing good deeds are being discussed, and the Talmud permits a scholar who wishes to do so, to maintain his studies rather than involve himself in such activities.
2. Tosafot (*in situ*, s.v. *Talmud gadol*) and R. Bezalel Ashkenazi (*Shitah Mekubetzet, Bava Kama* 17a) explain that the text is referring to a younger person who should devote his time to learning rather than actively engaging in charitable causes, no matter how worthy. However, after obtaining an education, the goal should be to promote welfare, as the Mishnah states: "not learning, but action, is the main thing" (*Avot* 1:17). In fact, the very wording in tractate *Kiddushin*, "study enables one to perform *mitzvot* properly," indicates that the only justification for studying is to eventually perform *mitzvot*, and precedence should be given to morally-oriented commands.
3. Based on another Talmudic source (BT *Mo'ed Katan* 9a-b), one may distinguish between the situation that there is nobody other than the scholar available to do the particular good deed, in which case performing that mitzvah overrides studying Torah, and the case where others can just as easily

perform the mitzvah, in which case the scholar is not required to interrupt his studies. Indeed, the halachic decisors accept this distinction as *halachah* (*Hilchot Talmud Torah* 3:3-4; *Yoreh De'ah* 246:18).[11]

Turning from Evil – a Task for Every Jew

At this stage, the idea suggested by R. Sacks mentioned earlier, namely that the first portions in the book of Numbers outline the special tasks assigned to each of the segments of the Jewish nation, will be re-examined. Although the functions of the priests and Levites are well-defined, the question that remains is how a simple Israelite can distinguish himself. R. Sacks suggests that this is the reason that Nazirism is described in the portion of *Naso*, since this is an avenue open to an Israelite who wishes to achieve greater holiness. Another option that was pointed out is to strive to be a Torah scholar. It was noted that a prerequisite to attaining that title is to perfect one's personality traits and erase any hint of corruption. There are two areas in which people are especially vulnerable—financial matters and sexual matters, which are both discussed in chapter 5 in *Naso*.

Financial Matters

The section in this portion concerning financial corruption is an addendum to a paragraph that appears at the beginning of Leviticus, which states:

> **21** If a person sins and commits a trespass against the Lord by dealing deceitfully with his fellow regarding a deposit [an item which he leaves with him to watch over] or a money transfer [Rashi: as an investment or loan], or

---
11. See Abba Engelberg, *The Ethics of Genesis* (2014), pp. 252-254.

Naso

through robbery, or by defrauding his fellow [Rashi: (by depriving him of his) wages]; **22** or he found that which was lost and denied it, and swore falsely regarding any of all the things that a man does to sin by them; **23** so it will be that he has sinned and is guilty [Rashi: when he realizes that he should repent—to know and admit that he has sinned and is guilty], then he must restore the item that he took by robbery, or the wages which he kept by defrauding, or the deposit which was deposited with him, or the lost item which he found, **24** or anything [any other financial matter] about which he swore falsely, he must pay it in full, and add one-fifth part to it; to him to whom it belongs should he give it, on the day of his being guilty [Rashbam: when he admits his guilt and repents for his sin]. **25** And he must bring his guilt offering to the Lord, an unblemished ram from the flock, [worth] the [proper] value for a guilt offering, to the priest (Lev. 5).

Here in the portion of *Naso*, this law is repeated in summary form (including an extra verse), perhaps as a first step for a non-Levite who seeks holiness:

6 Speak to the Children of Israel: When a man or woman commits any sin that men commit, to commit a trespass against the Lord, and that soul is guilty; **7** and when they confess the sin which they have done, then he must make restitution for his guilt in full, and add to it one-fifth part, and give it to the victim of his sin (Num. 5).

The first point to note is that in both texts it states that this person has committed "a trespass against the Lord." However, he has actually sinned against his neighbor by denying that he has either an item or money which belongs to him. The Midrash (*Sifra Chova* 22:4) explains that, generally, financial transactions are made in the presence of witnesses. Here, however, it was done between the two disputants exclusively, with the assumption that the only additional presence was that of the Eternal. When one of the two parties denies his involvement, he is thus betraying the Lord. More generally, the Torah stresses once more that moral behavior is Godly behavior and, more importantly, that immoral behavior is un-Godly behavior, in accordance with the view of Hillel, who says: "What is hateful to you, do not do to your neighbor; that is the whole Torah, while the rest is commentary thereof; go and learn it" (BT *Shabbat* 31a).[12]

Sexual Matters

The Torah strongly favors an emotional, sexual, and loving relationship between a man and a woman. According to the Bible, woman was created only when God said: "It is not good that the man should be alone; I will make for him a companion to help him" (Gen. 2:18). The sexual aspect of the relationship is clear from the very first command of the Torah,[13] which is to procreate, when God says: "Be fruitful and multiply, and fill the earth" (Gen. 1:28), since God wants the world to be populated, as Isaiah said: "He created it [the earth] not to be empty, [but rather] He formed it to be lived in" (Isa. 45:18).

In order to stimulate man to procreate, sexual activity was designed to be pleasurable (*Chovot ha-Levavot* 9:1). Specifically, one was advised to have relations on the Sabbath, as it was considered to be "one of the delights of the Sabbath" (*Orach Chaim* 280:1).

According to the Torah, how should men and women form a relationship? Rambam explains:

---

12. See Abba Engelberg, *The Ethics of Genesis* (2014), pp. 227–229.
13. *Sefer ha-Chinuch* 1; Rambam, *Sefer ha-Mitzvot,* positive command 212.

Naso

Before the Torah was given, a man would meet a woman in the marketplace and if they agreed to get married, he would bring her into his house and consummate the marriage between them privately, and she would be his wife. Once the Torah was given, Israel was commanded that if a man wanted to marry a woman, he would acquire her first in front of witnesses, and afterwards she would be his wife, as it says, "When a man takes [by performing a legal ceremony] a woman and has relations with her" (Deut. 22:13). And taking a wife in this manner is a positive commandment of the Torah (*Hilchot Ishut* 1:1-2).

Accordingly, Rambam counts as *mitzvot* the requirement to perform a legal marriage (*Sefer ha-Mitzvot*, positive command 213) and the prohibition (*Sefer ha-Mitzvot*, negative command 355) to engage in a sexual relationship without a religious ceremony and marriage contract (*ketubah*).[14] Although both Ra'avad (*Hilchot Ishut* 1:4) and Ramban (Deut. 23:18; Lev. 19:29; *Hasagot, Sefer ha-Mitzvot*, negative command 355) argue with Rambam and permit concubinal relationships on the Torah level, Rivash (responsum 395) explains that even Ra'avad requires a formal marriage with a *ketubah* (i.e., prohibits concubinal relationships) on a rabbinic level, as does Ramban (Rashba, Responsum 284 [ascribed to Ramban]).

Once married, a husband is required by *halachah* to have sexual relations regularly, based on the verse stating that "he must not withhold her food, her clothing, or her conjugal rights" (Exod. 21:10). Although stated with regard to a female slave's relationship to her owner, the oral law extends it to the normative situation (Rambam, *Sefer ha-Mitzvot*, negative command 262; *Sefer ha-Chinuch* 46), even specifying the frequency of intercourse based on the availability of the husband (*Ketubot* 5:6). Furthermore,

---

14. Commands 552 and 570 in *Sefer ha-Chinuch* parallel Rambam's count.

since having sexual relations is a mitzvah independent of the requirement to procreate, it is a requirement even when procreation is not possible, such as when a woman is pregnant or post-menopausal.

To summarize, the Torah favors sexual relations in the context of marriage, independent of procreation. In fact, the Talmud states: "Even if a man has numerous children, it is forbidden to remain without a wife" (BT *Yevamot* 61b), and this view is accepted by R. Yosef Karo (*Even ha-Ezer* 1:8).

Of course, the relationship is not confined to being sexual. On the contrary, it starts as being a loving emotional one, and progresses to being sexual, as is apparent from the text (BT *Yevamot* 62b): "The Sages taught: One who loves his wife as he loves himself, and who honors her more than himself... of him the verse states: 'And you will know that your tent is in peace'" (Job 5:24).

Ra'avad, in the introduction to his marital manual *Ba'alei ha-Nefesh*, rephrases the Talmudic dictum as follows: "Therefore, it behooves every man to love his wife as he loves his soul, to honor and deal compassionately with her, and to protect her as one would protect his own limbs." In short, a man must relate to his wife with love and empathy.

Although the above citations refer only to the husband, the expectation is that the feelings of love are mutual and highly gratifying to the extent that the Talmud feels that: "Any man who has no wife lives without joy, without blessing, and without goodness" (BT *Yevamot* 62b). With such an attitude on the part of both partners, it is clear why the Talmud characterizes such a home as one which will be devoid of quarrel and sin, and in which peace will reign.

Naso

LIMITATIONS

In order to maintain a loving mutual relationship between husband and wife, it was necessary for the Torah to impose restrictions in two areas of sexual behavior. First, it was necessary to prohibit incestuous relationships with close relatives. Second, it was necessary to prohibit adultery. The relevant laws are presented in the portions of *Acharei Mot* (Lev. 18) and *Ki Teitzei* (Deut. 22:22-27), and of course in the Ten Commandments (Exod. 20:13; Deut. 5:16).

It is clear that allowing a sexual relationship between a parent and child or two siblings would put at least one of them in an awkward situation and would not lead to a mutually beneficial association (*Guide for the Perplexed* 3:49). Although Ramban considered some of the incest laws to be in the category of statutes (Lev. 18:6), *Ba'al ha-Akeidah* notes that most civilized people view such liaisons as being repulsive (*Akeidat Yitzchak*, Lev. 64, *Acharei Mot*).

Although there seems to be an imbalance between the limitation of a wife to one husband, on the one hand, and the permissibility of polygamy in Jewish law on the other, it should be noted that post-Biblical history records very few cases of the latter. Eventually, polygamy was completely prohibited by the edict of R. Gershom (11th century). Even in the Bible, it seems to have generally been resorted to only in the case of infertility, and it is likely that the Torah permitted it initially only to inject a certain degree of flexibility into the Jewish laws of marriage and divorce by allowing a woman whose husband was dissatisfied with her to maintain the financial benefits of marriage.

In the portion of *Naso*, the ordeal of the adulterous woman is presented. Since it has been noted that the prohibition to commit adultery is mentioned numerous times in the Pentateuch, as well as the punishment for doing so, the question that arises is: why is an

The Ethics of Numbers

additional section necessary? For example, committing murder and worshipping idols are equally serious sins, yet no special portion with unusual ceremonies is devoted to defining and describing the treatment of the transgressor. The answer is that one must distinguish between two situations: either two witnesses observe the offender committing the sin, or two witnesses do not see the offender commit the sin, but there exists circumstantial evidence.

In the first case, all capital sins are treated identically. Based on the testimony of valid witnesses, the offender is executed. In the second case, the following (*Hilchot Sanhedrin* 20:1) is the law with regard to a person suspected of committing murder:

> A court does not exact punishment on the basis of circumstantial evidence, only on the basis of the testimony of [two] witnesses with clear proof. Even if witnesses saw a person pursuing someone and consequently warned the pursuer, but then diverted their attention; or, alternatively, if they followed the pursuer to the entrance of a [enclosed] ruin, entered after him and found the victim in his death throes, and saw the sword dripping blood in the hand of the [suspected] murderer, since they did not see him at the time that he struck him, the court does not execute the killer based on this testimony. Concerning this and the like, it is written: "Do not kill an innocent and righteous person" (Exod. 23:7).

What is the law with respect to circumstantial evidence in the case of adultery? That is what the section on the *sotah* (adulteress) in the portion of *Naso* presents. The Bible provides the following background:

Naso

12 Speak to the Children of Israel and say to them: If any man's wife goes astray, and is unfaithful to him, **13** and a man lies with her carnally, and it is hidden from the eyes of her husband, and she becomes impure secretly, and there is no witness against her, and she was not caught in the act. **14** Then, if a spirit of jealousy comes over him, and he is jealous of his wife, and she has become impure; or if the spirit of jealousy comes over him, and he is jealous of his wife, and she has not become impure.

At this point, the Torah describes the procedure of having the *sotah* drink the water of bitterness, which will cause her thighs to decay and her abdomen to swell if she is indeed guilty (Num. 5:21). On the other hand, if she is innocent, the potion will have no negative effect, and in addition, R. Akiva adds that if she was formerly barren, she will now become fertile (BT *Sotah* 26a, accepted by Ibn Ezra as the simple meaning of Num. 5:28), while according to R. Yishmael:

> If [in the past] she gave birth in pain, [from now on] she will give birth with ease; [if in the past she gave birth to] females, she will [now] give birth to males; [if her children were] short, she will [now] give birth to tall [children]; [if her children were] black, she will give birth to white [children] (BT *Sotah* 26a).

In determining exactly what evidence there is against the woman, the Talmud (BT *Sotah* 2b) analyzes the following phrases:

1. (Verse 14) A spirit of jealousy comes over him—the first stage is that the husband becomes jealous, called *kinnui* (jealousy).

The Ethics of Numbers

2. (Verse 13) She becomes impure secretly—the second stage is that the woman is seen entering a concealed room with the suspected adulterer, called *steera* (concealment).

3. (Verse 13) There is no witness against her, and she was not caught in the act—this verse refers to the third stage: performing a sexual act, where the first two stages are *kinnui* (jealousy) and *steera* (concealment), respectively. From the fact that the verse stresses that there are no witnesses to testify as regards the third stage, the Talmud (BT *Sotah* 2b) derives (according to R. Yehoshua in *Sotah* 1:1) that for the earlier stages two valid witnesses are required.[15]

4. The Mishnah (*Sotah* 6:2) further derives that the entire procedure only occurs if there is "no witness." But if there is a single witness that an act (coitus) was performed, even one who is normally not acceptable, such as a servant, then the procedure is not performed, and the husband divorces her without giving her the sum allocated in the *ketubah* (marriage contract), even though normally two valid witnesses are required to convict a person in Jewish law.

---

15. R. Eliezer, a minimalist, holds that verse 13 only teaches that two witnesses are needed for *kinnui* (jealousy warning). For *steera* (concealment), one is sufficient, even if it is the husband himself. A second version of the view of R. Eliezer, found in a *braita* (BT *Sotah* 2b), is that he holds the opposite, namely: that two witnesses are needed for *steera*. For *kinnui*, one is sufficient, even if it is the husband himself. R. Chanina says that nowadays, when there is no Sanhedrin to finalize which of the three opinions is accepted (R. Yehoshua and the two versions of R. Eliezer), one should never warn his wife not to seclude herself with a given man, since that could start the process that would eventually require drinking the waters of bitterness which are not available today, in which case she would be permanently prohibited io her husband. If he warns her and then sees her seclude herself, and if we adopt the stringency of each of the two versions of R. Eliezer, she would be required to drink, and that is the *halachah* (*Hilchot Ishut* 24:25; *Even ha-Ezer* 178:7). If a husband did so, he should immediately pardon her (Rema), but *Pitchei Teshuvah* sees R. Chanina as only issuing a non-actionable warning.

Naso

MODERN SENSIBILITIES

The procedure described undoubtedly grates on modern sensibilities, according to which equal rights independent of gender or sexual preference are the default. Certainly, any woman who underwent the *sotah* process was mortified to the essence of her soul. One would be justified in asking why there is no parallel ceremony for unfaithful husbands. Furthermore, the very permissibility of polygamy objectifies women, deprives them of the inherent respect which is the birthright of every human being, and introduces societal discrimination.

Of course, the Torah was given to the Jewish nation in an age when society was patriarchal. Nevertheless, it is clear that the oral law, as interpreted by the Sages, made a serious effort to lessen the negative impact of these seeming flaws.

First, it should be noted that the previously described gory punishment undergone by a guilty adulteress is extended in the Mishnah to the adulterer as well (*Sotah* 5:1). Second, as already mentioned, in the event that the suspected adulteress was innocent, she was supernaturally lavished with enhanced fertility. Third, the Rabbis fixated more on the potential unwarranted jealousy of the husband than on the supposed guilt of the wife, and it is for this reason that as part of the proceedings, the priest writes the Biblical words on a piece of parchment: "May the Lord make you for a curse and an oath among your people" (Num. 5:21), which are later blotted out (Num. 5:23, *Sotah* 2:3). Commenting on this segment, Rambam (based on BT *Sukkah* 53b) writes: "Even God's name is blotted out in order to create peace between a husband and his wife" (*Hilchot Chanukah* 4:14). In other words, the Rabbis were more focused on soothing the husband's jealousy and hopefully recreating a loving environment than on inflicting punishment on any of the parties.

Economic conditions in ancient times were such that the Sages accurately assumed that a woman preferred an unhappy marriage with its ensured physical sustenance to possibly happier singlehood, as is summarized by the Talmudic maxim: "*Tav le-meitav tan doo mi-lemeitav armalo*" (BT *Yevamot* 118b, BT *Ketubot* 75a, BT *Kiddushin* 7a, BT *Bava Kamma* 111a), meaning: It is better to dwell as two (Jastrow: in grief, with a load) than to dwell in widowhood. Since the wife would most probably have retained her marital status, the Rabbis were determined to make it as satisfying and pleasant as possible.

Perhaps with prescience as to later moral discernment, the entire ceremony was eventually abandoned towards the end of the Second Temple period, as stated in the Mishnah (*Sotah* 9:9):

> When adulterers increased, the [ceremony of] bitter waters ceased, and it was R. Yochanan b. Zakkai who discontinued it, for it says: "I will not punish your daughters when they commit harlotry, nor your daughters-in-law when they commit adultery, for they themselves join with harlots and they sacrifice with the prostitutes" (Hos. 4:14);

R. Yochanan b. Zakkai, in anticipation of later ethical conventions, disdained asymmetric demands with respect to the sexual behavior of the community.

On the Acceptability of Circumstantial Evidence in the Case of the Adulterous Woman

The portion of the *sotah* demonstrates that although circumstantial evidence is not generally acceptable, in the case of adultery it is. One may ask: why is this the case? To answer this, one might first question whether not accepting circumstantial evidence is an effective way to govern. A Mishnah states:

> A Sanhedrin that carries out an execution [as infrequently as] once in seven years is called a destructive tribunal.

Naso

> R. Eliezer b. Azariah says: "[as infrequently as] once in seventy years." R. Tarfon and R. Akiva say: "If we had been members of a Sanhedrin, no one would ever have been put to death." R. Gamliel remarked: "And [if their policy were applied] they would also have increased the number of murders in Israel (*Makkot* 1:10).

It is likely that the small number of executions, which is deplored by R. Gamliel, partially resulted from the halachically sanctioned refusal to accept circumstantial evidence. On the other hand, a solution to this problem is available, based on the following mitzvah, which gives the king the right to carry out executions of those who transgress his or the Torah's commands (called *mishpat ha-melech*), and to waive the normative requirements (*Sefer ha-Mitzvot*, positive command 173):

> The 173rd mitzvah is that He commanded us to appoint a king from Israel who will gather together our entire nation and lead us, and He said: "You are entitled to set a king over yourself" (Deut. 17:15).… And every time that this king makes a command which does not contradict one of the *mitzvot* of the Torah, we are required to obey it, and regarding he who transgresses his command and does not obey it, it is permissible for the king to kill him for any matter that he so chooses, and as our fathers said of themselves: "Any man who ignores your [Joshua's] desires and does not obey every order that you give him will be put to death" (Josh. 1:18).

Rambam uses the verse from the book of Joshua to shed light on the definition and authority accorded to the king whom the Torah allows the nation to appoint. Of course, the laws which the king is permitted to enact are not arbitrary, but must have a righteous purpose, as Rambam (*Hilchot Melachim* 4:10) derives from the book of Samuel:

> All the land which he conquers is his, and he is free to give his servants and warriors what he wishes, and to keep for himself what he wishes. All the laws he enacts concerning such affairs are valid. But in all such matters his actions should be for the sake of God; his chief aim should be to promote the true religion and to fill the world with righteousness and to weaken the strength of the wicked and fight the battles of the Lord; for a king is basically chosen to do justice and wage war, as it says: "And our king will judge us, and go before us and fight our battles" (1 Sam. 8:20).

As noted, the restrictions on imposing capital punishment could easily lead to a situation where murderers have free reign, and it is thus readily understandable why the king would wish to speedily remedy this situation, as described below:

> Whoever has committed murder, but there is no clear evidence to prove it, or if he was not warned, or if there is only one witness, or if one [seemingly] slew a person by accident whom he just happens to hate, [in all such cases] the king has the authority to kill him, in order to maintain the public welfare, in accordance with what the situation demands (*Hilchot Melachim* 3:10; see also *Hilchot Rotzeach* 2:4).

One might now suggest that circumstantial evidence is not accepted in criminal cases because there is a backup, namely *mishpat ha-melech*, which takes up the slack when normative law enforcement does not suffice. In the case of adultery, on the other

Naso

hand, that possibility does not exist, since the king's prerogative relates only to civil law (*bein adam le-chaveiro*), but not to laws between man and God (*bein adam la-Makom*), and adultery falls in the latter category (*Or Same'ach, Hilchot Melachim* 3:10).

One might ask, in what sense does *Or Same'ach* consider adultery to be *bein adam la-Makom*. It certainly would seem to represent a moral deficiency with respect to interpersonal relationships. The *Or Same'ach* undoubtedly bases himself on the following Talmudic segment: "R. Akiva expounded: When husband and wife are worthy [Rashi: they traverse the same path, (in the sense that) neither is he an adulterer, nor is she an adulteress], the *Shechinah* abides with them; when they are not worthy, fire consumes them" (BT *Sotah* 17b). R. Akiva bases this exegesis on the fact that the letters of the word for 'husband' in Hebrew are *aleph*, *yud*, and *shin*, and those for 'wife' are *aleph*, *shin,* and *heh*. The *yud* and *heh* form the Divine Name; but if omitted, only *aleph* and *shin* are left, which form the Hebrew word *aish* (fire).

Both peace and love are considered to be Godly virtues without which one is unable to fulfill the laws of the Torah, as emphasized in another Talmudic segment:

> R. Tanhum stated in the name of R. Hanilai: Any man who has no wife lives without joy, without blessing, and without goodness… without Torah and without a [protecting] wall… without peace (BT *Yevamot* 62b).

In fact, moral behavior is considered to be a prerequisite to properly obeying the laws of the Torah, as reflected in the maxim "*derech eretz kadmah la-Torah*" (*Yalkut Shimoni, Bereishit* 3:34), meaning that *derech eretz* must precede acceptance of the law. According to R. S.R. Hirsch (*Avot* 2:2), *derech eretz* refers to "the mores and considerations of courtesy and propriety arising from social living and also to things pertinent to good breeding and general education."

It is true that the king cannot intervene in laws between man and God. However, the Talmud states that the Sanhedrin can do so:

> R. Eliezer b. Ya'akov says: I heard that the court may administer lashes and [capital] punishment, [even] when not [required by] Torah [law]. And not [because they wish] to violate the Torah law; rather, to erect a fence around the Torah [to provide deterrence].
> And an incident [occurred] involving one who rode a horse on Shabbat in the days of the Greeks, and they brought him to court and stoned him, not because he deserved that [punishment, since the prohibition to ride a horse on Shabbat is rabbinical], but because the hour required it [people had become lax in their observance of the Shabbat]. Another incident occurred involving a man who engaged in intercourse with his wife under a fig tree, and they brought him to court and flogged him, not because it was fitting for him [such conduct is not expressly forbidden by the Torah], but because the hour required it [people had become lax in matters of modesty] (BT *Sanhedrin* 46a; BT *Yevamot* 90b).

Since a severe punishment could theoretically have been meted out by the Sanhedrin even based on circumstantial evidence, the initial question remains: why does the Torah find it necessary to change the rules, when it does not do so in the case of murder? One might answer that the option available in the case of murder (*mishpat ha-melech*) is much stronger, because the king may legislate his requirements into law. When Sanhedrin takes extraordinary steps, it is on an *ad hoc* basis, as the Talmud cited says: "because the hour

Naso

required it," and Rambam (*Hilchot Sanhedrin* 24:4) also calls it *hora'at sha'ah* (a one-time decision), and each case would have to be treated individually.

A preferable answer, however, is that the Torah wishes to focus attention on sexual transgression, just as it previously stressed financial corruption in this portion, since these are the two most common areas where man's lust leads him to sin, and it is upon these sins that man must concentrate when he starts to perfect himself by turning from evil.

Doing Good

As noted, achieving perfection requires two steps, turning from evil and doing good, and by doing so any Israelite can become even as worthy as the High Priest. *Naso* has provided guidelines by stressing how careful one must be regarding financial and sexual matters. As previously mentioned, the section in *Naso* dealing with monetary theft and embezzlement is a summary of what was already legislated in the book of Leviticus. There is, however, one verse which is added here, and which, according to the Midrash (*Sifrei Naso* 2; see Rashi, Num. 5:6), provides the justification for repeating the entire section. It is the verse stipulating what to do with the money that is to be returned if the person wronged was a convert who has died without relatives. The verse says:

> But if the man has no relative to whom restitution may be made for the guilt, the restitution for guilt which is made will go to the Lord, i.e., the priest, in addition to the ram of the atonement, through which atonement is made for him (Num. 5:8).

Note that the verse does not say that it is referring to a convert. The Talmud derives this as follows: "Is there any person in Israel who has no relatives? Rather, the verse speaks of robbery of a convert [who did not marry or have children as a Jew]" (BT *Bava Kamma* 109a; Rashi, Num. 5:8).

The question that arises is: why would the Torah repeat an entire section just to deal with a highly unusual and esoteric situation which occurs only as the result of three unlikely events:

(1) the victim of the crime was a convert,
(2) the convert died before remuneration was made,
(3) the convert had no Jewish children.

Perhaps the Torah relates this highly improbable scenario only to highlight the desecration of God's name which results from defrauding a proselyte—a person who was born a Gentile and became enthralled by the beauty of Judaism, only to be victimized by his new co-religionists (in whom he chose to place his trust), and was then appalled that a natural-born Jew could be guilty of such a deed. As one commentator notes:

> The robber who stole from him desecrates the name of God in the eyes of the proselyte who sought refuge under its [Judaism's] wings. This is why he is called "a trespasser on the sacred," and is obligated to bring a sin offering, which is the law regarding those who trespass on the sacred (Sforno, Num. 5:6).

The law cannot distinguish between the punishment for deceiving a Jew from birth or doing so to a proselyte. But the Torah definitely wishes to send the message that improper behavior is measured not

Naso

only by the severity of punishment, but also by the victim's place in society. Conversely, the Torah undoubtedly desires to stress the positive consequences which can flow from honest behavior in business transactions.

However, "doing good" appears in this portion not only by innuendo, when considering the sanctification of God's name that could have taken place had the offender acted with integrity. The restitution which the sinner makes must be preceded by his confession (Num. 5:7). According to Rambam (*Sefer ha-Mitzvot*, positive command 73), this is the source of the general command to repent, which includes accepting upon oneself not to commit the particular sin in the future (*Hilchot Teshuvah* 2:2). With respect to sins of passion, Rambam (*Hilchot Teshuvah* 7:2) stipulates that in order to avoid them one must learn to practice self-control, as described below:

> Do not say that one may only repent for sins that involve an action, such as adultery, robbery, and theft. Just as a person must repent for these, so too he must search out his bad character traits, and repent for them: for anger, hatred, jealousy, foolishness, pursuit of money and honor, gluttony, and so on. A person must repent for all of these. And these sins are harder than those which have an action, because once a person is immersed in them, it is difficult for him to free himself from them. Thus, the verse says: "Let the wicked forsake his way, and the unrighteous man his thoughts" (Isa. 55:7).

In other words, repentance involves not only "turning from evil," but also "doing good" by working on one's character traits for the purpose of developing an empathetic, merciful, charitable, and righteous personality.

The Ethics of Numbers

Summary

In this chapter, the question of whether asceticism has any place in Judaism was discussed. Although there are different opinions among the Tannaim, Amoraim, and Rishonim (early commentators), Rambam posits that fasting and Nazirism are not to be encouraged, and numerous citations were brought to show that Judaism is in favor of enjoying the world to the extent that *halachah* permits.

It should be pointed out that there are other laws of the Torah concerning which rabbinical opinion was not unanimous as to their advisability, such as the appointment of a king (Deut. 17:14-20 as opposed to 1 Sam. 8:4-22) and having sexual relations with a captive woman in times of war (Deut. 21:10-14, modified by the rabbinical dictum that Scripture makes this concession only in view of man's evil inclination - BT *Kiddushin* 21b). Especially in the latter case, many rabbis argued that God permitted such behavior only because He is aware of human nature and preferred to make available legal means of relief rather than see the warriors become sinners.

The second topic dealt with was how a Jew who is neither a *kohen* nor a Levite can distinguish himself. Although one possibility would be to take upon himself a vow to be a Nazirite, it was suggested that there are other options available as well, such as becoming a scholar in Torah, which seems to be the preference of the Sages. However, scholarship should be preceded by character development, which itself is composed of two stages: turning away from evil and doing good. The former involves controlling one's financial and sexual appetites, and it is thus appropriate that the portion of *Naso* discusses how one makes restitution for fraudulent financial dealings and how to treat an adulterous woman.

Naso

According to the view that Nazirism is not an especially cherished goal for the typical Jew, why is it mentioned in this portion, which deals with the desirable functioning of the various members of society? One might adopt the explanation provided in the Talmud and accepted by Rashi (Num. 6:2):

> Why was the portion of a Nazirite placed next to the portion of a *sotah*? [It was done] to tell you that anyone who sees a *sotah* in her disgrace will [have an urge to] renounce wine [as over-drinking easily leads to sexual promiscuity] (BT *Sotah* 2a).

Although Nazirism is not recommended, it might serve as a one-time remedy for a traumatic experience.

Beha'alotcha

The portion of *Beha'alotcha* touches upon many topics, including those introduced in other portions. While the making and lighting of the *menorah* were first portrayed in the book of Exodus (25:31-40; 27:20-21), and the installation of the Tabernacle was described in the book of Leviticus (in the portions of *Tzav* and *Shemini*), details are added and the Levites are dedicated for service in the present portion. Travelling arrangements were first broached in the portion of *Bamidbar* (Num. 2), but the implementation details occupy the second half of ch. 9 and all of ch. 10 in this portion, and the plaintive nature of the Israelites first encountered in the portion of *Beshallach* (Exod. 14:10-14, 15:22-26, 16:1-36, 17:1-7) appears again in ch. 11 of *Beha'alotcha*.

Two other topics, which also have antecedents in other locations of the Pentateuch, will be dealt with in this chapter. The first is the paschal lamb, the *korban pesach*, which is described in detail in the portion of *Bo* (Exod. 12). A new aspect is introduced in *Beha'alotcha*, namely the possibility of a compensatory sacrifice for those who were unable to bring it at the proper time. One might ask that since there are many time-constrained *mitzvot* in the Torah, especially those associated with the holidays, why was this specific command chosen as the one which could be redressed. The answer hinges upon the centrality of the Passover holiday in the ethos of the Jewish religion.

Beha'alotcha

A second topic which resurfaces here is the subject of the slander (*lashon ha-ra*) engaged in by Aaron and Miriam, leading to the latter being stricken with leprosy. Related prohibitions have already appeared (Lev. 19:16-18), while the subject of leprosy, considered to be a punishment for *lashon ha-ra*,[16] has been discussed at length (Lev. 13:1-59; 14:1-57). The manifold grievances of the Israelites, many of which bordered on libel, are thoroughly detailed in this portion as well as in the past. However, this seems to be the only place where dissension among the righteous leaders is described.

UNDERSTANDING THE TWO MOST SERIOUS POSITIVE COMMANDS

The Amorah R. Simlai (BT *Makkot* 23b) was the first to clearly state that there are 613 *mitzvot* in the Torah, 248 of which are positive commands (corresponding to the traditional number of limbs in the human body), and 365 of which are negative commands (corresponding to the days of the solar year). As opposed to the negative commands, whose transgressors are generally punished with lashes, nowhere does the Torah penalize one who neglects to fulfill one of the positive commands,[17] with the exception of the paschal lamb and circumcision, for which the Biblical text ordains excision (Num. 9:13; Gen. 17:14), which is considered a more severe punishment than lashes.

The aforementioned *mitzvot* are grouped together in a well-known Midrashic interpretation of ch. 16 in Ezekiel, where the prophet reviews the people's past history, showing how it led to

---

16. See Abba Engelberg, *The Ethics of Leviticus*, pp.125-156.
17. However, there is a rabinically ordained punishment (*makkot mardut*—flagellation for disobedience) for those who do not fulfill positive commands or rabbinically ordained commands, as recorded in various locations in the Talmud (BT *Ketubot* 45b, *Yevamot* 52b, *Menachot* 70a, *Nazir* 23a, *Shabbat* 40b).

the destruction of the Temple and the scattering of the nation. Israel is portrayed as a baby girl born in a field, abandoned, and saved by the Lord, Who nurtures her until she is a beautiful grown woman. He then betrothes her, lavishes upon her many gifts, and finally marries her. But in spite of God's graciousness, Israel is ungrateful and allows herself to be led astray by other gods. The verses which describe how God happens upon the deserted child and rehabilitates her read as follows:

> And when I passed by you, and saw you wallowing in your blood [referring metaphorically to their enslavement in Egypt], and I said to you: "In [spite of your wallowing in] your blood, [you will] live. In your blood, [you will] live" (Ezek. 16:6).

The next verse describes God's nursing of the foundling (Israel):

> I caused you to increase, like the plants of the field. And you increased and grew up and became adorned in the most precious jewelry; your breasts were full, and your [adult] hair was grown, *yet you were naked and bare* [spiritually and morally; Rashi: bereft of *mitzvot*] (Ezek. 16:7).[18]

God proceeds to provide physical and spiritual succor:

> And I passed you and saw you, and, behold, **your time was the time for love** [i.e., to marry], I spread the corner [of my garment, a reference to marriage] over you, and covered your nakedness; and I swore to you, and entered into a covenant with you, [these are] the words of the Lord your God, and you became Mine (Ezek. 16:8).

---

18. Verses 6 and 7 are quoted in reverse order in the Passover Haggadah.

Beha'alotcha

The Midrash understands the words "your time was the time for love" to mean that the time had come for God to fulfill his oath to Abraham that He would redeem his children after years of slavery (Gen. 15:14). Indeed, the young maiden (Israel) had physically matured, but she was still "naked and bare," meaning that she had not yet proven herself worthy of being redeemed. The Midrash explains how that situation is remedied:

> The Lord gave them two *mitzvot*: [those associated with] the blood of the paschal lamb and the blood of circumcision for them to engage in, in order that they be redeemed, as it says: "And when I passed by you, and saw you *wallowing in your blood*" (*Mechilta de-Rabbi Yishmael Bo, Mesechta de-Pascha, parsha* 5).

Rashi, in quoting the Midrash, explains that the word for "blood" in the verse is in the plural Hebrew form, implying the blood of two *mitzvot*, and this is spelled out further by a second Midrash which elucidates the final words of the verse as follows:

> And I said to you: "*In your blood*, [you will] *live*"—this refers to the blood of the paschal lamb; "*in your blood*, [you will] *live*"—this refers to the blood of circumcision (*Song of Songs Rabbah, parsha* 5, s.v. *kol dodi dofek*).

The two *mitzvot* of circumcision and sacrificing the paschal lamb share other similarities as well. The Torah creates an explicit connection between the two, when it says regarding *korban pesach*: "no uncircumcised person may eat of it" (Exod. 12:48). They are also each "firsts," circumcision being the first mitzvah given to Abraham (Gen. 17:10), as well as the first mitzvah that every male Jew fulfills with his body (literally), and *korban pesach* being the first mitzvah commanded to the Children of Israel as a nation (Exod. 12:3). Finally, both *mitzvot* are recalled at the same time of year, being that circumcision is mentioned in the portion of *Tazri'a*, which is always read in the early spring, and *korban pesach* is relevant on Passover.

However, the fact that these two commandments have various common aspects does not explain why transgressing them should carry a heavier punishment than other positive laws which appear numerous times and would seem to be of greater significance, such as Sabbath observance ("Observe the Sabbath day, to keep it holy" – Deut. 5:12; Exod. 20:8), which sanctifies time, or affixing *mezuzot* to door-posts ("And you should write them [the appropriate Biblical texts] on the door-posts of your house" – Deut. 6:9, 11:20), which sanctifies space.

Apparently, circumcision and *korban pesach* reflect the essence of Judaism more than other *mitzvot*, as implied by the commandment to circumcise all males at the time of revelation (BT *Kreitot* 9a, cited by Rashi, Exod. 24:6), as well as the requirement to do so in the future as part of the process of conversion to the Jewish faith (BT *Yevamot* 46a). Similar to the lesson of circumcision— that man was placed in this world in order to improve it (*tikkun olam*),[19] bringing the paschal lamb inculcates intrinsic values which affect the practicing Jew throughout his entire life, thereby enabling him to succeed in the task of *tikkun olam*.

However, it is impossible to fulfill the mission of improving the world unless one knows what facet is to be improved. One could concentrate on the physical aspect by building magnificent structures, cultivating untamed lands, and inventing more advanced machines. On the other hand, one could concentrate on the social aspect by tending to the ill and supporting the poverty-stricken. Bringing the *korban pesach* answers to this question, and

---

19. See Abba Engelberg, *Ethics of Leviticus*, p.119.

Beha'alotcha

as such is one of the most central *mitzvot*. The Jewish populace instinctively accepts the paramount importance of this law, which is commemorated today at the Passover Seder that opens the holiday. Surveys have consistently shown that as many as 90% of all Jews—religious, traditional, secular, and even assimilated—observe the festival to some extent.[20]

Obviously, fulfilling the mission has something to do with what is written in the Torah. After all, Rashi's comment (Gen. 1:1) on the first word in the book of Genesis, "*Bereishit*" ("In the beginning"), is: "God created the world for the sake of Torah (*Gen. Rabbah* 1:4) … and for the sake of Israel" (*Lev. Rabbah* 36:4). In other words, the world was created in order for Israel to proactively spread the message of the Torah. In fact, when God first appointed Moses to lead the nation out of Egypt, He made it quite clear what the next step would be when He said: "When you have brought out the people from Egypt, you will serve God on this mountain" (Exod. 3:12).

The Israelites were given the command to slaughter the paschal lamb on the first day of the Hebrew month of Nissan (Exod. 12:2). The actual slaughtering was on the 14th of Nissan (Exod. 12:6).[21] Interestingly, other than the sacrifice which they brought on the eve of their departure from Egypt, they brought the *korban pesach* only one more time before they arrived in the Land of Israel,[22]

---

20. Kobi Nahshoni, "Most Israelis Eat Kosher for Passover" (March 28, 2007), Ynet.News; Hana Levi Julian, "Majority of Israeli Jews Eat Kosher for Passover" (March 17, 2010), Ynet.News; Shoshana Schechter, "Freedom to… Not Freedom from: Pesach and the Road to Redemption" (April 2016), Torah To-Go.
21. This is the source for the command for future generations (*Sefer ha-Chinuch* 5; *Sefer ha-Mitzvot*, positive command 55).
22. Rashi, Num. 9:1, based on *Sifrei Beha'alotcha* 67. According to Ibn Ezra (Exod. 40:2), only upon arrival in Israel was the entire seven-day festival observed (based on Exod. 13:5, where the seven days are linked to arrival in the land). Until then, unleavened bread was required, and leavened bread forbidden, only on the night of the fifteenth.

since the majority of the Israelites were not circumcised in the desert for reasons of health (BT *Yevamot* 72a), and circumcision is a prerequisite to bringing the *korban pesach* (Exod. 12:48; BT *Kiddushin* 37b, Tosafot s.v. *ho'il*). Nevertheless, the effect of that experience was enough to lay the spiritual basis for the continued character of the nation until this very day.

Korban Pesach

The paschal lamb serves as a reminder of three elements which enable a Jew to lead a Torah-oriented life, hence the choice of *korban pesach* as one of the two major positive commandments. These elements are:

1. awareness of Torah law and *hashkafah* (*Weltanschauung*),
2. freedom to observe the laws of the Torah,
3. motivation to observe the laws of the Torah.

The command to bring the paschal lamb is contained in the following verse: "And they should eat the *flesh* on this night, roasted with fire, and with *unleavened bread* and *bitter herbs* they should eat it" (Exod. 12:8).

Note that the requirement is to eat three items—the paschal lamb (*pesach*), unleavened bread (*matzah*), and bitter herbs (*maror*). It will be demonstrated that each of these items stresses one of the three prerequisites to proper observance of the religion, as summarized in the following table:

Pesach	awareness of Torah law and *hashkafah*
Matzah	freedom to observe the laws of the Torah
Maror	motivation to observe the laws of the Torah

Beha'alotcha

Accordingly, Rabban Gamliel said in the Haggadah:

> Whoever does not mention the following three things on Passover has not fulfilled his duty, namely: **pesach** (the *korban pesach*), **matzah** (the unleavened bread), and **maror** (the bitter herbs).

PESACH: AWARENESS OF TORAH LAW AND HASHKAFAH

In addition to dividing the laws into positive and negative commands, one may divide them into those which are between man and his fellow-man (*bein adam le-chaveiro*) and those which are between man and God (*bein adam la-Makom*). Actually, each of the former is also considered to be one of the latter, since it is God who commanded the Jew to act in that way toward his fellow man. R. Eliezer Berkovits has explained that the main purpose of the ritual-oriented and God-oriented laws, as well as those restraining one's sexual and culinary appetites, is to train one in self-control, so that when he must control himself and his emotions in dealing with others, he will be well prepared to do so.[23] R. Berkovits has suggested that the ritual laws serve the same purpose as war games. One creates such games to teach the soldier how to attack and how to defend himself in a real war. The experience he gains is not as good as real war experience, but it serves, at a low cost, to reduce the casualty rate when the soldier is ordered into combat. Similarly, laws restraining a person's sexual and culinary appetites serve to train him in self-control, so that when it is necessary to control himself and his emotions when dealing with his compatriots, he will be well prepared.

The laws regarding the bringing of the paschal lamb emphasize both types of *mitzvot*.

---

23. Eliezer Berkovits, *God, Man, and History* (1965), p. 109.

The Ethics of Numbers

Ritual Laws

Since one of the laws associated with the *korban pesach* is that one should not have any leavened bread products in his possession when he slaughters the lamb, it will be included in this discussion.

The Passover sacrifice serves as a good introduction to the ritual laws, being that there is a myriad of *mitzvot* connected with it. Rambam lists sixteen commands in *Hilchot Korban Pesach*, and eight in *Hilchot Chametz u-Matzah*.

Social Laws

The Talmud (especially the tractate *Pesachim*) and codes of law discuss the halachic details of each of the three items mentioned, namely the paschal lamb, the unleavened bread, and the bitter herbs. At the same time, great stress is placed on the social aspects (*bein adam le-chaveiro*) of the festive meal in the following verse: "They should take for themselves for every man a lamb, according to their *fathers' houses*, a lamb for a household" (Exod. 12:3). R. Samson Raphael Hirsch explains that the father's house referred to might be a large number of families all stemming from the same patriarch, a situation that would obviously generate considerable fellowship. Furthermore, if the household is too small to consume the entire sheep, one might think that it could be finished the next day. But this has been explicitly prohibited (Exod. 12:10).

Why would the Torah require one to burn the left-overs? After all, there is a prohibition against wasting food (*ba'al tashchit*), based on Deut. 20:19. An answer which may be given is similar to that offered by *Ha'amek Davar* concerning the short period that was allotted for the eating of the thanksgiving offering (one day and one night, as opposed to two days and a night for a simple peace offering), namely: "So that there will be only one feast with many guests" (Lev. 7:16).

What should be done if the family is too small to consume the entire lamb? The Torah answers this explicitly: "If the household

Beha'alotcha

is too small for [consuming] a lamb, then *he and his neighbor next to his house* should take one [a lamb] proportionate [in size] to the number of souls" (Exod. 12:4).

The *Midrash Lekach Tov* explains that anyone, not necessarily a relative or a neighbor, may be invited to join, just that the verse mentions the most common occurrence. The Tosefta (BT *Pesachim* 8:13) says that the verse specifically mentions "neighbor" to clarify that if one has indigent neighbors, he should not join friends and let the neighbors fend for themselves, but he should go out of his way to bring the sacrifice with their participation.

The constant concern with the plight of the poor is reflected by the opening phrase of the Haggadah: "Let anyone who is hungry come and eat [with us]." This is just symbolic, because it is said within the house, not outdoors where the poor might be lurking. As noted, during the time of the Temple, the poor people were notified in advance of whose paschal lamb they would be partaking. This decision would not, and could not, be left to the last moment, since the Talmud states:

> [Then *he and his neighbor next to his house* should take one] proportionate to the number of the souls: this teaches that the paschal lamb is [permitted to be] slaughtered only for those who are registered [counted] for it (BT *Pesachim* 61a).

Another reminder of the importance of proper social behavior flows from the Talmudic discussion of the verse in Deut. (16:3) which refers to *matzah* as "bread of affliction." One of the explanations of that particular term is as follows:

> Just as a poor man stokes [the oven] and his wife bakes [without delay, since they cannot afford more fuel if the oven cools], so here as well, he heats and she bakes

> [i.e., even wealthy people must bake the unleavened bread without unnecessary delay, lest it rise and become *chametz*] (BT *Pesachim* 116a).

Although the Talmud is using the phrase to describe the way *matzah* should be baked, the very use of the simile referring to a poor person emphasizes the importance of having such people in mind whenever one speaks of unleavened bread.

Finally, the Torah stresses with regard to the paschal lamb—as well as in regard to all of the other *mitzvot*—the democratic nature of Judaism, and the equal treatment of all of its adherents, when it finalizes the portion dealing with *korban pesach* by concluding that: "One law should apply to citizens [from birth] and to the stranger [convert] that lives among you" (Exod. 12:49).

MATZAH: FREEDOM TO OBSERVE THE LAWS OF THE TORAH
One cannot even begin to think about setting goals for himself unless he possesses freedom of action, which the Hebrews were deprived of in Egypt, as the Bible states:

> And the Egyptians worked the Children of Israel very hard. And they made their lives bitter with hard service, in mortar and in brick, and in all manner of service in the field; all of the service [which they demanded of them], they made them work very hard [Rashi: work which crushes the body and shatters it] (Exod. 1:13-14).

The Israelites were enslaved until they departed from Egypt, as the verse says: "And it came to pass at the end of four hundred and thirty years, on that very day [Rashi: without delay], all of the

Beha'alotcha

soldiers of the Lord [the Children of Israel] left the land of Egypt" (Exod. 12:41).[24]

In what way does *matzah* represent freedom? An answer emerges from the exegesis of the following verse: "For seven days you should eat unleavened bread—bread of affliction, because you went out of the land of Egypt in haste" (Deut. 16:3). R. Hirsch explains that affliction is the exact opposite of freedom; hence, recalling past oppression accentuates present freedom. Sforno states: "'Bread of affliction' — bread which they ate in poverty, and for which they did not have enough free time to allow the dough to rise, because of the pressure of the taskmasters." Others say the unleavened bread was given to them purposely to save on food. According to the *Chatam Sofer* (BT *Pesachim* 115b), it more readily satiates, but would not have been chosen willingly; according to Abravanel, it is harder to digest, so less is consumed. Alternatively, because it is harder to digest, the Egyptians sadistically supplied only such bread to torture the Israelites (Malbim).

Sforno comments on his own explanation:[25] the first part of the verse implies that *matzah* is eaten because it is "bread of affliction," and hence reminds every Jew of the enslavement in Egypt, but the second half of the verse implies that it is eaten as a reminder of the fact that they left Egypt in a hurry and were unable to allow enough time for the dough to rise. He answers his question as follows:

> "Because you went out of the land of Egypt in haste" — the reason to record the haste in baking the bread is that in exchange for the haste caused by oppression [during the

---

24. Rashi (based on *Seder Olam Rabbah*, ch. 3) indicates in three locations (Exod. 12:40, 6:18; Gen. 15:13) that the total number of years they were in Egypt was 210. *Siftei Chachamim* on Exod. 6:16, based on Rashi, shows that they were actually enslaved for only 116 years.

25. The question is equally valid on the explanations of R. Hirsch, Malbim, and *Chatam Sofer*.

period of enslavement], you had afterwards the haste of redemption, as it says: "and I will turn their mourning into joy" (Jer. 31:12).

Matzah is thus seen to symbolize freedom, and it is an especially strong symbol specifically because it reminds one of the earlier state of oppression.

Support for the positive symbolism of *matzah* can be found in the Talmudic treatment of the expression "bread of affliction," which in the original Hebrew is *lechem oni*. The Talmud (BT *Pesachim* 115b) suggests three possible interpretations, one of which is *lechem she-onim alav devarim harbei*, literally, "bread over which we recite [*onim*] many words." What are these words? They are the words of the Haggadah in praise of, and in thanks to, the Almighty for redeeming the Jewish nation.

The Hebrew word for "freedom" is *chofesh*, which appears in a conjugated form five times in the Pentateuch,[26] always in connection with the freeing of slaves. One would accordingly think that an appropriate description for Passover would be "Festival of Freedom" (*chofesh*), but surprisingly the only alternative name which appears in the Bible is "Festival of *Matzot*" (Exod. 23:15, 34:18; Lev. 23:6; 2 Chron. 30:13, 30:21, 35:17), and this is the form which was adopted in prayer and grace after meals (once in the *ya'aleh ve-yavo* paragraph and thrice in the *musaf amidah*[27]) and sanctification over wine (*kiddush*). Three times (Exod. 23:15, 34:18; Deut. 16:1) the Torah mentions that Pesach occurs during the (initial) month of spring, so it is perhaps not surprising that another alias for Pesach, which developed in the Middle Ages,[28] is "Festival of Spring" (*Chag ha-Aviv*).

---

26. Exod. 21:5; Lev. 19:20 (twice); Deut. 15:12, 15:13.
27. In the following paragraphs: *va-titen lanu, ve-et musaf,* and *u-mipnei chata'einu*.
28. Shimon b. Tzemach Duran, *She'elot u-Teshuvot* 2:250; Shabtai b. Yosef Bass, *Siftei Chachamim,* Exod. 23:17.

Beha'alotcha

Interestingly, the Mishnah (*Pesachim* 10:5)[29] uses a different word for "freedom," when it states that at the Seder, the Jew thanks God for delivering him from "bondage to freedom [*cherut*]." One may ask, why is this Hebrew word for "freedom," rather than the Biblical word *chofesh*, utilized in the prayer service, appearing as part of the descriptive phrase which follows the reference to Passover as the "Festival of *Matzot*."

An Aramaicized derivative of *cherut* (freedom) is *ben chorin*, "a free person," and this usage appears at the beginning of the Passover Haggadah, where the reader is told (in the Aramaic vernacular): "*Hashata avdei, le-shana ha-ba'ah bnei chorin*" ("This year [we are still] slaves, next year [may we be] free men."). But isn't the Haggadah a narrative of gratitude expressed by the Jews upon their redemption from slavery?

The epithet *ben chorin* also appears in a Mishnah, which states: "No-one is free other than he who occupies himself with the study of Torah" (*Avot* 6:2). The obvious question is that burdening oneself with a constant regimen of Torah study would seem to resemble slavery more than freedom, so in what sense is such a person called free?

The first point which must be clarified is that the Mishnah is not advocating Torah study bereft of performing good deeds and perfecting one's positive traits, as is clear from the immediately preceding Mishnah:

> R. Meir said: He who occupies himself with the study of Torah for its own sake [i.e., not for personal aggrandizement] merits many things... *he delights mankind*. It [the Torah] clothes him with humility and

---

29. In parallel in the Jerusalem Talmud, e.g. *Pesachim* 10:4, and subsequently the various Midrashim, e.g., *Tanchuma Noach* 13 and *Sechel Tov, Bo* 12:2.

reverence, and prepares him to be a righteous, pious, honest, and loyal person.... *[People] benefit from his counsel and wisdom, understanding and strength.... He becomes modest, patient, and forgiving of insult* (Avot 6:1).

Clearly, the definition of Torah study is much broader than mere book study. It involves rigorous character development and intensified social integration.

This approach is evident in some of the other *Mishnayot* in *Avot*, such as:

1. Shammai said: "... say a little and do a lot" (*Avot* 1:15). The classic example of such behavior is that of Abraham, who told his guests: "I will fetch a morsel of bread" (Gen. 18:5), when in fact he told Sarah to prepare cakes while he brought butter, milk, and meat.
2. "Learning is not the most important thing, but rather doing" (*Avot* 1:17). When the nation found itself hemmed in by the sea in front and the Egyptian army behind, God told Moses: "Why are you crying [praying] to Me? Speak to the Children of Israel and let them travel [forward]" (Exod. 14:15).

It is now possible to explain in what sense constant Torah involvement enables a person to be free. The Talmud (BT *Kiddushin* 30b) states:

> My children! I created the evil inclination and I created the Torah as its antidote; if you occupy yourselves with the Torah [i.e., with Torah-sanctioned behavior], you will not be delivered into his hand, for it says [regarding Cain]: "If you improve yourself, you will overcome [your evil inclination]" (Gen. 4:7). But if you do not occupy

Beha'alotcha

yourselves with the Torah, you will be delivered into its hand, for it says: "sin crouches at the door" (ibid.). Furthermore, it [the evil inclination] is completely preoccupied with you [to make you sin], for it says: "and to mislead you is its longing" (ibid.). [But] if you wish, you can rule over it, for it says: "you may rule over it" (ibid.).

The point being made is that it is possible to be enslaved to Pharaoh, as were the Israelites in Egypt. It is also possible to be redeemed from slavery and yet remain enslaved to one's own nefarious desires, oblivious to the suffering of one's fellow men, and disinterested in easing the burden of mankind. King David compared being controlled by one's evil inclination to being imprisoned, when he begged of the Lord: "Free my soul from prison, so that I may express thanks to Your [holy] name" (Ps. 142:8). R. Hirsch writes:

> Even as the Torah ennobles us, so a truly devoted study of it also makes us free—free from error, free from the temptations of physical lusts and desires, and free from the crushing and degrading power of the multitude of worries and troubles of daily living.

In short, if *chofesh* refers to "freedom," it is only physical freedom, not the spiritual autonomy connoted by *cherut*. It is now clear why only the latter noun made its way into the holiday prayers, and why the Haggadah notes, when it says that only next year will we be free men, that we have not completely achieved the desired level of *cherut* which results from being totally immersed in the Torah way of life.

The Mishnah (BT *Pesachim* 116a) discusses the structure of the Haggadah, which starts with a number of questions, in answer to which the story of the exodus is related. According to the Mishnah: "He starts with shameful events and ends with praiseworthy events." On that phrase, the Talmud asks: "What are these shameful events?" and answers: "Rav said, he starts as follows: 'Originally our fathers were idol-worshippers,' and Shmuel said: 'We were slaves.'"

Based on the previous discussion, one might say that Rav suggests that the participants thank God immediately for their spiritual redemption (*cherut*), while Shmuel takes a more gradual approach, starting with physical redemption (*chofesh*) by mentioning the enslavement of the Hebrews, and only later moving on to Torah study and prayer (as described in the story of R. Elazar b. Azariah, which follows).

At a much later stage, the same distinction was perhaps alluded to by the liberal philosopher Sir Isaiah Berlin in an inaugural lecture at the University of Oxford, where he spoke of negative and positive liberty.[30] Negative liberty was defined as the absence of constraint, similar to *chofesh*, while positive liberty demanded, in addition to freedom from constraint, that one be embedded in a community which has a positive outlook concerning the purpose and goal of creation in general, and humanity in particular (*cherut*).

Maror: Motivation to Observe the Laws of the Torah

The third element needed to ensure proper observance of the *mitzvot* is motivation. Obviously, one must know their details in order to fulfill them, and must have the freedom to do so, but he must also have the will to do so.

In the Covenant of the Parts, God tells Abraham: "You should know that your descendants will be strangers in a land that is not theirs, and they will be enslaved and oppressed for 400 years" (Gen. 15:13). Rashi points out that although the verse seems to say that the Jews were in Egypt for 400 years, this is impossible, since the years of Kohath (130), Amram (137), and Moses (80)—

---

30. Isaiah Berlin, *Liberty* (2002).

Beha'alotcha

many of which overlapped—come to a total of only 347. Ramban helps solve the problem by explaining that the phrases are out of order, and the verse should be understood as follows: "You should know that your descendants will be strangers in a land that is not theirs [not necessarily Egypt] for 400 years and will be enslaved and persecuted."

Rashi also notes that the verse does not mention Egypt, but "a land that is not theirs." The reference is actually to the sojourning of Abraham after Isaac's birth in the land of the Philistines (Gen. 21:34), of Isaac in Canaan (Gen.26:3), of Jacob in the land of Ham (Ps. 105:23), and of his sons in Egypt (Gen. 47:4), and the 400 years start from the birth of Isaac, since Abraham left his home soon after.

In fact, the actual length of enslavement was only 116 years.[31] The 400 years may thus be divided into two segments: 284 years of exile and 116 years of slavery. This leads to three questions:

1. What did the Jews do to deserve such a long period of exile?
2. What did the Jews do to deserve such a long period of slavery (even 116 years is quite long)?
3. Why does the verse combine the two and speak of 400 years of affliction?

Before answering these questions, it should be recalled that, according to the Midrash (*Gen. Rabbah* 1:4), six entities existed in fact or potential before the creation of the world, two of them being the Nation of Israel and the Torah. This implies that the world was created in order for Israel to obey God's dictates as expressed in the Torah, which was to be accomplished in the Land of Israel (Lev. 20:24, 25:38). However, in order to fulfill the laws of the Torah, one must be on a high enough level to exercise sufficient self-control to

---

31. See Abba Engelberg, *The Ethics of Exodus* (2014), p. 45.

obey them, a level that the emerging tribes had not yet achieved. Furthermore, even after their arrival, if the nation did not meet the required standard, they would be spewed forth from their own land (Lev. 18: 28).

In answer to the first two questions, the periods of exile and slavery were necessary because the Jews were not yet good enough, and the Gentiles were not yet bad enough.

Starting with the Jews, it will be noted that already at the time of the patriarchs, the extended family exhibited serious character flaws, which allowed such atrocities as the destruction of Shechem (Gen. 34; Ramban, 34:13, 49:5) and the selling of Joseph (Gen. 37:12-36; *Midrash Mishlei* [Buber] 1). However, as long as the righteous forefathers were alive, God desisted from exacting serious punishment and only exiled them from their land, as Sforno explains:

> It [slavery] did not happen to them in the generations of the righteous people, so that all of the time that one of the tribal patriarchs was alive, the bondage did not start, but it transpired when they corrupted their ways (Sforno, Gen. 15:13).

How did Sforno know that this was in fact the case? He based himself on the following verse from Ezekiel, in which the prophet speaks of Israel's wickedness in Egypt and how God would accordingly punish them in Egypt proper:

> And they rebelled against Me and did not want to hearken to Me; [every] man did not cast away the detestable things [which they saw with] their eyes [i.e., icons], neither did they forsake the idols of Egypt. And I decided to pour out My fury on them, to spend My anger on them *in the midst of the land of Egypt* (Ezek. 20:8).

Beha'alotcha

Paganism, by allowing for more than one supernatural force in the world, leads to immorality. A multiplicity of gods does not transmit a code of behavior to human beings, for each god can contradict the opinion of any other god. In addition, they do not serve as role models, because they themselves are embroiled in arguments with each other and they do not behave in a moral fashion. They actually exhibit the traits of hedonism and selfishness, with no consideration for others.[32]

On the other hand, the Torah and its commandments can endure and flourish only if the belief in the oneness and uniqueness of God is strong enough for Israel to loyally adhere to His code of behavior, and not to that of any other god. The code that God wants Israel to fulfill is one that engenders love among brothers, as Rambam[33] writes: "Great is peace, since the entire Torah was given to make peace in the world, as it says: 'Her ways are ways of pleasantness, and all her paths are peace' (Prov. 3:17)."

The sin of Israel in Egypt was idol worship, but more importantly what flowed from it, namely hedonism, selfishness, narcissism, and egotism. Their punishment—enslavement—was meant to teach them humility, devotion, self-sacrifice, magnanimity, and, most importantly, empathy with the downtrodden. The people needed these character traits in order to be able to accept upon themselves the restraints which the Torah would impose, to develop a long-range vision, and to become a light unto the nations, a function which could only be achieved in the Land of Israel.

During the years of exile and slavery, a second process which involved the non-Jewish inhabitants of Israel was taking place. Indeed, the Bible states: "And in the fourth generation [Rashi: Judah entered Egypt and his great-grandson Caleb was freed] they will come back here [to the Land of Israel], *for the iniquity of the*

---

32. See Abba Engelberg, *The Ethics of Exodus* (2014), pp. 279-280.
33. *Hilchot Megillah ve-Chanukah* 4:14.

The Ethics of Numbers

Amorite is not yet full" (Gen. 15:15). In other words, it is apparently essential for the Children of Israel to dwell in the Land of Israel. On the other hand, this would require expelling its inhabitants, the Amorites. Rashi explains:

> The Almighty does not exact punishment from any nation until its measure [of sins] is full, as it says: "When its measure is full [here Isaiah is referring to the Northern Kingdom of Israel], it will be punished by exile" (Isa. 27:8).

God gives everyone freedom of choice, whether Jew or Gentile. Since the Amorites had sinned, but not to the degree which would justify exile, their community was permitted to continue to function, and the possibility of returning to the right path was still available. Eventually, however (specifically after four generations), their society became irretrievably corrupt, and needed to be destroyed, much like the antediluvian civilization, and that was when God (not co-incidentally) chose to redeem the Israelites from bondage.

As for the third question, the connection between exile and enslavement is that complete redemption would occur only with the establishment of a territorial entity enabling Israel to serve as a paradigm for the rest of mankind. For that reason, exile and slavery were grouped together as a 400-year preparatory period, since only then would the sins of the Canaanites be sufficient to be punishable by their total destruction, thus freeing the land for settlement by the Israelites. Only then could the fledgling nation fulfill its mission to serve as "a light unto the nations" (Isa. 49:6).

The suffering which led to the development of positive traits, to the motivation to be good, and to feelings of mercy for the unfortunate is recalled by the bitterness of the *maror*.

There is an additional element which stimulates one to behave properly, and this is the concept of reward and punishment. R.

Beha'alotcha

Yosef Albo includes this among the three basic principles of Judaism.[34] Although one is urged to do good for its own sake (*Avot* 1:3), nevertheless it is encouraging to know that the results of idealistic action will eventually be taken into account, and this knowledge adds to one's motivation to obey the law. This idea is emphasized by the words of the previously quoted verse: "*for the iniquity of the Amorite is not yet full*," from which one logically deduces that God is keeping track of their deeds, in this case to eventually exact punishment, but clearly to endow reward as well when merited.

Miriam's Leprosy

The story of Miriam's attack of leprosy is described in ch. 12 of *Beha'alotcha*. To appreciate this episode more thoroughly, it is helpful to be familiar with the different views with respect to Zipporah, the wife of Moses (see **Appendix I - Zipporah**):

> **1** And Miriam and Aaron *spoke against Moses* because of the Cushite woman whom he had married; for he had married a Cushite woman. **2** And they said: "Did the Lord indeed speak only with Moses? Did He not speak with us as well?" And the Lord heard [their conversation]. **3** Now the man Moses was very humble, more so than any man on the face of the earth. **4** And the Lord spoke unexpectedly to Moses, and to Aaron, and to Miriam, [saying]: "Go out, the three of you, [Ibn Ezra: from your respective tents] to the Tent of Meeting." And the three went out. **5** And the Lord came down in a pillar of cloud, and stood at the door of the Tent, and called Aaron and Miriam; and they both came forth. **6** And He said: "Please hear My words: if there

---
34. *Sefer ha-Ikkarim*, Introduction to the First Article.

is a prophet among you, [I,] the Lord, make Myself known to him in a vision, I speak with him in a dream. **7** [It is] not so [with] My servant Moses; he is trusted in all My house; **8** with him I speak mouth to mouth, clearly and not in riddles; and he sees the likeness of the Lord; why were you not afraid to speak against My servant Moses?" **9** And the Lord was angry at them, and He departed. **10** And when the cloud departed from over the Tent, behold Miriam was leprous, as white as snow; and Aaron turned toward Miriam and, behold, she was leprous.

From the Biblical account, it is clear that Miriam and Aaron sinned, as implied by the use of the words "spoke against Moses" in v. 1, and the more explicit message that their behavior angered God in v. 9. In addition, the word for talking used in v. 1 is "spoke." The Midrash (*Sifrei Beha'alotcha* 99) points out that conjugations of the word "speak" always indicate a harsh tone, while a milder tone is denoted by conjugations of the word "say." Rashi (12:1) notes that in v. 6, where God rebukes the pair, He does so gently and politely, using a form of the word "say," and also adding the courtesy "please."

But what was their sin? Two approaches are available: that of Rashbam, who generally adheres to the literal meaning of the text, and that of his grandfather Rashi, who tends toward the Midrashic narrative.

Rashbam (Num. 12:1) understands that Moses took a second wife, from Cush, as opposed to Zipporah, his first wife, who was from Midian. After all, if the reference is to the latter, why is she suddenly being slandered at this point, many years—and two children—after her marriage to Moses? The verse does not mention any negative trait or action on her part, only her existence

Beha'alotcha

as the wife of Moses. It is also clear why the phrase referring to the Cushite woman is repeated—the first time to note that she was being slandered and the second time to inform us that Moses had recently taken her as a second wife, since until now only one wife has been mentioned.

According to Rashbam, their criticism of Moses was that by taking a second wife, he was being inconsiderate of Zipporah, who had until now been Moses' only spouse, not to mention his only intimate. She was thus being hurt on both a practical and emotional level.

However, God deemed the approach of Miriam and Aaron sinful for a number of reasons. First, if they felt Moses was behaving improperly, they should have confronted him directly. Until they discussed it with him, they should have given him the benefit of the doubt, since even from their point of view, what he did was not a sin, just perhaps not in good taste.

However, there is one problem facing Rashbam, and that is the second verse, in which Aaron and Miriam stress that they are just as worthy as Moses, the implication being that it is unfair that he alone is considered the leader of the people and the recipient of all the honor and glory. Indeed, the Bible (Exod. 15:20) and the Talmud (BT *Megillah* 14a) classify Miriam as a prophetess, while the Midrash (*Exod. Rabbah* 3:16) speaks of Aaron as functioning as a prophet for the Hebrews in Egypt for eighty years prior to the return of Moses.

According to Rashbam, then, the second verse contains a completely different, and far more acrimonious, complaint than the first. Furthermore, when the Lord intervenes, He totally neglects the first grievance and refers only to the second. A better explanation would unite both verses into a single objection to which God responds.

The Ethics of Numbers

The first one to attempt combining the first two verses was Onkelos, who translated the first verse as follows:

> And Miriam and Aaron spoke about Moses on the subject of the beautiful woman whom he had married, for the beautiful woman that he had married *he distanced* [from himself, i.e., he separated from].

What motivated Onkelos to add the reference to Moses separating from Zipporah? He might have had the same question which bothered Rashbam. If the Cushite is Zipporah, why does the verse in Numbers mention that Moses married her at this stage, when that happened long ago? Instead of answering that the Cushite was a different wife, however, he answers that although formulated in terms of marriage, the verse actually refers to divorce.

It is now possible to see how the first and second verses combine to present an overall description of the siblings' objection. They complained out of concern for the well-being of Zipporah, from whom Moses had separated for unjustifiable reasons (in their eyes). The first verse informs the reader that they were separated, and the second points out that in the view of Miriam and Aaron, transmitting the word of God is not an adequate reason for divorce, being that they too served in the same capacity and yet were able to maintain routine family life.

The continuation of the portion fits in well now. God replies to them by explaining that the communication between Himself and Moses is continuous, sudden, and on a higher plane than with other prophets, and hence a higher degree of purity is required. Nevertheless, Moses, as any Jew, was obligated to marry and create a family. The Midrash (*Tanchuma Tzav* 13, cited by Rashi on v. 4) notes that God purposely appeared to them without warning (in v.

Beha'alotcha

4)—as He was wont to do with Moses, and when they were impure as a result of marital relations, to emphasize the need for Moses to always be in a state of purity.

There is still one verse which seems irrelevant, and that is v. 3, which describes Moses' extraordinary humility. R. Shlomo Levenstein (*U-Matok mi-Or*, Num., p. 382) gives an answer based on a Talmudic text (BT *Shabbat* 87a), which says that there were three cases where Moses acted of his own volition, one of them being his decision to separate from his wife. At the time of the giving of the Torah, the nation was told: "Do not come near a woman" (Exod. 19:15), from which Moses derived *a fortiori* that if it was required of the Israelites—to whom God spoke for such a short period of time—how much more so would this be required of he himself, to whom God spoke frequently and without advance notice. Miriam and Aaron might have refuted Moses' reasoning by saying that such abstinence may have been necessary for the simple people, but Moses was on such a high level that a sexual relationship would not diminish from his state of holiness. The text therefore notes that Moses was so humble that he did not consider himself spiritually superior to others, and that is why he felt it was necessary to separate from Zipporah.

Another possible question is: how did Miriam in fact know that Moses and Zipporah were separated? The Midrashic literature has numerous answers to this question.[35] The following teaching, adopted by Rashi (Num. 12:1), appears in both *Sifrei* and *Tanchuma* (*Tzav* 13):

> R. Natan says: Miriam was beside Zipporah when it was said [to Moses]: "Eldad and Meidad are prophesying in the camp" (11:27). When Zipporah heard this, she exclaimed:

---
35. *Tanchuma Tzav* 13; *Sifrei Beha'alotcha* 99; *Sifrei Zuta* 12:1.

The Ethics of Numbers

"Woe to the wives of these [Rashi (12:1): if they are to be prophets, for they will separate from their wives just as my husband has separated from me]." It is from this that Miriam knew [about it], and she told her brother, and both of them spoke against him (*Sifrei Beha'alotcha* 99).

Rashi chose this anecdote rather than other alternatives, since Miriam's protest in ch. 12 follows immediately upon the story of Eldad and Meidad at the end of ch. 11. This same Midrash notes that Miriam initiated the complaint, as is clear from the fact that it was she who had gleaned the information from Zipporah, and that explains why her name is mentioned first in v. 1. Being the initiator, as well as the fact that she was the older sibling (according to most viewpoints), explains why she was punished more than Aaron.

There is only one difficulty with the view of Onkelos, and it has to do with the lack of transparency, as well as the verbosity, of v. 1. First, he claimed that the purpose of the verse is to inform the reader that Moses and Zipporah are separated, but this particular fact is omitted from the verse. Second, the verse mentions twice that Zipporah is a Cushite, which Onkelos understands to mean that she was beautiful. This remark, however, has no direct relevance to the narrative at hand, and its overall importance is questionable. The Midrash (ibid.) attempts an answer by saying that the first mention refers to her looks and the second to her deeds. But why is it mentioned at all? In order to answer this question, Ibn Ezra (Num. 12:1) adopts the separation aspect introduced by Onkelos but rejects his translation of "Cushite" as beautiful, taking it to mean exactly the opposite—ugly. According to Ibn Ezra, Miriam and Aaron are saying that Moses ended his physical relationship with Zipporah because of her bad looks. If Moses were to justify his separation based on his prophetic ability, they could respond that they too were prophets but did not separate from their spouses

Beha'alotcha

(v. 2). God then answers that they may have the same vocation, but they are not in the same league.

Summary

This chapter focuses on the major aspects of Judaism symbolized by the paschal lamb, indicated by the severe punishment of excision meted out to one who neglects his obligation to bring this sacrifice on Passover, a penalty whose source is found in the portion of *Beha'alotcha*. Circumcision, the only other positive commandment punishable by excision, conveys the message that the purpose of man's creation is *tikkun olam*—improving the quality of life in this world—a message also taught by the paschal lamb. The laws associated with the paschal lamb—the earliest Biblical legislation—introduce the Jewish legal code by including a number of commands both of a ritual and social nature. The *matzah*, with which the sacrifice must be eaten, represents the prerequisite to fulfilling God's commands, namely the sensation of physical and spiritual freedom on the part of every Israelite. Finally, the bitter herbs—which must also accompany the sacrificial meat—underline the source of a Jew's motivation to accept upon himself the yolk of fulfilling the Torah's commands.

The end of the portion, which discusses the sin of Miriam, stresses the consequences of one of the most serious of the interpersonal commands, the prohibition to slander. Not only is transgressing this command an evil act on its own, but doing so eases the path to the performance of numerous other grave offenses, as noted in my commentary on the portion of *Meztora* in Leviticus where the nature of slander is examined more thoroughly.[36]

---

36. Abba Engelberg, *The Ethics of Leviticus*, pp.125-156.

Shlach

The most prominent subject in the portion of *Shlach* is the saga of the twelve spies, who were sent to investigate the Land of Israel shortly before the nation was scheduled to enter the land. Unfortunately, things did not work out as planned, and instead of spending a little over a year in the desert, the nation wandered for forty years before finally arriving at their destination. In the Torah text, the narrative of the spies is followed by laws concerning meal offerings and libations, and the dough offering given to a priest, subjects which might more appropriately be located in Leviticus. Although these laws were to take effect only after arriving in Israel, they may have been purposely included after the spying incident to reassure the community that although there would be a delay, and many individuals would not live to set foot in the Land of Israel, the overall design was intact and their descendants would eventually settle there (Rashi, Num. 15:2).

Towards the end of the portion, certain instances of inadvertent idol worship are discussed, the case of the Sabbath-desecrating wood gatherer is presented, and the laws of *tzitzit* (ritual fringes) are listed. Rashi explains that each of these is a very central, significant mitzvah, namely abstaining from idol worship, properly observing the Sabbath, and wearing *tzitzit*, because when one notices them, they remind him of all the 613 Biblical commands. In Rashi's words (Num. 15:41):

Shlach

> From the work of R. Moshe ha-Darshan I copied [the following]: Why is the section speaking of the wood gatherer juxtaposed with the section dealing with idolatry? In order to tell you that whoever desecrates the Sabbath it is as if he worshipped idols, for it [the law of the Sabbath] also is alone of equal importance to the entire sum of the commandments [just as is refraining from idol worship, see Rashi on 15:22].... And the section dealing with *tzitzit* is for the same reason juxtaposed with these two sections, because it, too, is of equal importance to the entire sum of the commandments, for it says: "[That you may remember] and do all of My commandments" (Num. 15:40).

In this chapter, the portion of the spies will be examined in detail, while the story of the wood gatherer, which posed certain questions that Moses was unable to answer, will be studied in the context of the relationship between the written and oral laws.

THE STORY OF THE SPIES: THE BASICS

One of the most serious sins in the Torah is that of *lashon ha-ra* (literally, "the evil tongue"), which is listed in the portion of *Kedoshim* (Lev. 19:16).[37] To stress its severity and to elucidate its rules and restrictions, R. Israel Meir Kagan wrote an entire book, which became the source of his moniker, the *Chafeitz Chaim*. A primary case study is presented in the portion of *Shlach* in connection with the story of the spies, who were sent to search out the land and returned with a negative report, and concerning which the Mishnah states: "We find that the judgment against our fathers in the wilderness was sealed only because of their evil tongue" (*Arachin* 3:5).

---

37. See Abba Engelberg, *The Ethics of Leviticus* (2019), pp. 140-154.

The Ethics of Numbers

The Biblical Text

According to Numbers 13, the spies were presented with the following mission:

> **18** And (A) see the land, what it is; and (B) the people that dwell there, are they strong or weak, are they few or many; **19** and (A) what is [the type of] the land they dwell in, is it good or bad; and (C) what is [the type of] the cities that they dwell in, are they in open places or in strongholds; **20** and (A) what is [the type of] the land, is it fat or lean, (D) is there a tree there or not. And you should be strong, and (E) you should take of the fruit of the land.

In other words, they were assigned five tasks: The first four were to answer questions about (A) the land, (B) the people, (C) the cities, and (D) the trees. The fifth was (E) to bring back specimens of the land's produce.

The results of their mission are described as follows:

> **26** ... they made their report to them and to the whole community, and (D, E) they showed them the fruit of the land. **27** And they told him: we came to the land where you sent us, and indeed (A) it flows with milk and honey, and this is its fruit. **28** However [in Hebrew, *efes*], (B) the people that dwell in the land are fierce, and (C) the cities are fortified and very large; moreover, (B) we saw the descendants of the giant there.... **30** And Caleb hushed the people before Moses and said, "Let us verily go up and possess it, for we can surely overcome it." **31** But the men that went up with him said: (F) "We cannot attack that nation, for it is stronger than we [are]."

Shlach

WHAT WAS THE SIN OF THE SPIES? — RAMBAN

Ramban (Num. 13:27-31) notes that they loyally fulfilled their mission, answering all of the questions truthfully. If so, what was their sin? He explains:

> Because he commanded them to see if it is fat or lean, they answered him that (A) it is fat and also flowing with milk and honey, and regarding his question is there a tree there or not, they answered him (D, E) this is its fruit, because so he commanded them to show him [by saying you should take of the fruit of the land]. And behold regarding all this they told the truth and replied as they were commanded and they had to say that (B) the nation that dwells on it is strong and (C) the cities are fortified, because they had to reply truthfully to their dispatcher, for so he commanded them [when he said]: are they strong or weak, are they in open places or in strongholds. *But their wickedness is in the word efes* ["however"], *which indicates something negative, removed from a person's ability, which is impossible in any case.*

Ramban says that in spite of telling the truth, they sinned by saying the word *efes* (however, v. 28). In what sense does saying *efes* constitute saying *lashon ha-ra*? To answer that one must understand the essence of *lashon ha-ra*. The tale-bearer tells the truth about a specific item. If his intention were to confine himself to that item exclusively, it would be perfectly legitimate to pass on such information, even if it is negative. For example, if someone is looking for a good doctor, it would be perfectly acceptable to express one's true opinion, and totally improper to praise a poor doctor, which would mislead the questioner. By doing so, one would surely transgress the prohibition of "you should not… place a stumbling-block before the blind" (Lev. 19:14). The problem arises when the information being passed on is not directly relevant, and its only purpose is to create an overall aversion. This is completely unfair, since nobody is perfect, especially the tale-bearer, and the only result of such speech is to create social friction, while the Torah strives for social harmony.

In the case of the spies, the word *efes*, "however," implies that it would be impossible for the Israelites to overcome a strong enemy—a judgment the spies were not requested to make. The spies were only asked to answer four specific questions and to perform one specific act.

What Was the Sin of the Spies? — *Akeidat Yitzchak*

In the words of *Akeidat Yitzchak* (*Sha'ar* 77), they were sent as researchers to retrieve facts, not as consultants to make decisions. Note that the index (F) in the report of the spies has no parallel in their original assignment. By supplying extraneous information in the form of their unsolicited opinion, they created a negative attitude, which could only have harmful repercussions with respect to the task at hand.

The conclusions of Ramban and *Akeidat Yitzchak* boil down to the same thing. The only difference is that Ramban feels that they sinned from the time that they said *efes* (however), which cast aspersions on the land, while *Akeidat Yitzchak* says that the sin occurred only in v. 31, when, in response to Caleb's assurances, the spies explicitly expressed a contradictory viewpoint.

Was It Necessary to Send Spies?

God had already informed the Israelites that He was bringing them "to a good and spacious land, a land flowing with milk and

Shlach

honey" (Exod. 3:8).[38] The question that arises is: if the decision to capture the land had already been made, why did Moses send the spies in the first place?

THE TALMUD'S ANSWER

According to the Midrash and Talmud, God did not command Moses to do so. With respect to the verse: "Send for yourself men to scout the land of Canaan, which I am giving to the Israelite people" (Num. 13:2), the Talmud states:

> Reish Lakish said: ["*Send for yourself*" means] at your own discretion [and not as a Divine command] because does anybody choose a bad portion for himself? [Rashi: Would God have commanded them to engage in an activity that in the end would lead them to stumble (by doubting God's ability to overcome their enemies)?] And that is [the meaning of] what is written [when Moses retold the story in the book of Deuteronomy]: "And it was good in my eyes" (Deut. 1:23). Reish Lakish said: in my eyes, but not in the eyes of the Omnipresent (BT *Sotah* 34b).

The Talmud does not say that God prohibited the sending of spies, because He allows freedom of choice in accordance with the adage: "On the road that a man is resolved to go, he is allowed to go" (BT *Makkot* 10b). Rather, it says that God would not have initiated such an idea, because He knew where it would lead, and encouraging such a move would have given them a push in the wrong direction, and that would also be unfair.

---

38. Cited by *Tanchuma Shlach* 5. Rashi (Num. 13:2) cites Exod. 3:17, possibly because the latter was said directly to Israel, while Exod. 3:8 is drawn from a conversation between God and Moses, which the Israelites were not privy to.

The Ethics of Numbers

Whose idea what is to send the spies? Scripture makes it quite clear that it was the nation that initiated the request, as the verse states: "Then all of you came near to me and said: 'Let us send men ahead to reconnoiter the land for us and bring back word on the route we will follow and the cities we will come to.' And I approved of the plan" (Deut. 1:22). There is no hint here of ill intentions. On the contrary, it sounds like the Israelites are eager to get going and wish to avidly participate in the planning process. The Talmud (BT *Sotah* 34b), however, suggests otherwise:

> R. Hiyya b. Abba said: The spies' only intention was to shame the Land of Israel. It is written here: to reconnoiter [*ve-yachperu*] the land for us, and it is written there: "Then the moon will be embarrassed [*ve-chafrah*] and the sun will be ashamed" (Isa. 24:23).

According to R. Hiyya, the spies had decided early on to do their best to foil the entire project, since there was apparently no need to check out the land, because God had already informed them of its superb quality and desirability. The Israelites did not even need to determine the exact route on their own, being that the Ark preceded them by a distance of a three-day journey (Num. 10:33), and closer to their convoy they were led by a cloud during the day and a pillar of fire by night (Exod. 13:21).

Another indication that the spies had ill intent is the order in which they answered the questions that Moses had posed. Answering questions in the order that they are asked is considered to be one of the signs of a wise person (*Avot* 5:7), and Rashi notes this behavior in several Biblical sources (e.g., Gen. 31:31, Exod. 3:12). Yet, as noted above, the questions were answered in the following order: D, E, A, B, C, B (with question B answered twice). Why was the order changed? Clearly, the spies wished to arrive

Shlach

at a negative conclusion. In order for their opinion to be taken seriously, it was necessary to be ostensibly objective, which could only be affected by starting out on a positive note and moving on to the negative. They therefore started off by displaying the fruit of the land to indicate that the land was indeed lush, and only afterwards revealed their fear of being unequal to the task of overcoming the inhabitants of the land.

Abravanel's Answer

Abravanel (Num. 13:1) is in complete agreement with the assumption that the entire mission was redundant and even problematic. As noted, God had assured the Israelites that the land was luxuriant and fertile, and there was no need to ascertain directions or enemy fortifications, since the cloud of glory and pillar of fire would lead them in the most efficient way to the enemy's most vulnerable spots. According to Abravanel, the spies were sent as the result of a misunderstanding. When Moses retold the nation's immediate history, he recalled making the following statements just before their request to send spies:

> **20** And I said to you, "You have come to the hill country of the Amorites, which the Lord our God is giving to us. **21** See, the Lord your God has placed the land before you. *Go up, take possession*, as the Lord, the God of your fathers, has spoken to you. Do not fear and do not be dismayed." **22** And all of you approached me and said, "*Let us send men ahead to reconnoiter the land for us* and bring us back word by which route we must go up, and to which cities we will come" (Deut. 1).

Abravanel explains that the people mistakenly thought that by saying "Go up, take possession," Moses meant by natural means, without the help of the cloud and the fire. That is why, in v. 22, they asked Moses for permission to send spies by saying, "Let us send men ahead to reconnoiter the land for us." They did not ask Moses to undertake the task, just to approve it, since they thought that the entire project had been transferred to them, and that the spies would report back to them and not to Moses.

At this point, if God prohibited sending the spies, the people would suspect that the land was not satisfactory. On the other hand, if He allowed the people to assume the leadership and neutralize Moses, this would create a power vacuum resulting in pandemonium. God's solution was not to oppose the mission, but to insist that the managing officer be Moses and not the nation itself. By doing so, Moses' leadership was reinforced, and the chance that the spies would present an unbiased report more in keeping with God's intentions was improved. It is now clear why the portion opens with the words "send for yourself men," since it was very important to stress that the entire operation was under the control of Moses.

In spite of his detailed explanation of the nation's mistaken understanding of Moses' words "go up, take possession," Abravanel apparently reconsiders, and concludes that the people really knew perfectly well what God's intentions were, and the supposed misunderstanding was an excuse rather than a real misapprehension. Accordingly, when they spoke of their desire "to reconnoiter the land for us and bring back word on the route we will follow and the cities we will come to," this was just a cover-up for their real intention to see if the land was as good as God had promised and vulnerable by natural means.

Ramban's Answer

It will be recalled that Moses had approved the spying mission. Ramban is bothered by the fact that if Israel was being criticized for sending spies, since God had already told them the land was good,

Shlach

why was Moses any more innocent than the rest of the nation? As far as the spies scaring the nation by saying that the enemies' cities are "fortified and very large" (13:28), Moses' words at a later stage would certainly have inspired even more fear in their grandchildren, who had not yet entered the Holy Land, when he said:

> You are about to cross the Jordan to go in and dispossess nations more populous and mightier than you; great cities fortified up to heaven; people great and tall, the Anakites, of whom you have knowledge, for you have heard it said: "Who can stand up to the children of Anak" (Deut. 9:1-2).

Ramban answers that although God had ensured them that the land was good, and had until that point directed them by means of the Ark and the cloud of glory, nevertheless the nation did not want to be totally dependent on God's supernatural intervention. Sending spies was a fully accepted preliminary act to waging war. Moses himself did so when conquering the Amorites (Num. 21:32), and Joshua did so before attacking Jericho (Josh. 2:1). Determining whether the people are strong would tell them how alert they must be and how much to arm themselves. Checking where enemy fortifications are located would enable them to determine whether to build ramparts and siege walls, or to seek out an exposed direction. Furthermore, rough terrain is harder to conquer, so maybe they would avoid such areas initially. It is also possible that Moses wanted them specifically to investigate the quality of the land even though he knew it was "good and spacious" (Exod. 3:8). In this way, the spies—and later the nation—would rejoice and renew their strength to go up to the Land of Israel in good spirits, and for that reason he also asked them to bring back fruit of the land, so that the entire nation could confirm the positive report of the spies. For all these reasons, Moses approved

The Ethics of Numbers

of the plan. By doing so, he also would have realized that he was training them to conduct a proper military campaign, which they would be required to do upon their arrival in the land, when it was suspected that there would be a cessation of the age of miracles. In short, Ramban justifies the necessity of the mission, but as previously indicated, deplores the adverse attitude of the spies and eventually the nation.

Compounding the Sin: Eventually They Lied

Even though initially the report of the spies was accurate, the tone was tainted. After Caleb stated that in spite of the difficulties, they would be able to overcome their enemies (13:30), the spies apparently panicked and expressed their unsolicited negative opinion as to the likelihood of success after seeing the inhabitants and cities, which was designated by *Akeidat Yitzchak* as their major sin. At this point, according to Ramban, they also told their first outright lies when they said that the land "devours its inhabitants" (13:32) and that they had seen *nephilim* (13:33), who were actually no longer extant, and the text rightly terms these statements as calumnies (*dibbat ha-aretz* 13:32).

Summary

Three approaches to the evolution of the sin in the story of the spies have been presented. The Talmudic approach (and the final view of Abravanel) is that the nation did not trust God's previous promises that the Land of Israel was a good land and that He would enable them to conquer it. God knew that the mission would lead to rebellion, but Moses did not, and so allowed it in a fatherly manner even if he thought it was unnecessary, so as not to be accused of being a dictator. Abravanel in his initial comments suggests that the nation misunderstood Moses and thought that God's intervention was

Shlach

about to cease and they would have to resort to natural means. God realized that this was not the intention of Moses, but He did not want Moses' leadership to dissipate, so He told Moses to assume control. Finally, Ramban believes that the mission was indeed justified, and consequently approved by Moses, because God's intervention would indeed cease upon the nation's crossing of the Jordan, and it was desirable that they become experienced in espionage.

WHY DID THE SPIES, AND THEN THE NATION, SIN?

A number of options have been offered regarding the sin of the spies. Did they lie? Was their negative tone of voice the incriminating factor? Did they present the evidence in a manner which was more likely to lead to rebellion? Or did they express their personal opinions, and very forcefully at that, when they had only been authorized to gather data? No matter which of these offenses they committed, the main question to be dealt with is what motivated them to develop such an attitude. After all, this is the generation which had seen the Egyptians stricken by the miraculous ten plagues and concerning which the Midrash states: "A servant girl saw at the [crossing of the Red] Sea what Isaiah and Ezekiel did not behold" (*Mechilta de-Shirah* 3), not to mention the miraculous supplies of food, water, and manna which had accompanied them on their trip so far.

The answer is that it was known that the age of miracles was not meant to last forever, as was eventually made clear in the book of Deuteronomy, when Moses stated: "The Lord your God will dislodge those peoples before you little by little; you will not be able to destroy them quickly, lest the beasts of the field outnumber you" (Deut. 7:22). In other words, God would not miraculously intervene and conquer their enemies or even the wild animals.

It was noted that according to Abravanel, immediately after Moses said, "Go up, take possession," the nation was either truly convinced or pretended to believe that they would be entirely on their own, without God's Providence. For a people who had been pampered from the day they left Egypt with supernatural occurrences, it must have been terrifying to imagine standing up to enemies all on their own, and that fear motivated them to resist having to face such a situation.

Their mistake was that although the level of miracles would be drastically reduced, and perhaps God would not as readily mow down the vicious animals, the same verse also says that He would accompany them in dislodging their enemies, even if it was to be "little by little." They had not yet developed enough self-confidence to rely on themselves, or even to have faith in God that the small dosage of succor which they could not mobilize on their own would be supplied by Him. After the spectacular miracles that they had witnessed, their inability to believe that God would always be there to rescue them was considered to be a sin. What the forty-year punishment accomplished was that it allowed a braver, more assertive generation to develop, one whose self-confidence had not been eroded by decades of slavery. Even in modern times, one might say that it took the Jewish nation almost two thousand years to gather the physical and spiritual strength to attempt to reconquer their homeland.

The Case of the Sabbath-Desecrating Wood Gatherer, and Moses' Apparent Lapse

The Written and the Oral Law
According to the traditional view, the Torah was revealed to Moses on Mt. Sinai. Were the general rules as well as the details of each

Shlach

of the laws of the Torah transmitted at Mt. Sinai, or were only the former given at Sinai, while the rest was filled in throughout the forty years of wandering in the desert? The following Tannaitic text (BT *Zevachim* 115b; *Chagigah* 6a) relates to this question:

> R. Yishmael says: The general laws were stated at Sinai [Rashi: e.g., "an altar of earth you should make for Me" (Exod. 20:21) and the laws of burnt offerings and peace offerings were not explained there], and the details [were stated] at the Tent of Meeting [Rashi: after the Tabernacle was set up, the laws dealing with priests were told to Moses, where it was explained "and he should flay the burnt offering and cut it into pieces" (Lev. 1:6)]. R. Akiva said: The general laws and the details were stated at Sinai, repeated in the Tent of Meeting, and said a third time on the plains of Moab (Deut. 1:5).

R. Yishmael's approach is that the process was gradual, a view which fits in with the slow accretion of *mitzvot* experienced by the fledgling nation. It has been noted that God first gave the seven Noahide laws, which Rambam has characterized as being such that "the mind tends to accept them instinctively" (*Hilchot Melachim* 9:1). These were followed by specific commands given to the patriarchs, to Amram the father of Moses, and at Marah. Most of the earlier laws were of a moral-ethical nature, although at Marah laws of a testimonial or even statutory nature may have been given as well.[39] It is thus reasonable to assume that Moses first received an outline of each law, which he would transmit to the congregation, and only at a later stage would the details be provided.

On the other hand, there are many Talmudic texts that accept the approach of R. Akiva that the Torah in its entirety was

---

39. Abba Engelberg, *The Ethics of Exodus* (2014), pp. 295-299.

transmitted to Moses at Sinai, as impossible as it would seem for a human being to absorb so much material even in a period of forty days. **Appendix II - R. Akiva's Opinion Regarding the Oral Law** cites a number of Talmudic and Midrashic extracts which support his approach.

R. Akiva's Definition of the "Details" of a Law

What is referred to by the "details" of a law? In order to answer this question, one must understand that the traditional belief (according to both R. Akiva and R. Yishmael) is that Moses received both the written and the oral law at Mt. Sinai. The written law refers to the laws which appear in the Pentateuch. The oral law refers to the oral transmission of clarifications and additional details concerning those laws. It also refers to totally new laws (such as *shechitah*, kosher slaughtering), or even non-derivable explanations of enigmatic words which appear in the Torah (such as *totafot* referring to *tefillin* in Exod. 13:16 and Deut. 6:8, 11:18) called *halachot le-Moshe mi-Sinai* (laws given to Moses at Sinai). Saying that the details as well were given at Sinai means that refinements which were implied in the written version of the Torah, as well as new rulings which became part of the oral law, were also transmitted to Moses at Sinai, as opposed to at a later stage, such as in the Tent of Meeting when travelling through the desert, or on the plains of Moab.

Questions on the View of R. Akiva

In a number of places, the Torah precedes a set of commands with information as to where or when God made the command. Consider the following examples:

1. "And He called to Moses, and God spoke to him from the Tent of Meeting, saying" (Lev. 1:1).

Shlach

2. "And the Lord spoke to Moses, after the death of the two sons of Aaron, when they drew too near to the Lord, and died" (Lev. 16:1).
3. "And the Lord spoke to Moses on the plains of Moab by the Jordan at Jericho, saying" (Num. 33:50).

According to R. Akiva, Moses was already acquainted with all the laws which God asked him to convey, from his stay on Mt. Sinai, so why did God have to re-appear to him? One might answer that God had indeed informed Moses of these laws, but then He had to communicate to Moses exactly which of the laws were to be taught to the Children of Israel at each specific time. Of course, one could ask: why was it not sufficient to just tell Moses the name of the subject to be taught?

There are four places, however, where the Torah seems to be describing a situation where Moses is unaware of the correct halachic answer and has to consult with God to obtain information which is part of the written or oral law, and accordingly should have already been taught to him during his stay on Mt. Sinai:

1. A number of people would have liked to sacrifice the paschal lamb at the proper time, but were unable to do so because they were unclean. They asked Moses if there was any method of compensation, and Moses requested of them to wait while he inquired of the Lord (Num. 9:1-14).
2. A man was caught gathering wood on the Sabbath. The members of the congregation were aware that such behavior was prohibited and they had warned him that carrying on the Sabbath is forbidden (BT *Sanhedrin* 41a), but they did not know the consequence. Moses did not know much more, because he placed the man in detention and waited for God to clarify how he was to be punished (Num. 15:32-34). The Talmud

The Ethics of Numbers

(BT *Sanhedrin* 78b) explains that Moses actually knew that desecrating the Sabbath was punishable by death, as is recorded explicitly in the book of Exodus, where it says: "He who profanes it [the Sabbath] will be put to death" (Exod. 31:14). Moses had been commanded by God to relay the content of that verse to the congregation (Exod. 31:13). His only question was which form of death penalty (stoning, burning, decapitation, or strangulation) was applicable, so it seems that in this matter the congregation knew as much as he did.

3. Toward the end of the forty-year trek in the desert, the Israelites began to discuss their future life in the Land of Israel, where they would engage in agricultural efforts. It was assumed that when a man passed on, his family plot would be divided among his sons, who would work the land. Although this might seem discriminatory with respect to his daughters, it was assumed that they would be provided for by their own husbands, or by their brothers if they did not marry. This logic broke down, however, if a man had no sons at all, only daughters. According to the extant laws of inheritance, the land of the deceased would then return to his father or to his own brothers and their families, and there would be no one to provide for the daughters of the deceased. This is the situation in which the daughters of Zelophehad found themselves, and concerning which they approached Moses. Being of a polite nature, they did not mention their own distress, but rather the fact that their father's possession would not endure, since it would become an integral part of another person's heritage. Again, Moses brought the matter before God, who made it clear that in such a case the daughters would indeed inherit their father's plot (Num. 27:1-11).

Once more, the Talmud alleviates the problem by saying that in principle Moses already knew that daughters inherit

Shlach

in the absence of sons. What he did not know was whether primogeniture applies. In other words, did Zelophehad, as the first-born, receive a double portion of his father's inheritance (since his father died before they entered Canaan, i.e., when the inheritance was only prospective)? And did his eldest daughter receive a double portion compared to the other daughters (BT *Bava Batra* 119a) or not? At any rate, Moses did not know the answers to these technical questions, even if he was aware of the general rule.

4. When a man uttered the four-letter name of God in a contemptuous manner, it was known that he was deserving of punishment, as it says: "You should not revile God" (Exod. 22:27). However, in this case (as opposed to the case of the wood gatherer), even the Talmud (BT *Sanhedrin* 78b) is of the opinion that Moses was uninformed as to what the punishment should be, and so he required the blasphemer to wait in detention until the issue was clarified by the Almighty (Lev. 24:10-16).

The simplest answer to these questions is that although Moses may have been taught almost all the details of the law, there were exceptions. Specifically, the halachic details which answer the four previously mentioned questions were withheld—either initially, or after forgetting (artificially) all of the Torah knowledge which he had acquired, and then miraculously receiving it back as a gift (see **Appendix II - R. Akiva's Opinion Regarding the Oral Law**). The Talmud explains why certain laws were given only in association with specific people when it says: "Merit is brought about by means of the meritorious and punishment by means of the guilty" (BT *Bava Batra* 119b).

The straightforward explanation of the above phrase is that those who are righteous receive an additional reward by having

The Ethics of Numbers

their names mentioned in conjunction with God's grace, and those who are evil suffer additional chastisement by having their names recorded in connection with the punishment meted out to them. However, *Peirush Yonatan* (Num. 15:32) says that even the wood gatherer, who was being punished, had some merits, and for that reason his transgression, and the new laws which it generated, are included in the Torah. This is especially understandable according to the view of Tosafot (BT *Bava Batra* 119b, s.v. *afilu*) that the wood gatherer was actually Zelophehad, who purposely violated the Sabbath restrictions in order to make the public aware of the fact that these laws had to be obeyed even by those who would not enter Israel as a result of the sin of the spies. In other words, he sinned seriously, but his intentions were positive.

Similarly, with regard to the blasphemer, the Midrash makes it clear that he was the son of the woman who was molested by the Egyptian killed by Moses (Exod. 2:12).[40] Apparently, the son considered himself to be part of the Jewish nation, which Rashi derives from the words "among the Children of Israel" used in describing his background. The Midrash[41] even says that he converted. The issue that arises is that since his mother was Jewish, conversion should have been unnecessary. Accordingly, Ramban (Lev. 24:10) understands this to mean that he took part in the mass conversion of all of the Israelites before they were able to receive the Torah (BT *Kreitot* 9a). Ramban does, however, cite the view of the French rabbis that before the Torah was given, Jewishness was transmitted patrilineally, so he might have indeed needed conversion. Either way, he obviously looked upon himself as a member of the community. The Midrash further mentions that he had grown up among the tribe of Dan and expected to receive a plot of land as a member of the tribe. His blasphemy resulted from his disappointment at

---

40. *Tanchuma Emor* 24; *Lev. Rabbah* 32:4.
41. *Sifra Emor* 14:1, quoted by Rashi on Lev. 24:10.

Shlach

his lack of entitlement to the land due to not being considered a member of the community because of his non-Jewish father.

The Difference between R. Yishmael and R. Akiva

R. Yishmael and R. Akiva agree that in the end, the entire written and oral Torah were revealed to Moses by God. They only argue as to whether the Torah was given entirely on Mt. Sinai or whether it was given in installments.[42]

Revelation is by definition a supernatural occurrence. Whether it occurs in one place or many does not make much difference conceptually. Nevertheless, one might say that by spreading out the transmission of an encyclopedic amount of information, R. Yishmael is implying that, at least on the part of Moses, the process was more natural. It has been pointed out in the past that the *mitzvot* were imposed on Israel in a gradual fashion, starting with the Noahide laws and continuing through the patriarchs, Amram, Marah, the Ten Commandments, and finally the remainder of the Torah.[43] R. Yishmael transforms the Torah's transmission to Moses into a similarly gradual operation.

Summary

Two topics have been examined in this portion, that of the ill-fated spying mission and that of the wood gatherer who transgressed the law of the Sabbath. Regarding the first, the discussion revolved around whether the sin was initiated by the nation as a whole (Talmud and Abravanel) or whether it started with the negative connotations of the report returned by the spies (Ramban and

---

42. Of course, the Talmudic segment passage which speaks of even "the innovations which would be introduced by the Scribes" (BT *Megillah* 19b) being given at Sinai was proposed exclusively according to the view of R. Akiva, and thus had to be justified only by him, and not by R. Yishmael.
43. Abba Engelberg, *The Ethics of Exodus* (2014), pp. 287-309.

Akeidat Yitzchak). What seems to be common to all commentators is that in the end, the spies lied and the Israelites readily accepted their pessimistic outlook, thereby displaying ingratitude for all of God's miracles, and a grievous lack of faith.

The case of the wood gatherer might be looked upon as an independent event, although a suggestion linking the two was cited by Tosafot, who said that the righteous Zelophehad was the wood gatherer, who sacrificed his life in order to demonstrate that the law was to be obeyed even by those males over the age of twenty, who had been condemned to perish in the desert.

Korach

The portion of *Korach* describes the rebellion of Korah and his compatriots against the leadership of Moses. The Bible describes how the main perpetrators were swallowed up by the ground, while their 250 followers, who were told to prepare censers containing incense, were devoured by a fire that descended miraculously. The copper censers were beaten into plates which served as a covering for the altar, a permanent reminder that incense was to be offered exclusively by priests. In the meantime, Aaron used his own incense-filled fire-pan to rescue the Israelites from a noxious plague, although not before there were 14,700 victims. To vindicate Aaron's priesthood, God requested Moses to take a rod from the prince of each tribe and inscribe the latter's name on it, with Aaron's name inscribed on the rod of Levi. The next morning, the rod of Aaron alone had blossomed with ripe almonds. The princes retrieved their bare rods, but Aaron's was placed next to the Holy Ark.

The portion ends with a description of the obligations of the priests (and the Levites), and a list of the 24 priestly gifts which they were entitled to receive from the Israelites. Rashi explains the juxtaposition of these items with the story of Korah as follows:

> This may be compared to a king who gave a field to his friend but did not write or seal [a deed], nor did he record

it in court. A man came and claimed ownership of the field. The king said to him [his friend]: "Anyone can come and claim against you. Behold, I am writing and sealing a deed for you, and recording it in the court." So too, here. Because Korah came and made a claim against Aaron to the priesthood, Scripture came and gave him [i.e., recorded] the twenty-four priestly gifts as an everlasting covenant of salt (Rashi, Num. 18:8).

Participants in the Rebellion of Korah

In order to provide the reader with a better understanding of the motivation for Korah's rebellion, Scripture (Num. 16:1) enumerates the people involved:

Korah of the Tribe of Levi

Korah's family tree traces back to Jacob as follows: Korah, Izhar, Kohath, Levi, Jacob. Interestingly, in enumerating the genealogy, the verse omits the name of Jacob (Num. 16:1). The Midrash (*Tanchuma* (Buber) *Korah* 7) states that God acquiesced to the special request of Jacob not to highlight the familial relationship with Korah, which he had prophetically expressed in his (muted) blessing to Levi: "Let my glory not be associated with their [evil] congregation" (Gen. 49:6).

In addition to Izhar, Kohath had three other sons: Amram, Hebron, and Uzziel (Exod. 6:18). Since Moses was the son of Amram (6:20), he and Korah were first cousins.

The name "Korah" is akin to the Hebrew word *karachat*, which means baldness. The *Zohar* (*Tazria* 3:49a) says he was given that name based on his past history as a Levite, in light of the fact that part of the Levitical inauguration ceremony involved shaving the entire body. The Talmud (BT *Sanhedrin* 109b), on the other hand, derives the name "Korah" from events yet to transpire, explaining that he caused a baldness in the Israeli populace in that he was swallowed up together with his associates (Num. 16:32). Maharsha explains the Talmudic text to mean that the list of potential names for newborn boys was to become sparser, since the name of a wicked person is not reused among Jews (BT *Yoma* 38b), although the same name had been given to a supposedly wicked son of Esau (Gen. 36:5).

Korah was considered to be exceptional in terms of his qualities and abilities. The *Zohar* (ibid.) considers him to have the greatest potential of all the Levites (perhaps including Moses and Aaron), having been endowed by God with superhuman qualities. The Sages describe him as a great *talmid chacham* (scholar) who was chosen as one of the bearers of the Ark in its travels through the desert (Num. 7:9), an honor bestowed only on great scholars (*Tanchuma* (Buber) *Korach* 5; *Num. Rabbah* 18:3 and Radal 6 thereon). However, Korah utilized his knowledge and intelligence to foment rebellion. The Midrash states:

> What is written before this episode [of Korah]? "[And the Lord spoke to Moses saying:] 'Speak to the Children of Israel and tell them to make ritual fringes (*tzitzit*) for themselves on the corners of their garments [throughout their generations, and they should affix a thread of blue (wool) on the fringe of each corner]'" (Num. 15:37-38). Korah said to Moses our Master: "Moses, regarding a prayer shawl (*tallit*) which is all blue, is it exempt from [the requirement to make] ritual fringes?" Moses said to him: "It is required to have ritual fringes." Korah said to him: "A prayer shawl which is all blue does not exempt itself, but four [blue] strings exempt it?"

"Regarding a house which is full of Scriptural books, is it exempt from [the requirement to have] a *mezuzah* [doorpost parchment, which contains only two Scriptural passages]?" He [Moses] said to him: "It is required to have a *mezuzah*." He [Korah] said to him: "The whole Torah has 275 sections in it, and they do not exempt the house [from having a *mezuzah*], and the two sections which are in the *mezuzah* exempt the house?" He [Korah, then] said to him: "These are things about which you have not been commanded. Rather you are inventing them from your own heart" (*Tanchuma* (Buber) *Korach* 4).

The *Kli Yakar* (Num. 16:1) notes that the Midrash's suggestion that Korah argued about the laws of *tzitzit* is based on the story's contiguity to those laws, which are presented at the end of the previous portion of *Shlach* (Num. 16:37-41). That he argued about the laws of *mezuzah* is derived from the redundant words describing how Dathan and Abiram stood "at the entrance of their tent" (Num. 16:27). According to the *Kli Yakar*, the exact location where they stood indicates that they joined the argument about the ritual object (the *mezuzah*) which is placed in the entrance.

Another provocation engineered by Korah was the making of a large banquet, to which he invited the members of his rebellion with orders to dress in pure blue shawls (devoid of *tzitzit*), at which he served the meat of peace offerings. When Aaron's sons came to receive the breast and right thigh of each animal, as delineated in Scripture (Lev. 7:31-32), Korah refused, claiming that Moses had legislated that law on his own for the benefit of his brother's family (*Tanchuma* (Buber) *Korach* 5).

Korah attempted to convince the populace of his own generosity and Moses' miserliness, as seen from the following Midrash, which praises the person who does not spend time with scoffers, by presenting a sample of Korah's perversity:

Korach

Korah would belittle Moses and Aaron. What did he do? He gathered together the entire congregation, for it says: "Korah gathered the whole community against them" (Num. 16:19). He began speaking words of cynicism and said: "There is a widow in my neighborhood with two orphan daughters, and she owns one field. She went to plow [the field]. Moses told her, 'You may not plow with an ox and a donkey together' (Deut. 22:10). [When] she went to sow, he told her: 'you may not sow your field with two kinds of seed' (Lev. 19:19). [When] she went to harvest and stack it, he said to her: '[you must forfeit for the indigent] gleanings, forgotten sheaves, and [the produce of] the corner of the field.' When she went to ingather [the grain] to the threshing floor, he told her: 'Give me the heave offering, and the first and second tithes.'[44] She sadly conceded and gave it to him. What did the poverty-stricken lady do? She sold the field and bought two sheep, in order to wear clothing from their wool and benefit from their offspring. When they gave birth, Aaron appeared and said: 'Give me the firstborn, for so said the Almighty: 'You must consecrate to the Lord your God all male firstborns that are born in your herd and in your flock; you must not work your firstborn ox nor shear your firstling sheep' (Deut. 15:19). She sadly conceded and gave him the newborns. Shearing time arrived, and she sheared them. Aaron approached and told her: 'Give me the first of the fleece' (Deut. 18:4). She said: 'I have no strength to hold out against this man, so I will slaughter them and

---

44. Actually, Moses would have only gotten the first tithe, since the heave offering is for the priest and the second tithe is eaten in Jerusalem by the field owner. But Korah's intention was to paint a sordid picture, and he felt no need to adhere to the truth.

eat them. Having slaughtered them, Aaron neared her and said: 'Give me the shoulder, the cheeks, and the stomach' (Deut.18:3). She said: 'After I slaughtered them I was not saved from you, behold I consecrate them.' He said to her: 'If they are consecrated, they all belong to me, for it says: 'Everything that has been consecrated in Israel is to be yours' (Num. 18:14). He took them and departed, and he left her weeping with her two daughters. It is apparently acceptable to oppress the unfortunate. They all do so and blame it on God's law" (*Midrash Shocher Tov*, Ps. 1).

This story depicts Korah as demonstrating to the uninitiated that the ritual laws are seemingly nonsensical and the moral laws are ostensibly unethical.

Korah was also said to be excessively wealthy, with just the keys for his treasure houses filling many wagons (BT *Sanhedrin* 110a). To this very day, there is a common expression in Israel that a wealthy person is said to be "as rich as Korah."

The source of his riches was said to be his discovery of one of the three treasures hidden by Joseph, who had collected all the money in the land of Egypt in exchange for the grain which had been bought during the years of famine (Gen. 47:14). During the years of slavery, Korah had been the manager of Pharaoh's palace and had access to the keys to Pharaoh's treasure stores (*Gen. Rabbah* 18:15). These riches were actually meant for the nation as a whole, to fulfill God's promise to Abraham: "and afterward they will go free with great wealth" (Gen. 15:14), but they were appropriated by Korah, i.e., they were not obtained legally (*Gen. Rabbah* 22:7).

This Midrash may explain Moses' seemingly irrelevant comment when addressing God concerning Korah: "I have not taken [even] one donkey from any one of them" (Num. 16:15),

Korach

which Rashi, based on Midrash *Tanchuma Korach* 7, explains: "Even when I went from Midian to Egypt and enabled my wife and my sons to ride on a donkey (Exod. 4:20), when I would have been entitled [at a later stage] to take the price of that donkey from them [as a business expense]. Nevertheless, I only took it [the donkey] from my own [belongings]." This approach strongly contrasts with Korah's behavior in taking for himself great stores of goods which had been intended for the Children of Israel.

THE BROTHERS DATHAN AND ABIRAM OF THE TRIBE OF REUBEN

The brothers' family tree traces back to Jacob as follows: Dathan and Abiram, Eliab, Pallu, Reuben, Jacob (Num. 26:5-9). Dathan and Abiram were inveterate troublemakers. The Talmud (BT *Nedarim* 64b) states that they were the two Hebrew combatants who Moses encountered in Egypt at the beginning of his career, and who answered him very insolently (Exod. 2:13-14). According to the Midrash (*Exod. Rabbah* 1:28), this took place after Moses saved Dathan from being beaten to death by the Egyptian taskmaster who had ravished Dathan's wife, which explains how Dathan knew that Moses killed the Egyptian. Dathan exhibits not only brazenness, but a lack of gratitude as well. In fact, when God told Moses that he could return from Midian to Egypt because "all the men who sought to kill you are dead" (Exod. 4:19), according to the Talmud (BT *Nedarim* 64b), He was referring to Dathan and Abiram, who had become impoverished (comparable to being dead) and were thus unable to execute their nefarious intentions.

Later, at the start of Moses' leadership role, when Pharaoh worsened the conditions of the Israelites as a result of Moses' initial efforts to obtain their release, Dathan and Abiram impertinently addressed Moses, saying: "May the Lord look upon you and punish

The Ethics of Numbers

you for making us loathsome to Pharaoh and his servants, to the point that they would take a sword in their hands to slay us" (Exod. 5:21).[45] According to *Targum Yonatan*,[46] Dathan and Abiram did not even depart from Egypt together with the rest of the nation, because they wished to emphasize their attachment to Israel as being nationalistic in nature and not religious.

According to the Midrash (*Exod. Rabbah* 25:10), it was they who displayed their distrust in God by attempting to preserve the manna overnight, although the nation had received express orders not to do so, but to have faith that God would supply more the next day (Exod. 16:20). The congregation was also told that they would receive a double portion of manna on Friday, so that there would be no need to collect it on the Sabbath (Exod. 16:22-26). The Bible notes, however, that in spite of the instructions not to do so on the Sabbath, "some people went out to gather, but they found none" (Exod. 16:27). The Midrash (*Minhagei Yeshurun* 71:37, p. 255) wonders why the verse says "they found none," implying that there had been some manna, but it was not found, rather than "there was none." The Midrash answers that Dathan and Abiram had purposely spread manna in the fields on Friday night, so that it would be found on Sabbath morning, thus impugning Moses' credibility. The birds ate that manna, and they are rewarded on *Shabbat Shirah*, when the story of the manna is read from the Torah in synagogues.

The Talmud (BT *Sanhedrin* 109b) sees their evil characters as being embedded in their very names, with Dathan containing the Hebrew word *dat* ("religion"), which he rebelled against, and Abiram being close to the Hebrew word *eebair* ("strengthened"), because he hardened his heart against considering the possibility of repentance. No wonder the Midrash states: "Whatever you can blame on these criminals, do so" (*Yalkut Shimoni*, Exod. 167).

---

45. BT *Nedarim* 64b, and Me'iri thereon, as well as Rashi, Exod. 5:20.
46. Abba Engelberg, *The Ethics of Exodus* (2014), pp. 127-129.

Korach

ON BEN PELET

On ben Pelet was also of the tribe of Reuben (Rashi, Num. 16:1, s.v. *bnei*). The only problem is that the name "Pelet" does not appear among Reuben's descendants mentioned in the portion of *Pinchas* (Num. 26:5-10). *Da'at Mikra* (p. 191, comment 1b) suggests that Pelet is actually Palu, in which case On's genealogy going back to Reuben would be: On, Palu, Reuben—making On an uncle of Dathan and Abiram (who were grandsons of Palu), which is reasonable, since it is very likely that he was swept into the rebellion under the adverse influence of his nephews (or vice versa). There is linguistic support for this theory, since a literal translation of the verse in *Pinchas* is: "And the sons of Palu were Eliab" (Num. 26:8). Although the word "sons" is in the plural form, only Eliab is mentioned. One may thus assume that there was an additional son, namely On, who is not mentioned by name.

The Midrash (*Midrash ha-Gadol*, Num. 16:32) notes that although On may have been closely related to Dathan and Abiram, his name does not appear again in this story. This is explained in the Talmud as follows:

> Rav said: On ben Pelet's wife saved him. Said she to him, "What difference does it make to you [who is greater]? If one [Moses] is greater, you are [just] his disciple; if the other [Korah] is greater, you are [still just] his disciple." He said to her: "What can I do? I took part in their counsel, and I have sworn to them to join them [Rashi: if they call me]." She said: "I know that they are all a holy community, as it is written: 'for the entire congregation is holy' (Num. 16:3)." [So,] she said to him: "Sit [here], for I will save you." She gave him wine to drink, intoxicated him and laid him down [in the tent, so that he would not transgress the oath he had taken upon himself, in the event that they call

him from the outside]. Then she sat down at the entrance [of the tent] and loosened her hair. Whoever came [to summon On] saw her and retreated [since it was improper to see her uncovered hair] (BT *Sanhedrin* 109b-110a).

This narrative indicates the importance of choosing a wife who is imbued with strong ethical values. Of course, On himself deserves much of the credit for listening to his wife and realizing that the conspiracy was unjust and that her approach was preferable. The Talmud (ibid.) explains that the Hebrew etymology of the name "On" is connected with the word for "regret," which according to Rashi shows that On repented for initially agreeing to participate in the rebellion, while *Eitz Yosef* explains that it refers to his disappointment at not being the one who took the initiative to cancel his participation.

The Midrash relates two more instances in which On's wife came to his rescue. The first was when the earth opened its mouth to swallow the camps of Dathan and Abiram and Korah. On ben Pelet was still in bed recovering from his inebriation. The ground (to be taken metaphorically), which had apparently not been updated as to On's recantation, exerted great pressure on On's bed in an effort to suck him in together with the other conspirators, whereupon On's wife held on to the bed with all her strength and exclaimed loudly that On had resolved nevermore to be an accessory to an argument and was thus innocent of wrongdoing. The third time she intervened was at a later stage, when On was embarrassed to emerge from his tent for fear of encountering Moses. When On's wife made Moses aware of the situation, Moses himself stood at the entrance of On's tent and urged him to come out, assuring him that God would forgive him *(Midrash ha-Gadol*, Num. 16:32).

The wife of Korah, in contrast to the wife of On, encouraged Korah to carry on his malicious behavior, as described in the continuation of the Talmudic text:

Korach

Korah's wife said to him: "See what Moses has done. He has become king; his brother he appointed high priest; his brother's sons he has made assistants to the high priest. If *terumah* is brought, he decrees: 'Let it be for the priest'; if the tithe is brought, which belongs to you [Korah, since you are a Levite], he says: 'Give one tenth [of it] to the priest.' Furthermore, he has had your hair cut off [at the purification of the Levites in Num. 8:7] and belittles you as though you were dirt, for he was envious of your hair."[47] He said to her: "But he has done likewise!" She said to him: "Since all the greatness was his [he is the absolute ruler who initiated the demeaning activities which you perform], Moses has also said: 'Let me die with the Philistines' (Judg. 16:30) [he is willing to do the same to himself]" (BT *Sanhedrin* 110a).

The Talmud continues to say that his wife even originated the provocation of wearing an all-blue prayer shawl. Although her ploy exhibited her intelligence and Torah knowledge, it also manifested the danger of being married to an unethical spouse. Nevertheless, although Korah's wife is depicted as encouraging his negative behavior, the ultimate guilt remains with him, as the maxim says: "One cannot be appointed a messenger to commit a sin [i.e., the sin is associated with the one who performs it, not the one who urged another to do it] (BT *Kiddushin* 42b).

250 Men

Korah, Dathan and Abiram, and On were joined by 250 men. Who were these men? No names are mentioned, but the Bible describes

---

47. *Tanchuma* (Buber) *Korach* 6 points out that as part of the incitement, it was noted that Korah was shaved first, and sitting right next to him was Aaron, adorned like a bride in the beautiful priestly vestments.

them as "princes of the congregation, the elect men of the assembly, men of renown" (Num. 16:2). Since this description closely parallels that given to the tribal leaders in Num. 1:16, who were in fact the princes of their tribes (see Num. 7), it is likely that they were men of the highest caliber. The Midrash (*Tanchuma* (Buber) *Korach* 5) is more precise, saying that they were Elitzur b. Shedeur, the prince of the tribe of Reuben (Num. 1:5), and his companions. On what basis did the Midrash single out these men as being from the trube of Reuben? The answer is that in a different location, the Midrash (*Tanchuma* (Buber) *Korach* 8) explains that the reason the three conspirators who joined Korah (Dathan, Abiram, and On) were all from the tribe of Reuben was that the tribe of Reuben was located on the southern edge of the encampment, while Korah's extended family (Kohath) was adjacently situated on the southern edge of the Tabernacle. The Midrash applies a poetic maxim to describe how Korah served as a bad influence: "Woe to the wicked one, woe to his neighbor." Dathan and Abiram did not need too much encouragement to join Korah. In fact, this maxim would seem more appropriate if it were used to explain Korah's effect on the 250 men. Rashi (Num. 16:1), when paraphrasing the Midrash, seems to have taken this into account when he wrote that Korah had assembled 250 men [on the level of] heads of the Sanhedrin, most of them of the tribe of Reuben, who were his neighbors.

What Was the Sin of Korah?

It is quite clear from the severe punishments described in the portion of *Korach* that Korah sinned. The question is: who did he sin against and what was the sin? Was it a sin against God, or against Moses, or against both? From the continuation of the story, it is quite clear that Moses had made all of the appointments at God's behest. Did Korah know that? If he did, then just as the nation had been faulted for requesting that spies be sent when God had previously informed them that He was leading them to "a land flowing with milk and honey" (Exod. 3:8), similarly, Korah deserved to be punished for attempting to second-guess God's decisions. On the other hand, if Korah was unaware that Moses was only acting as God's messenger, then his sin must be based on his behavior toward Moses and Aaron. In the latter case, one must distinguish between the immediate and the long-range cause. The immediate cause, dealt with by the classical commentators, will be discussed later. As for the long-range cause, the text makes it quite clear what was bothering Korah. He is quoted as saying:

> And they assembled themselves against Moses and Aaron, and said to them: "You have gone too far! For the whole community is holy, and the Lord dwells in the midst of all of them. Why then do you lift yourselves above the Lord's congregation?" (Num. 16:3)

Korah, apparently unaware that the appointments were issued by God, speaks in favor of democracy. The Midrash puts the following words in the mouth of Korah:

> He said to them: "The entire congregation—they are all holy, and they all heard at Sinai 'I am the Lord your God' (Exod. 20:2), so 'why then do you raise yourselves above the Lord's congregation?' (Num. 16:3). If you alone had heard, and they had not heard, then you could say [*Eitz Yosef*: that you are better than them]. Now they all heard, so why do you raise yourself [above them]? *(Num. Rabbah* 18:6)

Korah is implying that all of the Israelites were on a high enough level to make crucial decisions, because they jointly experienced revelation. But Scripture makes it quite clear that the nation was not really capable of extended communication with God, as the following verses from Moses' description of Revelation indicate:

> When you heard the voice out of the darkness, while the mountain was ablaze with fire, you came up to me, all your tribal heads and elders, and said: "The Lord our God has shown us His glory and His greatness, and we have heard His voice emanate from the fire; we have seen this day that God may speak with man and he can remain alive. Now therefore, why should we die, for this great fire will consume us; if we hear the voice of the Lord our God any longer, we will die. For what mortal ever heard the voice of the living God speak out of the fire, as we did, and lived? You go closer and hear all that the Lord our God says, and then you tell us everything that the Lord our God tells you, and we will hear it and do it." The Lord heard your words that you said to me, and the Lord said to me, "I have heard the words that this people said to you; everything they have said is good" (Deut. 5:20-25).

The text itself makes it clear that the nation was not capable of prolonged exposure to the Divine Presence. The Talmud specifies exactly how much they were capable of hearing directly from the Almighty:

> R. Yishmael stated: [The first two commands:] "I am the Lord your God" (Exod. 20:2) and "You may have no other gods" (Exod. 20:3) were heard from the mouth of the Almighty (BT *Horayot* 8a).[48]

---

48. See also Rashi, Num. 15:22.

Korach

With respect to the verse: "Moses commanded us [the laws of] the Torah" (Deut. 33:4), the Talmud (BT *Makkot* 23b) explains that the numerical value (*gematriya*) of the letters composing the Hebrew word *Torah* equals 611, because that number of *mitzvot* was passed on by Moses to the Israelites, after initially being given by God to Moses alone. Only the first two commandments were transmitted directly to the entire nation, leading to the traditional total of 613.

Since Korah obviously knew that God continued the presentation of the Ten Commandments as well as the remaining laws in direct communication with Moses exclusively, his claim that everyone had achieved the same level of spirituality was pure demagoguery. Being aware of Moses' spiritual superiority and open line of communication with the Lord, he certainly should have at least considered the possibility (if not the certainty) that Aaron's appointment was of Divine origin before making an accusation. Korah, however, was quite shrewd. He very craftily said to Moses "You have gone too far" (Num. 16:3). In other words, he said, "I am not challenging your position as leader, which is understandable and acceptable for the reasons stated. I am only disputing your choice of your brother—of all people—as high priest" (Rashi, Num. 16:3).

MOSES' HANDLING OF KORAH'S REBELLIOUS BEHAVIOR

Moses was certain that Korah was perfectly aware that the appointment was ordered by God. It is instructive to see how Moses reacted. The first thing to notice is that Moses did not get angry, nor did he become defensive. After all, he was "the meekest of all men on the face of the earth" (Num. 12:3) and would certainly have behaved in accordance with Rambam's description of a modest person as being one who "hears himself reproached but does not retort" (*Hilchot De'ot* 2:3). In fact, since Moses knew Korah's congregation had sinned, his first instinct must have been to beseech God for forgiveness. However, he realized that God might not accede to his prayers, as indicated by the Midrash on the following verse: "And when Moses heard it [their public murmuring], he fell upon his face" (Num. 16:4):

> Moses instantly became shocked because of the rebellion, for this was already the fourth offence on their part. A parable! This may be compared to the case of a prince who sinned against his father and for whom his [the father's] beloved friend gained forgiveness once, twice, three times. When he offended for the fourth time, the friend felt himself powerless, for he said, "How long can I trouble the king?" Also here, when they sinned by worshipping the golden calf [it states]: "And Moses besought [the Lord]" (Exod. 32:11); in the case of "and the people complained" (Num. 11:1), it states: "and Moses prayed" (Num. 11:2); at the incident of the spies, it says: "And Moses said to the Lord, 'When the Egyptians will hear this .... [and now I beseech You, etc.]'" (Num.14:13); [but now] at the rebellion of Korah, he said: "How long can I trouble the king? [Perhaps he will not again accept advocacy from me!]" (*Num. Rabbah* 18:6; Rashi, Num. 16:4).

At this stage, when Moses realized that begging God to relent was not an option, he very calmly suggested a means for determining who the rightful priests were, and so he continued in Num. 16:

> **5** ... *Tomorrow* God will let it be known who are His and who is holy... **6** ... take your censers, Korah, and all his company, **7** and put fire [coals] in them and place incense upon them before the Lord tomorrow, and it will be that the man whom the Lord chooses will be holy. You have gone

Korach

too far, sons of Levi! **8** And Moses said to Korah: Hear me, I pray you, sons of Levi. **9** ... Is it not enough for you that the God of Israel has set you apart from the community of Israel to bring you near to Him, to perform the service of the Lord's Tabernacle and to stand before the community to minister to them? **10** ... do you seek the priesthood too? **11** Truly, it is against the Lord that you and all your company have convened. For *who is Aaron that you should rail against him*? **12** And Moses sent for Dathan and Abiram, sons of Eliab; but they said, "We will not come!"

These verses demonstrate Moses' unlimited patience and unmitigated efforts in attempting to prevent the congregation from going astray. The important word in v. 5 is "tomorrow," which the Midrash (*Tanchuma Korach* 5; Rashi, Num. 16:5) explains as an attempt by Moses to let them sleep on their request, in the hope that they would come to their senses by morning. A similar tactic was taken by Aaron when the congregation demanded the idol which materialized as the golden calf (Rashi, Exod. 32:5).

In v. 6, Moses continues his conciliatory efforts by telling each of the priestly aspirants to prepare to bring the incense offering, which is generally brought by the high priest. The Midrash once more fills in the details:

> He said to them: according to the custom of the heathens, there are numerous forms of divine worship [and consequently numerous priests], and they do not all assemble in one temple; we, however, have only one God, one Torah, one [system of] law, one Altar, [all constituting one form of worship, and therefore we only need] one high

priest and one Temple; and you, 250 men,[49] all demand the high priesthood?! I would like this myself. Therefore, you and your congregation [please] present yourselves before God, take censers, and put fire in them. Here you have a [priestly] rite which is dearer to God than all the sacrifices (*Tanchuma Korach* 5; Rashi, Num. 16:6). [50]

In v. 7, Moses makes it clear to the rebels, in an implicit manner, that they are literally "playing with fire." According to the Midrash, he reminds them of the demise of Nadab and Abihu as a result of bringing an incense offering when they were not designated to do so. The Midrash then asks why Moses added "the man whom the Lord chooses will be holy." In the words of the Midrash:

Do we not know that he whom God chooses will be holy? But this, in effect, is what Moses said to them: "I am telling you this in order that you not imperil your lives. You are 250 men who are offering [the sacrifice]. Only the one whom He chooses will come out of this alive, and all [the rest] of you will perish (*Tanchuma Korach* 5; Rashi, Num. 16:6).

In vv. 8-10, Moses once more cajoles the rebellious group in an attempt to dissuade them from engaging in the experimental incense offering, having just explained to them the danger which it entails.

---

49. The Midrash portrays Moses as addressing himself only to the 250 princes, perhaps because the leaders were deemed to be incorrigible, or because the Midrash assumed that Moses prophetically knew that a different form of death awaited the leaders, or because the leaders were not present at this point (see verse 12).

50. The Midrash states: "Of all the sacrifices which you bring, none is dearer to me than the incense offering" (*Tanchuma Tetzaveh* 15).

Korach

Verse 8 is a bit strange. Moses starts by addressing Korah and continues by asking the Levites to listen. In the words of the Midrash: "Would a person who speaks to Joseph tell Simeon to please listen?" (*Tanchuma Korach* 6). The Midrash answers that Moses spoke gently at first to Korah (as implied by the word "said," used for softer tones; see Rashi, Exod. 19:3, s.v. *tomar*). When he noticed that Korah did not relate to his words seriously, he began to fear that Korah could be a bad influence on his entire tribe, whom Moses then invited to join the conversation. V. 9 is accordingly addressed to the whole tribe of Levi, whom he assures that they have a vital function even if they are not priests, while in v. 10 Moses reverts back to Korah, who was after all a leading member of his tribe.

It has been noted that even if the congregation had not been told explicitly that Moses' and Aaron's commissions were God-ordained, Korah was expected to know that this was the case. In order to remove any doubt on this account, in v. 11 Moses clarifies to everyone present that Korah's protest is basically against the Lord, meaning that all of Moses' administrative acts were commanded by God. Furthermore, since Korah knew that God installed Moses as his plenipotentiary, then Aaron's appointment must have been made by Moses, so "who is Aaron that you should rail against him" (v. 11)?

During the entire debate, apparently Dathan and Abiram were not in attendance, since in v. 12 Moses sends for them, thereby disregarding his own dignity as a leader, especially since Dathan and Abiram were known scoundrels. On the basis of this verse, Reish Lakish stated:

> This teaches that one must not maintain a quarrel, for Rav said: "He who maintains a dispute violates a negative command, as it is written: 'And let him not be as Korah and as his company' (Num. 17:5)" (BT *Sanhedrin* 110a).

The Ethics of Numbers

At this stage, then, one might say that Korah's sin was that he did not accept, or at least did not acquiesce to, God's authority to appoint Moses as the guide and instructor of the nation.

A number of later commentators greatly minimize the sin of Korah, while the classical exegetes adhere more closely to the simple meaning of the text. Three relatively modern commentators will be presented first, followed by the classical commentators.

Modern Commentators

The Izhbitzer

The question that arises is: granted that God appointed both Moses and his brother Aaron to their respective positions, does that mean that Korah had no right to express his own opinion, especially if it was based on a moral principle? Did Abraham not chastise God at the time of the destruction of Sodom, when he feared that innocent people would be killed, by impertinently asking: "Will the Judge of the entire earth not act justly" (Gen. 18:25)?[51] Similarly, Korah presented the following basic moral principle: "For the whole community is holy, and the Lord dwells in the midst of all of them" (Num. 16:3).

Korah's request for equal opportunity for all members of the congregation may be understood in two ways. It may mean that *leaders* should be chosen, but in a democratic fashion in which every citizen has a vote, and not by diktat, even if the dictator is God Himself. Alternately, it may mean that every *decision* should be made by a referendum which takes into account the opinion of every individual citizen. The first approach was later used when the earliest kings were chosen. Although Saul (1 Sam. 10:1) and David (1 Sam. 16:13) were initially anointed by Samuel, they were not officially accepted until approved by the nation as a whole. In

---

51. See Abba Engelberg, *The Ethics of Genesis* (2014), pp. 66-70

Korach

the case of Saul, this occurred (1 Sam. 11:15) after the defeat of Nahash the Ammonite (1 Sam. 11:11), and in the case of David (2 Sam. 5:3), after defeating the Philistines on numerous occasions (1 Sam. 17:49, 18:27, 23:5, 30:17) and achieving great renown (1 Sam. 18:7, 30).

The Izhbitzer (*Mei ha-Shiloach* 2, *Korach*, s.v. *ki kol ha-edah*) adopts the approach of the *Zohar* that intemperate language in defense of an intrinsic Torah value is justified and even recommended (see **Appendix III – Anger Management**). He certainly bases himself on the fact that Korah was considered to be a Torah scholar and was justified in expressing himself in a harsh and threatening manner (*rugza de-rabbanan*). He also says that the very fact that the Torah cites Korah's claim that "the whole community is holy and the Lord dwells in the midst of all of them" must mean that it has eternal validity, otherwise God would not have included it in the Biblical text.

So, what in fact was Korah's great sin? The Izhbitzer says that there is a very thin line between justified wrath (*rugza de-rabbanan*) and invalid anger, and Korah and his sons crossed that line, although the latter soon realized their error and repented (Num. 26:11). The Izhbitzer implies that as a great scholar, Korah was being held to a higher standard.

The Izhbitzer does not spell out how Korah crossed the line in unjustified anger. Perhaps it is similar to the case of Phinehas, concerning which *Torah Temimah* says that normal people may not practice zealotry, because they may be zealous for ulterior motives (see **Appendix III – Anger Management**). Another possibility is that even justified anger in defense of Torah principles must have some boundaries, and when it lapsed into *ad hominem* attacks, as when Korah said, "Why then do you lift yourselves above the Lord's congregation," then it became forbidden. Or perhaps they sinned when they spoke disrespectfully to Moses by saying "you have gone too far," since certainly Moses was a greater scholar than Korah. Finally, it may have been the tone of voice, which admittedly cannot be determined from the written text alone, that went beyond what is dictated by good taste.

RAV KOOK

Like the Izhbitzer, R. Kook (*Orot*, "*Yisrael u-Tchiyato*," ch. 15, p. 32) focuses on Korah's saying: "For the whole community is holy, and the Lord dwells in the midst of all of them" (Num. 16:3). The Izhbitzer understood that Korah put the stress on the words "whole community," with the implication that nobody is superior to anyone else, and so leaders should be chosen democratically or, alternatively, governance should be shared equally among the populace. According to R. Kook, Korah's emphasis was on the word "holy," which implies that everyone is holy, and therefore there is no need to observe *mitzvot*, whether between man and man or man and God, since mankind has already reached its epitome, or is sufficiently holy to eliminate the necessity for self-improvement. This is a serious breach of the principles of Judaism, as it negates the relevance of the entire Torah to everyday life and relegates it to an academic exercise.

Korah is taking the approach of Cain, whom God had long before rejected. The Bible states:

> In the course of time, Cain brought an offering to the Lord from the fruit of the soil, and Abel, for his part, brought the choicest of his flock and the fattest among them. The Lord turned to Abel and his offering, but to Cain and his offering He paid no heed. Cain was much distressed and his face fell. And the Lord said to Cain, "Why are you annoyed, and why is your face fallen? Is it not so that if you improve, it will be forgiven you? If you do not improve,

Korach

however, sin awaits at the door, and it wishes to ensnare you, but you can rule over it." And Cain said [Rashi: words of contention] to his brother Abel… and when they were in the field, Cain rose up against his brother Abel and killed him (Gen. 4:3-8).

The obvious question is: Why was Cain's offering rejected, especially since the whole idea of expressing gratitude by bringing a gift to their Creator was his and it was he who in fact brought the initial sacrifice, while Abel only followed in his footsteps? Clearly, Cain wanted to draw close to God, and it was for that reason that he was dejected by his lack of success in doing so.

R. Kook was apparently bewildered by this question, but he deduced from the words of God that Cain needed to "improve," and from Cain's immoral actions afterwards in killing Abel, that he had a misconception that drawing near to God did not entail any serious transformation on his part because, as Korah said, "the whole community is holy." Although it is true that the whole community has the potential to achieve holiness through its members working on themselves to observe God's laws and improve their character, Cain, as well as Korah, assumed that no transformation was necessary.

Rashi provides a basis for the rejection of Cain's offering by noting that the words "from the fruit of the soil" imply "of the worst fruits," while the text states explicitly that Abel brought "the choicest of his flock," i.e., he invested time and effort to bring a superlative sacrifice, as opposed to Cain, who was unwilling to trouble himself to expend more energy to accomplish the task in the best manner, and this reflected his general indolence and disinclination to engage in self-improvement.

R. Kook takes aim at faith-based religions, not in the sense that belief in God is not a necessary ingredient for a religious person, but in the sense that faith without making a concerted effort at purification of the individual and the community misses the target. Such religions make the same mistake as Cain, and do not succeed in refining their adherents' personalities. R. Yehuda Levi (*Mul Etgarei ha-Tekufah*, p. 49), in contrast to R. Kook, believes that Gentiles have by nature more refined personalities and do not require as many commandments. He bases himself on a Talmudic phrase which states that the Torah was given to Israel because they are strong-willed, which Rashi interprets to mean that they are stubborn in their wickedness, and only by observing and studying the laws of the Torah are they subdued (*Ein Ya'akov, Beitzah* 25b).

The Alter Rebbe

The Alter Rebbe (R. Shneur Zalman of Liady, *Likutei Torah* 4, *Shlach*, p. 36b[52]) believes that the confrontation between Moses and Korah occurred soon after and as a reaction to the spy episode described in the previous portion, *Shlach*. The spies were sent at the end of the Hebrew month of Sivan (BT *Ta'anit* 29a), and the episode of Korah took place shortly afterward (Rashbam and Tosafot, BT *Bava Batra* 119a). The spies believed that the involvement with the material and physical demanded by life in the Land of Israel would detract from their ability to cleave spiritually to the Almighty, but Moses corrected them by pointing out that in Judaism spirituality is subordinate to the fulfillment of *mitzvot*, and the best place to do that is in the Land of Israel.

Until that point Korah, who was himself a great scholar, accepted Moses' and Aaron's transcendence and authority unquestioningly, since he realized that it was Moses who received instruction directly from God, and it was Aaron who was then inculcated immediately by Moses. Only afterwards was Korah,

---

52. Summarized in *Shulchan Shabbat, Korach*, "*Madu'a Titnassu al Kehal Hashem*."

Korach

together with the elders and the entire congregation, exposed to the word of God (BT *Eruvin* 54b). However, after hearing the outcome of the spying debacle, which stressed that the actions involved in performing the commands is of greater importance than striving to cling to the Almighty, Korah concluded that he, as well as any Jew, as simple as he might be, could fulfill the *mitzvot* to the same extent, implying that Moses and Aaron were not superior in that sense to any other member of the nation.

Korah's mistake was that he went to an extreme, just as the spies had. While the spies only appreciated the contemplative and spiritual aspects of Judaism, and decried the physical fulfillment of the *mitzvot*, Korah elevated the significance of the latter, but belittled the importance of intention (*kavanah*) when fulfilling the commands, and the significance of endeavoring to develop a close relationship to the Almighty.

The truth lies between the extremes. While God treasures deep study, building a spiritual attachment between man and his Creator, and *kavanah* when fulfilling *mitzvot*, He also demands particularity. As with regard to many other areas, the golden mean is the preferred option (*Hilchot De'ot* 1:4). While the spies did not understand that the entire benefit of spiritual elevation is when it accompanies the fulfillment of *mitzvot*, Korah did not understand that performing a mitzvah without the proper intention and frame of mind makes it into a rote activity, since emotion and spiritual communication, which Moses was capable of instilling in the Israelites, form an integral part of every mitzvah.

The Classical Commentaries

Ibn Ezra

According to Ibn Ezra (Num. 16:1), Korah thought that the various appointments made by Moses were done of his own volition, and that he clearly favored his closest relatives and friends. The Izhbitzer (*Mei ha-Shiloach* 2, *Korach*, s.v. *va-yikach*) points out that even though he must have realized that Moses was implementing the Divine mandate, the jealousy generated by his *yetzer ha-ra* (evil inclination) induced him to act as if he were oblivious to the true origin of these assignments.

Initially, the priestly duties were performed by the first-borns, as stated by Rashi regarding the sacrifices which were brought before Moses ascended Mt. Sinai (Exod. 24:5, 19:22), and it was they who offered sacrifices to the golden calf (Exod. 32:6), as Ibn Ezra notes (Exod. 32:29). Based on their behavior, God transferred the priestly duties to the tribe of Levi (Rashi, Deut. 10:8). Although God made His decision then, it may not have been announced; but it became evident at the time of the inauguration of the Tabernacle, when Aaron and his sons performed the priestly duties (Lev. 8), and it was already at that point that Korah organized his rebellion (Ibn Ezra, Exod. 32:29), being that he himself was a first-born (Exod. 6:21).

Although Korah was also a Levite, and thus among those exclusively chosen to bring all of the communal sacrifices in the wilderness (BT *Chagigah* 6b), chant the accompanying prayers (Rashi, Num. 6:9), and carry the Tabernacle and its holiest appurtenances (Num. 4:1-36, 7:9), as a first-born he would have achieved the higher rank of priest. His feeling was that Moses had favored his brother Aaron, and accordingly appointed him and his sons as high priest and priests, respectively. Aaron's influential position apparently perturbed many of the Levites, which would explain why Moses specifically addressed them when he said: "Please listen, sons of Levi. Is it not enough that the God of Israel has distinguished you from the congregation of Israel to draw you near to Him, to perform the service in the Tabernacle of the Lord and to stand before the congregation to minister to them" (Num. 16:8-9).

Korach

It is now evident how Korah was able to mobilize many others from his own tribe of Levi to join the rebellion, after convincing them that they were being deprived of the priesthood as a result of Moses' nepotism. The question that remains is: Why did the perpetual troublemakers, Dathan and Abiram, join the conflict? They do not seem to have desired any specific office. What motivated them?

Dathan and Abiram were great-grandchildren of Reuben (Num. 26:5-9), the eldest child of Jacob. Although kingship had been promised to Judah (Gen. 49:10), Reuben's primacy was still evident, and he was indeed the leading tribe of one of the four tribal groupings called "flags" (Num. 2:10). Nevertheless, there was a feeling that Reuben had already lost his primogeniture from the time that Jacob declared with respect to Joseph's sons Ephraim and Manasseh "that you will be to me as Reuben and Simeon" (Gen. 48:5). In other words, instead of one tribe developing from Joseph's offspring, as was the case with the other brothers, two tribes would stem from him, one from each of his sons. Nevertheless, only Joseph was mentioned together with Jacob's other sons when he blessed them all (Gen. 49:22-26), and it was not until Moses appointed separate princes for Ephraim and Manasseh (Num. 1:10) that they were seen to have the same status as the other brothers, and this carried on to the division of the land[53] and also to the blessings that Moses bestowed upon the tribes (Deut. 33:17). At that point, Joseph had, in effect, received the benefits of primogeniture.

As previously mentioned, the tribe of Reuben camped on the southern side of the encampment (Num. 2:10), as did the family of Kohath (Num. 3:29), which provided ample opportunity for Korah to be a bad influence on Dathan and Abiram, not that they needed

---

53. According to Ramban (Num. 26:54), Joseph's descendants thus ended up with twice as much as the other tribes, but Rashi (ibid.) says the per capita amount of land was equal for all Israelites.

too much stimulation to generate contention. Nevertheless, since they did not seem to have any personal vested interest, it is possible that the proximity to Korah's camp played a role in their behavior. Korah, being envious by nature, may have been jealous of Joshua as well as of Moses, and he may have imagined that Moses had given extra privileges to the tribe of Ephraim, to which Joshua belonged (1 Chron. 7:27).

In summary, according to Ibn Ezra, Korah was jealous of Aaron and angry that the priesthood had been removed from first-borns like him, and Dathan and Abiram joined because they thought that the tribe of Reuben, to which they belonged, was being discriminated against in favor of the two tribes which emanated from Joseph. In both cases, the complaint was the absence of preferential treatment for first-borns. Of course, it never entered their minds that perhaps there is no justification for first-borns receiving special privileges in the first place.

Ramban

Ramban (Num. 16:1) cites Ibn Ezra and immediately disputes his claim that Korah's jealousy traced itself to the time of the golden calf, when the decision was made to relieve the first-borns (including Korah) of the priesthood, and that the actual confrontation took place the first time Aaron officiated, which was at the dedication of the Tabernacle. One of Ramban's long-standing guidelines is that the Torah is arranged in chronological order, except where the text specifically states otherwise. It follows that, according to Ramban, the episode occurred exactly where the text places it, which is after the ill-fated mission of the spies. Korah and his cohorts each had their own motivation.

As the Midrash (*Tanchuma Korach* 1) explains, Korah was upset that Elizaphan b. Uziel was chosen as the prince of the Levitical branch of Kohath (Num. 3:30). Elizaphan was the son of

Korach

the youngest of Kohath's four children, Moses and Aaron were the sons of his oldest son Amram, and Korah was the son of the second oldest (Exod. 6:18-22). According to Korah's logic, appointments should be based on external factors such as birth order, rather than ability, character, innate qualities, or even the word of the Lord. In conformity with his own approach, Korah felt that he should take precedence over Elizaphan, and he considered it to be a malicious act of ill-will on the part of Moses not to choose him for that function as soon as Amram's children had been properly placed. Furthermore, from Moses' mentioning that in addition to serving as a Levite, Korah sought the priesthood (Num. 16:10), it is apparent that Korah felt that before even awarding a second appointment to one of the children (Aaron) of the eldest son (Amram), Moses should have offered it to the eldest of the second son, namely Korah himself. Of course, if Korah had been a son of Amram, and Aaron had been a son of Kohath's second son Yitzhar, Korah might have thought otherwise.

Ramban notes that Dathan and Abiram were not disputing the transfer of Reuben's primogeniture to Joseph, because (as mentioned previously) Jacob had already made that decision (Gen. 48:5), so Moses could certainly not be blamed. Actually, they stated very clearly what was irritating them: "Neither have you brought us to a land flowing with milk and honey, nor have you given us an inheritance of fields and vineyards" (Num. 16:14). The ones who protested the transferal of the priesthood to the family of Aaron, according to Ramban, were the non-Levitical first-borns, who were its main victims, and not Korah.

As for the timing, there is a reason that it took place at this point. After the sin of the golden calf, the Israelites loved Moses intensely, for he had prayed on their behalf, leading to a relatively small loss of life (Exod. 32:28). In the light of the adulatory attitude of the multitudes, Korah was willing to tolerate the greatness of

The Ethics of Numbers

Moses and Aaron, and the first-borns were willing to tolerate the elevation of the Levites. However, when they entered the Wilderness of Paran and sinned, and suffered losses at Taberah (Num. 11:1), Kibroth ha-Ta'avah (Num. 11:33), and later in conjunction with the libelous report of the spies; and Moses' prayers were not as effective as in the past and the tribal princes all died (Num. 14:37); and it was decreed that the entire adult male population was destined to die in the desert (Num. 14:29), Korah sensed a window of opportunity which he utilized by rousing the rabble and instigating a rebellion.

In review, while Ibn Ezra related both Korah's and Dathan and Abiram's complaints to the rights of the first-borns, dating their insubordination to the installation of the priests, Ramban takes a wider view, with each party having its own ulterior motives—Korah being jealous of Moses and Aaron, the first-borns being upset at the transfer of their rights to the Levites, and Dathan and Abiram actually angry at God for not allowing the nation to remain in the "Egyptian paradise" and not delivering on His promises to bring them to a better land.

Ramban's differentiation between the sins of the various transgressors enables one to answer the following basic questions:

1. Since Korah seems to be the main instigator, why is Moses' ire directed in large part at Dathan and Abiram? Moses is saddened when he hears Korah's words (16:4 – "Moses heard and fell on his face") and he tries to reason with him (16:9 – "Is it not enough that the God of Israel has distinguished you from the congregation of Israel to draw you near to Him?"). However, only after he hears Dathan and Abiram does he actually get angry (16:15 – "Moses was exceedingly distressed").

   One might answer that as impertinent as Korah was, the words of Dathan and Abiram must have been especially

Korach

galling to Moses when they referred to Egypt by the honored appellation that had been reserved for Israel (16:13 – "a land flowing with milk and honey"). And it was they who came "standing upright… with their wives, their children, and their infants" (16:27), which Rashi interprets to mean "with a haughty bearing, to curse and to blaspheme." Those words must have especially incensed Moses, who almost immediately declaimed one of his most foreboding statements:

If these men die in the same way that all men die, and the [typical] fate of all men is visited upon them, then the Lord has not sent me. But if the Lord creates a [unique] creation, and the earth opens its mouth and swallows them and all that is theirs, and they descend alive into the grave, you will know that these men have provoked the Lord (Num. 16:29-30).

God also seems to have meted out punishment more severely to Dathan and Abiram, since concerning them the verse states that the earth swallowed up "them and their houses," which would imply their entire families, while with regard to Korah it was only "all the men who were with Korah" (16:32), and in fact the Torah states later "and the sons of Korah did not die" (26:11). Nevertheless, one may question whether the difference in treatment of Dathan and Abiram by both Moses and God was reflective of their personality flaws alone, or perhaps of more intrinsic issues.

2. The Torah refers extensively in the book of Deuteronomy to the sins of the spies (1:19-40) and the golden calf (9:8-21), but devotes only one verse—mentioned in passing—to the story of Korah, where it speaks of "what He did to Dathan and Abiram, sons of Eliab, the son of Reuben, that the earth opened

its mouth and swallowed them up and their households and their tents, and all the possessions at their feet" (11:6). Korah himself is not even mentioned.

In the portion of *Pinchas* a second census is taken and, in describing the genealogy of the tribe of Reuben, the earth swallowing incident is mentioned (Num. 26:9). Although Korah is also mentioned (26:10), it seems to be as an afterthought, with the main focus again being on Dathan and Abiram.

The episode is also referred to in the book of Psalms, when describing the poor behavior of the Israelites in their travels through the desert, where it states: "The earth opened up and swallowed Dathan and covered the congregation of Abiram" (Ps. 106:17). Once more, Korah himself is not even mentioned.

These questions may be answered by accepting the view of Ramban, who distinguishes between the sins of the various actors. Korah and the congregation of 250 sinned by being jealous and not accepting God's decisions, which was serious enough, but Dathan and Abiram denied the foundation of the faith, and the verse describes them alone as "inciting against the Lord" (Num. 26:9).

The difference between Korah and Dathan and Abiram is that Korah may have had bad traits, but he himself was, according to the traditional commentaries, a scholar, and was not attempting to undermine the entire Jewish (Zionist) project, which was to create a morally superior civilization in the Land of Israel that would serve as a model for the Gentile world, which would eventually be influenced in the right direction and join the Jewish nation in preparing for the arrival of the Messiah. Dathan and Abiram, on the other hand, when beckoned by Moses, actually praised the land of Egypt (Num. 16:13). After the spying disaster, the Bible states: "One said to another, 'Let us appoint a leader and return to

Korach

Egypt'" (Num. 14:4). The Midrash (*Tanchuma Shemot* 10) says that these men are Dathan and Abiram, and another Midrash (*Midrash Tehillim* 106:5) says that the people wished to appoint Dathan to replace Moses, and Abiram instead of Aaron. The word used in the verse for "leader" is *rosh,* which the Talmud (BT *Sanhedrin* 107a) points out can be used to refer to idols, and according to various Midrashim (*Midrash ha-Gadol, Otiot de-Rabbi Akiva,* version 2) that is indeed its meaning in this verse.

In conclusion, Dathan and Abiram wanted to abandon the quest to settle in the Land of Israel and to live in accordance with the guidelines provided by the written and oral law. Rather, they wished to return to Egypt and re-adopt the immoral and corrupt lifestyle prevalent in that land, in total ingratitude for the miracles God had wrought for them and the mercy He had shown them during their emancipation from slavery and their escape from Egypt.

Summary

The Talmud views Korah as a respected scholar. Modern exegetes accordingly conclude that his sin must have been one that only a very righteous person would be accountable for, since he is held to a higher standard. According to the Izhbitzer, Korah's emphasis on democracy was a worthy idea, but his harsh presentation was unacceptable. Rav Kook believes that by calling the entire congregation holy, Korah lessened the importance of self-improvement, instead implying that everyone may accept himself as he is, and God should do the same. The Alter Rebbe (Shneur Zalman of Liadi, the first Lubavitcher Rebbe) felt that in reaction to the spying episode, Korah believed that Torah study, prayer, and attempts at coming close to the Almighty were not incumbent, and God requires only routine performance of the commandments.

The Ethics of Numbers

The classical commentaries, on the other hand, focus on more prevalent human failures, such as jealousy, lack of gratitude, and the failure to believe in God and His commandments. According to Ibn Ezra, the main complaint concerned the transfer of power from first-born entities—whether it be a tribe or an individual. In the view of Ramban, although Korah and the princes were also upset by the loss of primogeniture, Dathan and Abiram rejected the foundations of the religion, which were based on faith in God and gratitude for His beneficence to the Children of Israel, and it was their approach which had to be seriously combated and totally uprooted.

Chukat

At the beginning of the portion of *Chukat*, the subject introduced at the end of the previous portion—namely the functions and benefits of the priests and Levites—is continued with the description of the red heifer, whose ashes were sprinkled on those who had made contact with a dead body in order to remove their defilement. The portion proceeds to describe the fortieth and last year of the Israelites' journey through the desert, during which time Miriam dies, and Moses and Aaron are informed that because they did not sanctify God's name at a place called Mei Merivah (literally, "Waters of Strife"), they would not be allowed to lead the assembly into the Land of Israel. Soon after, Aaron dies, while the death of Moses is delayed until the end of the Torah (Deut. 34:5).

There are some who find a parallel between the portions of *Shlach* and *Korach,* because they both describe a rebellion against Moses and his Sender—the Almighty. I would like to suggest a parallel between the previous portion of *Korach* and the present one of *Chukat*. In the former, one is exposed to a disease, while in the latter one becomes aware of its treatment. The disease is jealousy: between man and his compatriot in general, and within the family in particular (Moses, the son of Amram, was a first cousin of Korah, the son of Amram's younger brother Yitzhar). The proper treatment of this disease is intimated in the portion of *Chukat*, which reminds one of the glorious cooperation among the siblings Moses, Aaron, and Miriam. Each of them had a function and felt comfortable with it: Moses as the source of Torah knowledge, Aaron as the facilitator of harmony within the nation, and Miriam as a wellspring of spirituality and culture. The contribution of each member complemented that of the others and together they formed a completed leadership team, as the prophet says: "And I sent before you [*Targum Yonatan* (TY): three prophets] Moses [TY: who taught tradition and law; Ibn Ezra: and confronted Pharaoh], Aaron [TY: who led the nation to repent; Ibn Ezra: and prophesied before Moses' arrival in Egypt], and Miriam [TY: who instructed the women; Ibn Ezra: and prophesied for them]" (Mic. 6:4).

Moses and Aaron

The great mutual love and respect that prevailed between Moses and Aaron, his senior by three years (Exod. 6:7), is exhibited from the first mention of Aaron in the book of Exodus. It will be recalled that Moses, displaying his typical modesty, at first declined to accept God's offer to lead the nation out of Egypt by saying, "Who am I [to assume such a position]?" (Exod. 3:11). After a week of negotiations, during which all of his objections were exhausted (Rashi, Exod. 4:14), Moses finally said: "Send [this message] by the hand of whomever You wish" (Exod. 4:13). The verse does not say whether Moses was referring to any specific person, but apparently God instantly picked up on the cue, when He referred to the heretofore unmentioned Aaron in the next verse, stimulating Rashi to write: "All of this [reluctance] was because he was unwilling to assume any greatness making him superior to his brother Aaron, who was older than he and [also] a prophet."

Chukat

As previously cited in the name of Ibn Ezra, Aaron served as the principal prophet from the time he was three years old until the arrival of Moses in Egypt, when Aaron was eighty-three. The Midrash (*Exod. Rabbah* 3:16) quotes the prophet Ezekiel, "And I made myself known to them in the land of Egypt… and I said to them: 'Every man should cast away the despicable idols from before his eyes'" (Ezek. 20:5-7), to derive that there was a tradition of prophecy during the period of slavery. That the prophet conveying this message was Aaron is deduced from the message of the man of God to Eli the high priest: "Surely, I revealed Myself to your father's house in Egypt when they were subject to the House of Pharaoh, and I chose them from among all the tribes of Israel to be My priests—to ascend My altar, to burn incense, [and] to carry an *ephod* before Me, and I gave your father's house all of the offerings of the Israelites" (1 Sam. 2:27-28). Eli's father's house during the period of subjugation could only refer to the single progenitor of the priestly clan, namely Aaron.

After Moses noted that he was "slow of speech and slow of tongue" (Exod. 2:10), the Almighty replied:

> Certainly, I know that your brother Aaron the Levite speaks well. Even now he is setting out to meet you, and he will be happy to see you. You will speak to him and place the words in his mouth… and he will speak for you to the people. Thus, he will serve as your spokesman, and you will play the role of God to him (Exod. 4:14-16).

Upon the arrival of Moses, Aaron was to be demoted from a recipient of high-level communication from the Lord to a mere spokesman utilized to convey God's message as transmitted to Moses, who was to be the true leader of the nation. In addition, at Revelation, Moses alone would ascend Mt. Sinai (Exod. 19:20;

Rashi, 19:24). As a seasoned prophet, Aaron doubtless knew all of this in advance. Nevertheless, God tells Moses that "he will be happy to see you," and indeed Aaron warmly welcomes Moses upon his arrival in Egypt, and eagerly carries out his new mission, as is clearly indicated by the continuing narrative:

> The Lord said to Aaron, "Go to meet Moses in the wilderness." He went and met him at the mountain of God, and he kissed him. And Moses told Aaron about all of the words of the Lord which He had sent him [to communicate] and all of the signs about which He had instructed him. Then Moses and Aaron went and assembled all of the elders of the Israelites. Aaron repeated [to the nation] all of the words that the Lord had spoken to Moses, and he [Moses] performed the signs in the sight of the people (Exod. 4:27-30).

The kiss reveals Aaron's sincere joy at reuniting with his brother and having the opportunity to spend quality time with him. And Moses, certainly aware that he would be undertaking some of Aaron's tasks, does not display an ounce of haughtiness or distance, but openly relates to Aaron "all of the words of the Lord which He had sent him [to communicate] and all of the signs about which He had instructed him." Furthermore, their passionate relationship was on display for everyone to see when Aaron repeated all of God's words, but Moses performed all of God's signs.

Aaron's attitude toward Moses correlates with the Mishnah in *Avot* (2:10), which states: "Let the honor of your friend be as dear to you as your own," interpreted by Rabbeinu Yonah to mean that one should seek to honor his friend and desire that his friend attain honor no less than if he himself were being feted.

Chukat

This is not to say that Aaron lost his ability to prophesy after the arrival of Moses. On the contrary, the Torah henceforth records numerous instances of God speaking to Aaron alone,[54] or together with Moses.[55] That Aaron remained a prophet follows from Rambam's statement that "if a person, perfect in his intellectual and moral faculties, and also perfect, as far as possible, in his imaginative faculty, prepares himself in the manner which will be described," and if such is the will of God, then he will be a prophet, "for prophecy is a natural faculty of man" (*Guide for the Perplexed* 2:32). If Aaron had achieved the level prerequisite for prophecy before the arrival of Moses in Egypt, certainly his subsequent steady exposure to him could have only increased his prophetic aptitude. Although one might conjecture that God would have withheld prophecy from Aaron after the golden calf incident, the overall view of both the Midrash and Biblical exegetes is that he was guiltless, having made the best out of a difficult situation.[56]

The felicitous relationship between Moses (the younger brother) and Aaron contrasts sharply with the many parallel instances found in the book of Genesis, where the older brother or brothers are jealous or discriminated against, starting with Cain, who murders Abel (Gen. 4:8), and continuing with Ishmael, who is expelled as a result of Isaac's being chosen (Gen. 21:10); Esau's plans to murder Jacob, who attained the designated successor's blessing by devious means (Gen. 27:41); Joseph's brothers, who conspired against him in consequence of their father's proffering him preferential treatment (Gen. 37:18); and Jacob's switching his hands and declaring that the younger Ephraim will be greater than the first-born Manasseh (Gen. 48:19). Only in the latter instance was the older brother able to accept his situation amicably, as

---

54. Lev. 10:8; Num. 18:8, 20.
55. Exod. 6:13, 7:8, 12:1; Lev. 11:1, 14:33, 15:1; Num. 4:1, 4:17, 12:4, 14:26, 16:20, 19:1, 20:12, 20:23.
56. See Abba Engelberg, *The Ethics of Exodus* (2014), pp. 224-232.

explicated by R. Yehudah Levenberg (*Imrei Chen, Vayechi*, "Jacob's Blessing to His Grandchildren"):

> Between Ephraim and Manasseh there was no jealousy. Manasseh was not jealous of Ephraim in consequence of his grandfather placing his right hand on his [Ephraim's] head, and also Ephraim did not become vainglorious as a result of meriting that the right hand of his illustrious grandfather be placed on his head.

This was the paradigm adopted by Moses and Aaron. It is no coincidence that such a positive attitude led to significant roles for the junior partner both in the case of Ephraim and Manasseh, and that of Moses and Aaron. The tribe of Manasseh became proficient as legislators and Torah scholars. *Ha'amek Davar* (Deut. 3:16) explains that when the tribes of Reuben and Gad asked permission to settle on the eastern side of the Jordan, their request was granted only when the tribe of Manasseh acquiesced to join them to ensure that they observed the Torah, since they were known to be very learned and righteous, as the prophetess Deborah notes concerning them in her song of victory: "from Machir [Manasseh] there came [to join the battle effort] legislators" (Judg. 5:14).

The Talmud (BT *Sanhedrin* 6b) contrasts the method used by Moses to settle civil disagreements, which was by means of a halachic decision, with Aaron's preferred method— arbitration. The latter is defined as a process for settling a disagreement by having both parties present their opinions to a third party, who then tries to find a formula acceptable to all concerned. The Talmud states (BT *Sanhedrin* 6b):

> Moses used to say: "Let the law cut through the mountain, as is written, 'For the judgment is God's'" (Deut. 1:17).

Chukat

> But Aaron loved peace and pursued peace and made peace between one man and his friend, as it is written: "Instruction of truth was in his mouth and injustice was not found in his lips; he walked with Me in peace and integrity and returned many from sin" (Mal. 2:6).

Although arbitration would seem to lead to peace and harmony, Moses looked upon arbitration as a means of neglecting to seek a decision based on the letter of the law, and instead looking for a solution that satisfies both disputants. By arbitrating, one is in a certain sense slighting the law, and in another sense weakening the motivation, as well as the benefit, of studying the law, which is an important pillar of the Jewish religion.

The Talmud continues:

> R. Yehoshua b. Korcha says: Settlement by arbitration is a mitzvah, for it is written: "Truth and peaceful judgment should be executed in your gates" (Zech. 8:16). Surely, where there is strict justice there is no peace, and where there is peace, there is no strict justice! But what is that kind of justice which is also peaceful? One must say it is arbitration… Rav says: The *halachah* is in agreement with R. Yehoshua b. Korcha.

The Talmud has arrived at a strange conclusion. On the one hand, the accepted law is that even after arriving in court, it is not only permitted, but recommended, that the judges inform the litigants of the possibility of arbitration. On the other hand, Moses is said to have looked askance at this option. Would the Rabbis negate the opinion of Moses? The Netziv explains that once the basic outline of the final decision is clear, then even according to R. Yehoshua arbitration is not acceptable. But Moses was so knowledgeable that once the litigants presented their arguments, he immediately knew the appropriate decision, and therefore arbitration was improper. Almost nobody else had that clarity, and there is thus ample opportunity to resort to arbitration.[57]

Both Moses and Aaron appreciated and highly respected the cardinal values of peaceful arbitration on the one hand, and strict adherence to *halachah* on the other. The only difference between them was in their respective areas of expertise, with Moses excelling in the latter and Aaron in the former.

Moses, who spent forty days on Mt. Sinai after receiving the first set of tablets (Exod. 24:18) and another forty days upon receiving the second set (Exod. 34:28), fully immersed in the study of the written and oral law, and in direct communication with the Almighty, was certainly the greatest expert in Torah law to ever live. Furthermore, according to tradition, at the conclusion of the allotted time, any minutiae which were initially beyond his comprehension, he miraculously absorbed when God presented them to him as a parting gift (*Exod. Rabbah* [Vilna] 41:6).

Nevertheless, it would be incorrect to say that Moses lacked compassion. In fact, the first reference to Moses as an adult was when "he went out to his brothers and saw their burdens and saw an Egyptian beating a Hebrew, one of his kinsmen" (Exod. 2:11), which moved him to save the Hebrew by smiting the taskmaster. Later, when the local shepherds attempted to overpower the daughters of Jethro who had already filled the troughs with water for their own sheep to drink, Moses once more took the part of the injured side and drove the villains away (Exod. 2:16-17). Subsequently to Moses becoming Jethro's shepherd, the Midrash (*Exod. Rabbah* [Vilna] 2:2) tells of a kid that had escaped from the flock. After tracking it down and realizing that it was exhausted,

---

57. Netziv, *Harchev Davar*, Exod. 18:23. For a fuller discussion of this topic, see Abba Engelberg, *The Ethics of Exodus* (2014), pp. 355-364.

Chukat

Moses mounted it on his shoulders and carried it back to the herd. Noting his compassion, God told Moses, "If you display such a degree of mercy when caring for the sheep of a human being, how much more so will you be merciful in dealing with My sheep."

As the transmitter of the many beneficent laws of the Torah, such as those legislating kindness toward the stranger, orphan, and widow (Exod. 22:20-23; Deut. 14:28-29, 16:9-14, 24:17-22), and interest-free loans under the most considerate conditions to the poverty-stricken (Exod. 22:24-26; Deut. 24:6, 10-13), there is no question that Moses, no less than Aaron, was thoroughly devoted to social welfare, although in marginal cases, Moses had a tendency to adhere to the legalistic approach, while Aaron would seek compromise (BT *Sanhedrin* 6b-7a). Furthermore, Moses used his intuition in implementing ethically-oriented laws on the communal level. This is indicated by a Midrash (*Sifrei Shoftim*, par. 199) which calls Moses, as well as Aaron, a peace-lover (*ohev shalom*), based on his retelling the story of his battle against Sihon the Amorite king, where he says: "Then I sent messengers from the wilderness of Kedemoth to King Sihon of Heshbon with an offer of peace" (Deut. 2:26). Apparently, God acquiesced to Moses' initiative when He later commanded: "When you approach a city to attack it, you should offer it terms of peace" (Deut. 20:10). Based on this verse, Rambam ruled: "One does not engage in battle with anyone in the world unless he [first] makes a peace offer, whether it be an optional war or a compulsory war" (*Hilchot Melachim* 6:1).

Aaron was renowned for seeking peace and harmony. The Midrash (*Avot de-Rabbi Natan* A:12) describes how in cases of interpersonal disputes Aaron would privately tell each party how distraught his antagonist is, since he realized that it is actually he who is at fault, just that he is too embarrassed to step forward and openly confess his guilt. When the disputants would meet, they would lovingly embrace and forget that they had ever argued. Since it was frequently a husband and wife who were at odds until Aaron facilitated their reconciliation, there were many little "Aarons" running around, named after the *tzaddik* who was successful in stimulating them to renew their primal love and re-establish their family unit.

On the other hand, in addition to being merciful and loving, Aaron was a well-versed competent Torah scholar as well. He was the first to be taught each and every law by Moses after hearing it from the Almighty. Aaron then heard Moses repeat the lesson to Aaron's sons, the elders, and the whole nation, at which point Aaron reviewed the lesson for the entire congregation (BT *Eruvin* 54b). He was thus exposed to each Torah law five times.

The Midrash (*Tanchuma* [Buber] *Chukat, hosafah*) notes that when Moses died, the Torah states: "And the *Children of Israel* [just the men] wept for Moses at the plains of Moab thirty days" (Deut. 34:8), while regarding Aaron's demise the verse states: "And they wept for Aaron thirty days, the *entire house of Israel* [men and women]" (Num. 20:29). As noted, since Aaron dealt lovingly with familial problems and specifically with marital discord, his death was felt by the women no less than by the men.

Interestingly, a second Midrash (*Avot de-Rabbi Natan* A:12) relates Aaron's intense popularity not to his social graces but specifically to his judicial adeptness, noting that the populace felt that his verdicts reflected the absolute truth inherent in the law without prejudice, and he refrained from censuring the culpable side. Moses, on the other hand, would harshly rebuke the guilty party, possibly because his deeply honest nature did not allow any form of dissimulation. Properly reproaching others without seriously embarrassing them is an immensely difficult task, a realization which stimulated the Tanna R. Elazar b. Azariah to contemplate: "I wonder if there exists anyone in this generation who knows how to reprimand [honorably, without giving offense]" (BT *Arachin* 16b).

Chukat

Aaron's method of minimizing sin was prescriptive rather than reactive. The Midrash (*Avot de-Rabbi Natan* A:12) tells how he would consciously proffer a very warm welcome whenever he happened upon a known sinner. The next time an opportunity to sin arose, the sinner would say to himself: "If I perform this transgression, I will be so embarrassed when I meet Aaron and he extends his friendly and approving greeting." As a result, he would restrain himself from sinning. Another Midrash (*Tanchuma* [Buber] *Chukat, hosafah*) speaks of cases where Aaron became aware of one who left his house at night to perform a (presumably sexual) sin. Aaron would leave his home and find the potential sinner and tell him: "My son, why are you out at this time of night? People might suspect that you are planning to perform evil acts, which would certainly be slanderous, you being a good person from a distinguished family." Upon being praised and reminded of his family's illustrious ancestry, the person would find the inner strength to overcome his evil inclination. These stories were used to illustrate the meaning of the prophet's words (which were understood to be referring to Aaron): "he walked with Me in peace and integrity and *returned many from sin*" (Mal. 2:6), which were later encapsulated in the Mishnah's description of Aaron as one who "loved people *and drew them near to the Torah*" (Avot 1:12).

Aaron's approach was to cherish every person as a creation of God, independent of his level of observance, and such an approach frequently drew each one closer to Torah in the long run. Not technically a leader, he permitted himself the luxury of relating to every person as being totally righteous, and to each disputant as being completely in the right, even if he knew that was not the case, and by doing so, he was able to solve many conflicts. Moses, on the other hand, who was formally designated as the chief decision-maker, had to uncompromisingly lay down the law, allowing it to "cut through the mountain" even when it was painful to certain individuals, who went on to develop an aversion to him to the extent that they might not even mourn his passing.[58]

The Torah stresses the balanced relation between the brothers by sometimes giving precedence to Moses, and at other times to Aaron. With regard to the verse: "These are Aaron and Moses, to whom the Lord said: 'Take out the Children of Israel from the land of Egypt according to their tribes'" (Exod. 6:26), Rashi comments:

> There are some places where [the name of] Aaron precedes Moses [as here] and there are [other] places where [the name of] Moses precedes Aaron. [This was done] to tell you that they were of equal weight.

In summary, while they appreciated each other's strengths, Aaron may be typified as a pursuer of peace and Moses as a pursuer of truth. The Midrash (*Exod. Rabbah* 5:10) metaphorically interprets the verse: "Mercy and truth have *met*; justice and peace have *kissed* each other" (Ps. 85:11) as referring to Moses and Aaron, by citing verses which describe Moses as representing truth and justice, and Aaron as exemplifying mercy and peace. The Midrash then uses this explanation to bring out the deeper meaning of the verse describing how Aaron "*met* him [Moses] at the mountain of God and *kissed* him" (Exod. 4:27).

Moses and Miriam

Miriam is first mentioned, although not by name, in the beginning of Exodus as the sister of Moses, who arranged for him to be nursed by his own mother, Jochebed. She is first identified by her name Miriam as the sister of Aaron (and hence of Moses) later in

---

58. Meir Nehorai, "*Ha-Eivel be-Ait Petirat Aharon*," skamigdaloz/2016/06/28.

Exodus (15:20), where she is termed a prophetess, when she leads the women in song and dance in celebration of their escape from slavery and their successful crossing of the Red Sea. That she is the same sister who saved Moses follows from Num. 26:59, where she is listed as the only sister of Moses and Aaron.

Miriam's leadership of the women while still in Egypt was so successful that the Talmud states in the section dealing with Miriam's actions: "As a reward for the righteous women who lived in that generation, the Israelites were delivered from Egypt" (BT *Sotah* 11b). In other words, if not for the exceptional behavior of the women in Egypt, God would not have redeemed the Jews from slavery, because He would have concluded that the situation was hopeless, much as He did with regard to the generation of the Great Flood. The Talmud proceeds to describe how that righteousness was manifested in Egypt.[59] Furthermore, the women maintained their high standard at the time of the crossing of the sea, concerning which the Talmud (ibid.) states: "When the Lord revealed Himself by the Red Sea, they [the women and their young children] recognized Him first."

Throughout the Israelites' sojournings in the desert, the women's behavior continued to be exemplary. The Midrash (*Num. Rabbah* 21:10) suggests that women did not take part in the sin of the golden calf, nor in the sin of the spies. As a result, the punishment of dying in the desert was only meted out to the men, as the verse states: "And no *man* of them was left, save Caleb the son of Jephuneh and Joshua the son of Nun" (Num. 26:65), from which the Midrash deduces that the men of that generation were not left, but the women were.

In trying to understand why the women were less prone to sin, as revealed by their lack of participation in the golden calf and spying fiascos, it may be suggested that men are more affected

---

59. See Abba Engelberg, *The Ethics of Exodus* (2014), pp. 245-269.

by external appearances and passing whims, and were thus more readily attracted by the glitter of the golden calf on the one hand, but more easily frightened by the physical looks of the Canaanite inhabitants of Israel on the other hand.[60]

Based on the Midrash's claim that the women survived the forty-year trek in the desert, R. S.R. Hirsch (Num. 20:1) concludes:

> [If they] as mothers and grandmothers could bring over into the new generation personal recollections of the past in Egypt and the glorious personal experiences of the exodus and the subsequent living under the direct protection and guidance of God, and impregnate their grandchildren and great-grandchildren with the spirit of these God-revealing experiences, then no small part of their being endowed with the true Jewish spirit must be ascribed to their brilliant leader and prophetess Miriam and her shining example ever before them.

R. Hirsch explains that after Miriam imbued the women with the proper religious outlook, her task was completed, and so she died with the satisfaction that her mission was accomplished. A minority opinion holds that Miriam died soon after the exodus, when she was eighty-six years old[61] (*Seder Olam Rabbah* 3). The more commonly held viewpoint, however, is that she died at the end of the forty-year journey (*Sifrei, Nitzavim*), at the age of 127 (*Sefer ha-Dorot*).

---

60. This has been shown to be true with respect to sexual stimuli. See Heather A. Rupp; Kim Wallen. *Sex Differences in Response to Visual Sexual Stimuli: A Review,* "Archives of Sexual Behavior" 37, 2 (Apr 2008) pp. 206-218.
61. The Torah states that Aaron was three years the senior of Moses (Exod. 7:7). According to *Exod. Rabbah* (1:13), Miriam was the eldest, so she would have been eighty-six at the time of the exodus or before. But Ramban holds that she was younger, so she would have only reached that age a couple of years after leaving Egypt.

Chukat

Miriam appears in the Midrashic literature in a number of contexts. According to one view in the Talmud (BT *Sotah* 11b), Miriam and her mother Jochebed were the midwives who were instructed by Pharaoh to kill the newborn male children, and who rightfully and righteously disobeyed his edict, thereby risking their lives by declaring that the Jewish women gave birth before the midwives were able to seize the babies (Exod. 1:15-19). Although the Bible identifies them as Shifra (Jochebed) and Puah (Miriam), the Midrash takes these names to be adjectival rather than proper nouns, with Puah derived from a Hebrew word which, according Rashi, indicates that she spoke lovingly and soothingly to the infants. The Biblical text states that "they enabled the boys to live" (Exod. 1:17). The Talmud comments that the verse could have simply said "they did not kill the boys" (Rashi) or "they did not fulfill the king's order" (*Torah Temimah*, Exod. 1:29). By saying that they enabled them to live, it implies that they made additional efforts, specifically "they supplied them with water and food" (BT *Sotah* 11b). The Midrash explains that if the mother was poor, the midwives went to the houses of rich women, collected adequate sustenance, and delivered it to them. They further prayed that the babies should survive the birthing process and be born without blemish, and that their mothers should not die in childbirth (*Gen. Rabbah* 1:15). Rashi adds that they also provided the cultural environment necessary to maintain a spiritual life by raising them in their own home.

The Talmud (BT *Sotah* 12a) continues in a Midrashic vein, noting the peculiar phrase: "And a man from the house of Levi went, and he took [as a wife] a daughter of Levi" (Exod. 2:1). The normal way of conveying this idea would have been to write: "And a man from the house of Levi took [as a wife] a daughter of Levi." The verse instead says that "he went," but it does not say where he went or why it is important to know that he went. The Midrash proposes that "went" be understood not in the sense of physically going, but in the sense of acquiescing, i.e., going along with something. The advice was that which the young Miriam proffered to her father. When Miriam's father Amram heard Pharaoh's decree to cast all male babies into the river, he divorced his wife in order to prevent wanton loss of life. All of the men of Israel followed in his footsteps, since he was known to be the greatest sage of the generation. Miriam then confronted her father, telling him that his decree was even harsher than that of Pharaoh, since he would be preventing not only the birth of males, but also females, not to mention that in many cases Pharaoh's decree might be circumvented. He thereupon took his wife back, and the rest of the congregation followed in his footsteps.[62] The Talmud, however, expresses skepticism with regard to this narrative, noting that the verse says that "a man from the house of Levi [Amram] took [as a wife] a daughter of Levi." If the Talmudic tale is true, it should have said that he "took *back* [as a wife] a daughter of Levi." The Talmud answers:

> He acted towards her as though it had been their first marriage; he seated her in a palanquin, Aaron and Miriam danced before her, and the ministering angels proclaimed: "a joyful mother of children" (Ps. 113:9).

Combining the straightforward meaning with the Midrashic legends, Miriam is seen to be totally responsible for Moses' coming into the world and surviving. It was she who convinced her father to resume his marriage, enabling Moses to be conceived; it must have been she who served as the midwife at his birth, being that the other midwife, Jochebed, was the one giving birth; and it was she who arranged for his mother Jochebed to serve as his wet-nurse. Aaron also, at the tender age of three, was already displaying

---

62. See Abba Engelberg, *The Ethics of Exodus* (2014), pp. 25-27.

Chukat

his loving, indulgent, and warm personality. From the time that Moses was in his cradle, the sibling trio was united, manifesting true potential for eventual leadership, in which the leaders would complement each other.

The Triumvirate

In summary, although Moses and his siblings were exemplary in all of their areas of endeavor, each stood out with regard to a specific characteristic for which they served as a symbol and positive influence on the members of the community. Moses, who received and promulgated the Torah, represented the centrality of the written and oral law in the life of the Jewish nation. Aaron, through his behavior and peace-making efforts, signified the importance of people (and peoples) living in harmony with each other. Finally, Miriam—the loving and merciful older sister who instilled confidence and gratitude not only in her younger brothers but in all of the women initially, and in the entire community eventually—symbolized the important values of charity and loving-kindness.

The leading roles of these three luminaries is part of the Jewish tradition and is reflected in the previously quoted words of rebuke of the prophet Micah, who rails against Israel's lack of gratitude: "For I brought you up out of the land of Egypt, and I redeemed you from the house of bondage, and I sent before you Moses, Aaron, and Miriam" (Mic. 6:4). The prophecy continues with Micah informing the nation that God does not crave animal, and most certainly not human, sacrifice. Micah proceeds: "He has told you, O man, what is good, and what the Lord requires of you: only to do justice and to love goodness and to walk modestly with your God" (Mic. 6:8). The verse indicates that God has told man "what is good"—which refers to laws between man and his fellow man (*bein adam le-chaveiro*), and "what the Lord requires of you"—which refers to laws between man and God (*bein adam la-Makom*). An alternative explanation is that the beginning of the verse refers to what men have told other men ("He" refers to men), namely that sacrifices are good, and this is contrasted with what God really expects.[63]

The verse spells out exactly what God requires. By first mentioning "doing justice," the prophet defines the desired goal for decisors of Jewish law (*poskim*). Radak says that the phrase is specifically referring to enforcing social laws such as torts and sexual prohibitions, and Ibn Ezra adds that it also includes not hurting others verbally or physically. The Talmud (BT *Sukkah* 49b) implies that all halachic decisions are being referred to, and one may thus associate "doing justice" with the expert in that area—Moses our teacher.

The verse then says "to love goodness," which the Talmud (ibid.) explains as referring to the performance of acts of loving-kindness (*gemilut chassadim*). The Talmud goes on to elaborate that charity is superior to bringing sacrifices, and *gemilut chassadim* is superior to charity for the following three reasons:

> Charity can be done only with one's money, but *gemilut chassadim* can be done with one's person or one's money. Charity can be given only to the poor, *gemilut chassadim* [can be done] both to the rich and to the poor. Charity can be given to the living only, *gemilut chassadim* can be done both for the living and the dead.

Recalling Miriam's biography, this phrase may easily be referring to her special area of expertise.

---

63. Abraham Cohen, *The Twelve Prophets* (1948), p. 181.

Chukat

The difference between the first phrase ("doing justice") and the second ("loving goodness") is basically the difference between "turning away from evil," i.e., preventing, refraining from, and punishing negative actions, and "doing good" (Ps. 34:15)—proactively engaging in beneficent works.

The third phrase in the verse, to "walk modestly with your God," might be interpreted as referring to laws between man and God. But to which laws would it be referring? If the reference is to all of the laws of the Torah, in what sense is Micah epitomizing God's demands? Additionally, one may ask the same question as the Talmud asks regarding a similar verse:

> Is it, then, possible for a human being to walk with the *Shechinah*? Has it not been said: "For the Lord your God is a devouring fire" (Deut. 4:24). But [the meaning is] to adopt the attributes of the Holy One, blessed be He (BT *Sotah* 14a).

In fact, the Talmud relegates this phrase specifically to "attending to funerals and dowering a bride for her wedding" (BT *Sukkah* 49b). But would this not be included in acts of loving-kindness, already dealt with in the second phrase? Rashi was apparently bothered by this question, because he relates this phrase to exceptional acts beyond the normal purvey of good deeds. He says:

> "Walk modestly": The Lord's behavior is not like that of a human being. If a person wishes to appease his friend after embarrassing him, the friend will tell him, "I am not willing to be reconciled unless those people present when you embarrassed me also attend." But for the Lord, it is sufficient that only the perpetrator be present at the reconciliation (Rashi, Mic. 8:6).

The Ethics of Numbers

"Walking modestly with God" is being interpreted as following in the footsteps of the Almighty by conducting all aspects of one's life with an aura of modesty. One can be good to others for selfish reasons, for example because he wishes to eventually receive favors from them and he looks upon his charitableness as an investment in the future. Alternatively, one can be good to others because he is a humble person who respects and loves others with no ulterior motives. Such was Aaron, and because of this outstanding personality trait he was loved by all, and people were willing to acquiesce to his entreaties when he attempted to reconcile feuding parties. The third phrase in the verse is thus a good fit for Aaron.

It will be noted that the verse in Micah starts off with the words: "He has told you, O man, what is good, and what the Lord requires of you," which is past tense. Indeed, there is nothing new in this prophecy. God's preference for obeying the law over sacrifices had already been proclaimed by Samuel, when he asked: "Does the Lord desire burnt offerings and sacrifices as much as obedience to the Lord's voice" (1 Sam. 15:22). As far as obeying the laws of the Torah, certainly Moses had already spoken to the nation, saying: "I have taught you statutes and ordinances as the Lord my God has commanded me…. Observe them faithfully" (Deut. 4:5-6). Finally, practicing acts of loving-kindness formed the content of many of the commands, and was specifically derived from the phrase: "You should follow [in the footsteps of] the Lord your God" (Deut. 13:5; BT *Sotah* 14a). The prophet's contribution was accordingly summarized by the orientalist John Merlin Powis Smith, who wrote that the greatness of the statement is based on the fact that it "lays hold of the essential elements of religion and, detaching them from all else, sets them in clear relief. It links ethics with piety, duty towards men with duty towards God, and makes them both co-equal factors in religion."[64]

---

64. Abraham Cohen, *The Twelve Prophets* (1948), p. 181.

Chukat

The three siblings have been shown to represent not only three leaders, but three areas of functionality which are central to Judaism. This subdivision can be read into Mishnaic sources as well. Regarding functionaries, *Avot* (4:13) speaks of three crowns, that of Torah scholarship, priesthood, and royalty. Scholarship certainly pertains to Moses, Aaron became the high priest, and Miriam was the progenitor of King David (*Sifrei Beha'alotcha* 78; *Exod. Rabbah* 48:4). The high priests were clerics who, in addition to their ritual tasks, would certainly have maintained Aaron's involvement in magnanimous arbitration, while one of the functions of a king was the promotion of social welfare.

Another Mishnah speaks in terms of functional areas, saying that "The world stands on three things: On Torah, divine worship, and acts of loving-kindness" (*Avot* 1:2). Once again, Moses may be looked upon as the representative of Torah, and Miriam of loving-kindness. Divine worship may clearly be associated with Aaron the priest. However, the Hebrew word used in the Mishnah is *avodah*, which literally means "work." It of course refers to divine service, but as a principle for existence in this world, it must certainly include fruitful labor as well, for if people did not work, they would not be in a position to study Torah or engage in beneficent activities. Working productively and efficiently demands intensive cooperation, which can frequently lead to inter-personal friction, which would once again require Aaron's conciliatory expertise.

THE PASSING OF MOSES, AARON, AND MIRIAM

In the portion of *Chukat*, the demise of Miriam and Aaron is recorded, while the actual passing of Moses is only mentioned in the last chapter of the Torah (Deut. 34:5), although its immediate cause is found in *Chukat* (Num. 20:12). They die in the same order in which they were born, according to the majority viewpoint.

The Ethics of Numbers

Regarding Miriam, the Torah states:

> And the entire congregation of the Children of Israel came to the wilderness of Zin in the first month, and the people dwelt in Kadesh; and Miriam died there and was buried there. And there was no water for the congregation; and they assembled themselves together against Moses and against Aaron (Num. 20:1-2).

The verse states that Miriam died in the first month, i.e., the Hebrew month of Nissan, without mentioning an exact date. *Seder Olam Rabbah* states in one place (ch. 9) that it occurred on the first of the month (*rosh chodesh*), and in another place that it occurred on the tenth of the month, and the latter seems to be the generally accepted date.

Immediately after Miriam's passing, there was a dearth of water and the nation protested against Moses and Aaron, causing Moses to lose his temper and refer to the congregation as rebels, which in turn led to God chastising Moses and Aaron,[65] telling them:

> Because you did not trust Me enough to sanctify Me in the eyes of the Children of Israel, therefore you will not bring this congregation into the land that I have given them (Num. 20:12).

Shortly afterwards, Aaron dies.

The Midrash (*Song of Songs Rabbah* 4:2) allegorically interprets the verse "and I cut off the three shepherds in one month" (Zech. 11:8) to be referring to Moses, Aaron, and Miriam, with Rashi

---

[65]. According to Rambam (Introduction to *Avot*, ch. 4). Rashi (Num. 20:12), on the other hand, relates the chastisement to Moses' hitting of the rock.

Chukat

(BT *Ta'anit* 9a) explaining that it must relate to them, since there was no other triumvirate of leaders (shepherds) who functioned simultaneously.[66] The Midrash proceeds to question the claim that the three died in the same month, since regarding Aaron it says explicitly in the Torah that he died on the first day of the Hebrew month of Av (Num. 33:38), and regarding Moses the Talmud (BT *Kiddushin* 38a) derives from an analysis of various verses at the end of Deuteronomy and the beginning of the book of Joshua that he died on the seventh of Adar. In fact, they all died in different months.

The Midrash answers that indeed they died in different months, however it was shown previously that immediately after Miriam's death the incident which culminated in God decreeing that Moses and Aaron would not enter the land occurred, and so one might say that the future for all three was terminated in the same month—Nissan.

A second answer is that the month being referred to is Adar, since in that month the positive effect of all three personalities expired. The Talmud states:

> R. Yosi the son of R. Yehuda says: Three good leaders arose in Israel—namely, Moses, Aaron, and Miriam—and for their sake three gifts were conferred [upon Israel], namely the well, the [pillar of] cloud, and the manna; the well [a sieve-like rock that accompanied the Israelites throughout their wanderings in the wilderness; see Rashi,

---

66. This is not, however, the simple interpretation given by the commentators in the book of Zechariah. Rashi says the three leaders refers to the House of Ahab, the House of Ahaziah King of Judea, and the remaining members of the House of David (excepting Joash), the latter of whom were killed by Ataliah. Ibn Ezra says it might be referring to Haggai, Zechariah, and Malachi (even though the verse appears in the book of Zechariah). Radak says the reference is to the three sons of Josiah: Jehoahaz, Jehoiakim, and Zedekiah.

BT *Shabbat* 35a] for the merit of Miriam; the [pillar of] cloud for the merit of Aaron; the manna for the merit of Moses. When Miriam died, the well disappeared, for it says, "And Miriam died there" (Num. 20:1), and [it says immediately] afterwards, "And there was no water for the congregation;" and it [the well] returned for the merit of the [latter] two. When Aaron died, the clouds of glory disappeared, as it is written, "And the Canaanite, the king of Arad heard" (Num. 21:1). What news did he hear? He heard that Aaron had died, and [as a result] that the clouds of glory had disappeared; he thought that he was free to make war on Israel. Therefore, it is written: "And all the congregation saw that Aaron was dead" (Num. 20:29), with reference to which R. Abahu said: "Do not read 'they saw,' but 'they were seen' [i.e., the congregation was seen by the enemy, because of the disappearance of the pillar of cloud, because Aaron had died]." ... The two [the well and the cloud] returned because of the merit of Moses. When Moses died, all of them disappeared, for it says: "And I cut off the three shepherds in one month" (Zech. 11:8). Did they all die in one month? Did not Miriam die in Nissan, Aaron in Av, and Moses in Adar? It teaches that the three good gifts given because of their merit were nullified, and they all disappeared in one month (BT *Ta'anit* 9a).

A number of questions may be raised concerning this segment:

1. Why were those specific miracles chosen?

    According to *Iyun Ya'akov* (BT *Yoma* 74b), manna taught the Israelites the self-control necessary to pursue Torah studies, while R. S.R. Hirsch (Deut. 8) sees it as providing spiritual preparation for observing the law, both traits which

Chukat

may be associated with Moses the lawgiver. In fact, *Midrash Tanchuma* (*Beshallach* 20) says that those who ate manna and did not need to devote time to supporting themselves were able to master the intricacies of the Torah. Furthermore, as leader of his generation, Moses was responsible for providing not only spiritual sustenance, but physical sustenance as well, as embodied in the manna (Maharal, *Netzach Yisrael* 54).

The clouds, associated with Aaron, represent a tent which covers and unites. On the one hand, clouds manifest the Divine Presence in this world, as it says: "for I appear in the cloud enclosing the Ark's cover" (Lev. 16:2),[67] and Aaron the high priest nurtured this connection between man and the Almighty (Maharal). On the other hand, Aaron, in his personal capacity, cultivated close relations between man and his fellow man, allowing them to live together peacefully "under the same tent."

Finally, the well that quenched their thirst was provided in the merit of Miriam, who embodied the virtue of beneficence, as the Bible says of the midwives: "they caused them to live" (Exod. 1:17), to which the Talmud adds: "not only did they not put them to death [as Pharaoh had commanded in Exod. 1:16], but they supplied them with food and water" (BT *Sotah* 11b).

2. Why did the well and the cloud disappear in the first place, if the merit of Moses was sufficient to cause them to return? One may answer that they disappeared to show that their initial appearance was in Miriam's and Aaron's merit, respectively (*Eitz Yosef, Ein Ya'akov, Ta'anit* 9a).

3. Since all three returned because of the merit of Moses, why were they not initially instituted in his merit alone without

---

67. God's revelation in a cloud is mentioned in numerous locations in the Pentateuch, such as Exod. 19:17, 40:34; Deut. 31:15.

reference to Aaron and Miriam? The *Shlah* (*Pesachim Matzah Ashirah* 2:307) answers that there is a difference between retrieving something that already existed but disappeared and creating something new. Moses may have had sufficient merit to reincarnate pre-existing phenomena, but not enough to create them *ex nihilo*. This approach corroborates what has previously been noted, namely that each of the siblings was proficient in all of the areas symbolized by the manna, the well, and the cloud, but each had his/her own area of special distinction.

Equivalence in Death

The Talmud (BT *Bava Batra* 17a; see also BT *Mo'ed Katan* 28a) states:

> Our Rabbis taught: There were six [righteous people] over whom the Angel of Death had no dominion, namely, Abraham, Isaac, and Jacob; Moses, Aaron, and Miriam…. Moses, Aaron, and Miriam because it is written in connection with them [that they died] "by the mouth of the Lord."

The Talmud creates equivalence between the three siblings, and at the same time places them spiritually on the same level as the patriarchs. These people had reached a degree of holiness so far above the average that their mortality was not in the realm of the Angel of Death, who exclusively reigned over normal human beings. Their service as supporting pillars of earthly life was so great that their presence in this world could not be terminated routinely, but needed special approval, so to say, from the Lord himself, which He performed by lovingly bestowing upon them the kiss of death. The Talmud derives this from the following verses:

Chukat

- **With regard to Aaron:** "Aaron the priest ascended Mount Hor by the mouth of the Lord and died there" (Num. 33:38).
- **With regard to Moses:** "And Moses the servant of the Lord died *there* [*va-yamot sham*], in the land of Moab, by the mouth of the Lord" (Deut. 34:5).
- **With regard to Miriam:** "and the people dwelt in Kadesh; and Miriam died *there* [*va-tamot sham*], and was buried there" (Num. 20:1).

The Talmud immediately notes that the Bible in fact does not use the phrase "by the mouth of the Lord" with respect to Miriam, contrary to what was stated. The following answer is provided: "Miriam also died by a kiss, as we learn from the use of the word *sham* [meaning 'there'—in connection both with her death] and with that of Moses." In what way does the use of the word "there" indicate that Miriam, like Moses, died "by the mouth of the Lord?" The *Or ha-Chaim* (Num. 20:1) explains:

> It seems that since He mentioned "death," [the verse] took into consideration the respect due to a righteous woman, for the Sages stated (BT *Berachot* 18a) that the righteous in their death are called living [and since Miriam was a righteous woman, why is "death" mentioned with respect to her]. Therefore, the Talmud punctiliously noted that "there" is [properly] interpreted to mean "there she died and did not remain among them. However, she rests in a different place among the righteous," for the righteous are comparable before the Almighty to precious stones which lay in a vault. When He wants one of them, He removes it from the vault and embeds it in one of his pieces of jewelry.

The Talmud is positing that one concerning whom the Torah uses the phrase "died there"—implying that the person died only there (i.e. in this world), but is now in a holier and higher place (i.e. in the next world)—is one who died "by the mouth of the Lord."

However, the Talmud is not yet satisfied, for it proceeds to ask why dying "by the mouth of the Lord" is stated explicitly with regard to Moses and Aaron, and only indicated by implication with regard to Miriam. The Talmud answers: "Because such an expression would be disrespectful." Now one might ask: since the Almighty is neither male nor female, why is it any different for God to be kissing a woman than a man? The answer is that the Talmud means to say that Miriam would be presented in an unseemly manner, since for a woman more than a man, kissing is considered to be a sexually-oriented act, and this is not the facet of Miriam which the Torah wishes to accentuate. Rashi (Num. 20:1), however, says explicitly that the meaning of the phrase refers to speaking disrespectfully "about the Most High God." Apparently, Rashi believes that "the Torah employs human phraseology" (BT *Bava Metzia* 31b); i.e., since many people relate to God as a male figure (perhaps especially the God of the Torah, who takes on the role of the lawgiver), it would be inappropriate to speak of him giving Miriam the "kiss of death."

Summary

The portion of *Chukat* records the deaths of Miriam and Aaron, and describes the incident termed "the waters of strife," where Aaron and Moses erred and were informed that the punishment for their sin would be that they would not enter the Holy Land. The demise or near demise of the three siblings was taken advantage of to delineate each one's contribution to the overall leadership of the

Chukat

nation—Moses as the lawgiver, Aaron as the pacifier, and Miriam as the benefactor. It was noted how each of the three was adept in all of the important areas, but exhibited exceptional expertise in his/her specialization.

An additional point of interest is that the Bible seems to be implying that no matter how exceptional a person is, it is better for the functioning of an organization to undergo a turnover in its leadership after the elapse of a reasonable period of time and upon entering a new environment unfamiliar to the previous administrators.

Balak

The portion of *Balak* describes events which occurred as the Israelites entered the last stage of their journey to the Promised Land. Coming from the south, they had reached Kadesh, south of Edom and the Dead Sea, where Miriam died (Num. 20:1). Their eventual destination was the land of Canaan, on the other side of the Jordan. The most efficient route would have been to traverse Edom, for which they requested permission, as stated in the portion of *Chukat* (Num. 20):

> **14** And Moses sent messengers from Kadesh to the king of Edom: "So says your brother, Israel, 'You know of all the hardship that has befallen us… **17** Please let us pass through your land; we will not pass through fields or vineyards, nor will we drink well water. We will walk along the king's road, and we will turn neither to the right nor to the left until we have passed your border.'" **18** And Edom said to him, "You may not pass through me, lest I go out towards you with the sword!" **19** The Children of Israel said to him, "We will keep to the highway, and if we drink your water, either I or my cattle, we will pay its price. It is really nothing; I will pass through on foot."

Permission was not granted, and so the convoy was forced to go out of its way and skirt Edom from the east, even though the intention

Balak

was to move westward. To the north of Edom and to the east of the Dead Sea lay Moab, and the procession would then arrive at its eastern border. Efficiency would dictate that the congregation traverse Moab diagonally from southeast to northwest in order to arrive opposite Jericho, but the Pentateuch does not record any attempt being made to do so. In the book of Judges, however, Jephthah—in his message to the Ammonites, in which he presents a concise summary of the passage of the nation—makes it clear that Moab as well was entreated, when he states:

> And Israel sent messengers to the king of Edom saying, "May I please pass through your land," and the king of Edom did not acquiesce, and also to the king of Moab he sent, and he was unwilling; and Israel stayed in Kadesh (Judg. 11:17).

The last phrase indicates that as befits a properly planned trip, the dialogue with Edom and Moab took place while the congregation was still encamped in Kadesh. Having received two negative replies, it was clear that the procession would have to travel along the eastern border of Edom and continue northward along the eastern border of Moab, which is exactly what they did. They ended up in the valley of Arnon (Num. 21:13), which stretches from the east westward to the Dead Sea and served in the past to delineate the border between the Moabite kingdom and the Amorite kingdom to the north. The Jordan River served as the western border of the Amorite country, and beyond the Jordan lay the land which had been designated as the homeland for the Nation of Israel.

Although the Pentateuch does not explicitly tell of Moses requesting permission to pass through Moab, Rashi (Num. 21:13) is of the opinion that he hinted at having done so when he compared his interaction with the Moabites with that of the Edomites (Deut.

2:29). Based on the same verse, Ibn Ezra understands that there was one group of Moabites, those who lived in Ar, who granted the Israelites passage, implying that they must have been asked to do so, from which it may be deduced that the remaining Moabites denied such a request.

At this stage, Moses had to decide how to proceed, and the situation was somewhat more delicate than it had been with regard to Edom and Moab for the following reasons:

1. Although traversing Edom and Moab from south to north would have considerably reduced the length of the voyage, these countries were not across from the heartland of Israel. In fact, to the west of Moab lay the Dead Sea, so it would not have been possible to cross over into the future Land of Israel from there. The land of the Amorites, on the other hand, lay directly across from Canaan, separated only by the very narrow Jordan River.

2. The book of Deuteronomy retells the story of the journey through the desert, occasionally adding details. In particular, with regard to the Edomites (Deut. 2:5) and the Moabites (Deut. 2:9), the Torah states explicitly not to provoke them, so there was no option of invading their countries by force when they refused to accommodate the request for right of passage. The Ammonites were not even asked, since their country was not adjacent to the future homeland, but east of the land of the Amorites, and the Israelites had also been told explicitly not to antagonize them (Deut. 2:19). Regarding the Amorites, not only was there no command not to provoke them, but there was apparently an order specifically to do so (Deut. 2:24).

    The nation was very meticulous in observing the command not to attack Moab and Ammon. Regarding the verse: "For

Balak

Heshbon was the city of Sihon, king of the Amorites, and he had fought against the first king of Moab, taking all his land from his possession [from Heshbon in the north] to Arnon" (Num. 21:26), the Talmud (cited by Rashi *in situ*) asks:

What difference does this make [to us, i.e., that Heshbon was captured by the Amorites from Moab]? [The answer is that since] the Holy One, blessed be He, had commanded Israel: "Do not distress the Moabites" (Deut. 2:9), the Holy One, blessed be He [therefore] said: "Let Sihon come and take away [the land] from Moab, and Israel will come and take it [from Sihon]." And this is what R. Papa said: "Ammon and Moab were purified [made acceptable for capture by Israel] by Sihon" (BT *Chullin* 60b).

In other words, Israel was careful not to take Moabite land, but Heshbon was different, because although it had once belonged to the Moabites, it was subsequently captured by the Amorites, and was thus accessible to Israel.

The Talmudic text implies that the Amorites had also conquered land formerly owned by the Ammonites, which Israel was allowed to capture since it was no longer under Ammonite dominion. Although no such territory is mentioned in the book of Numbers, Ramban (Num. 21:26) cites a verse in Joshua describing the land allocated to the tribe of Gad which makes it clear that that is exactly what happened: "And their border was Jazer, and all the cities of Gilead, and half the land of the Ammonites, to Aro'er that is before [to the west of] Rabbah [Rabbat Ammon]… the rest of the kingdom of Sihon, king of Heshbon" (Josh. 13:25-27). Although the king of Ammon had physically relinquished his land to the Amorites, he apparently was not reconciled to the loss. This explains his claims against Israel in his tirade before Jephthah: "Because Israel took away my land, when they came out of Egypt, from Arnon and up to the Jabbok, and up to the Jordan" (Judg. 11:13). Since the formerly Moabite city of Heshbon was within these borders, it may be assumed that the Ammonite king was slightly exaggerating, or perhaps empathizing with the Moabites. Jephthah may have answered him tongue in cheek, when he said: "Is it not that which Chemosh your god gives you to possess, that you may possess" (Judg. 11:24). According to Ralbag *in situ*, Chemosh was the god of both the Moabites and the Ammonites. Radak, however, says only the Moabites worshipped Chemosh, and Jephthah may have been telling the king of Ammon that if he is weeping over Moabite land, he must accept the fact that the Moabite god had apparently acquiesced to this taking place.

3. The Amorites are among the seven nations that Israel was ordered to destroy (Deut. 20:17). Nevertheless, Moses initiated contact with them by merely requesting passage (Num. 21:22, Deut. 2:26-29). Rashi in both locations, based on *Sifrei* 199, clarifies that Moses was not commanded to do so,[68] and it is not clear what would have happened if the Amorites had agreed, since their land was eventually allocated to the tribes of Reuben and Gad (Num. 32:33). Rashi (Deut. 2:26) does say that Moses was quite certain that the Amorites would reject his offer, although the text (Deut. 2:30) says that Sihon king of the Amorites did so only as a result of God's hardening his heart, since accepting it would not have suited the Divine plan. In contrast to Rashi, Rambam (*Hilchot Melachim* 6:1), as well as Ramban (Deut. 20:10), based on the

---

68. Rashi formalizes his view in Deut. 20:10, which speaks of "calling out in peace" by explaining that the verse refers to optional wars only, as opposed to the war against the seven nations, which was obligatory.

Balak

Talmud (JT *Shevi'it* 6:1), say that in all cases one must offer peace. However, the peace offer is only conditional, based on the following very restrictive requirements:

a. acceptance of the seven Noahide commands,
b. willingness to pay tribute,
c. willingness to live under subjugation.

It is clear that it would be very difficult for most nations to accept these conditions, although the Gibeonites did (Josh. 9), and so the result of both Rashi's and Rambam's approaches would probably be the same in most cases.

In the end, Moses' proposition to the Amorites went beyond what would normally be offered even in Rambam's view, since none of his requirements were demanded and Moses limited the Hebrews' inroads to traversing their territory. Since God intervened in Sihon's decision-making process, perhaps the rules formulated for the conquest of the land of Canaan, which was to be accomplished by the Israelites in a totally natural manner without Divine intervention, were not yet relevant.

Another possibility is that there is a difference between the land to the west of the Jordan, which would become mainland Israel and would be under absolute Israelite sovereignty, and the land to the east of the Jordan, which would be conquered only if the Amorites did not acquiesce to the request for free passage. This approach is taken by Ramban (Num. 21:21) and the *Or ha-Chaim* (Num. 32:7), who say that Moses had not originally intended to conquer territories east of the Jordan, which he associated with the lands of the Kenites, Kenizzites, and Kadmonites, that were to be inherited only in the distant future (Rashi, Gen. 15:19). Ramban explains that the intention was for the tribes to live in consummate intimacy, which was possible only if they were all situated on the same side of the Jordan, specifically the west side, which was the only expanse to which the appellation "a land flowing with milk and honey"[69] was applicable (JT *Bikkurim* 1:8). Even after conquering the Amorite region, Moses would have allowed it to remain in its desolation had not the tribes of Reuben and Gad determinedly entreated him.

Both Ramban and *Or ha-Chaim* cite two sources for the diminished holiness of the land on the eastern side of the Jordan:

1. The view of R. Shimon in *Sifrei* (*Ki Tavo* 299) is that one does not bring *bikkurim* (the first fruit offering) grown east of the Jordan, because one cannot properly say the accompanying prayer: "I have come to the land which the Lord swore to our forefathers to give us" (Deut. 26:3), since the land on the east was taken by the tribes of Reuben and Gad of their own volition, and not given by God. R. Yosi ha-Glili finds difficulty with a different phrase: "He gave us this land, a land flowing with milk and honey" (Deut. 26:9). As previously noted, this sobriquet refers only to the Land of Israel proper, west of the Jordan (JT *Bikkurim* 1:8).
2. The Midrash, in enumerating the ten virtues of Jerusalem, states that: "The land of Canaan is holier than the Transjordan. The land of Canaan is valid [as a location] for the House of God [a tabernacle or temple], but the Transjordan is not valid for the House of God (*Num. Rabbah*, *Naso* 7:8).

---

69. Used in the Pentateuch numerous times to refer to the Land of Israel, specifically in: Exod. 3:8, 3:17, 13:5, 33:3; Lev. 20:24; Num. 13:27, 14:8; Deut. 6:3, 11:9, 26:9, 26:15; 27:3, 31:20, and in a negative sense by Dathan and Abiram in Num. 16: 13-14.

Balak

Balak's Fears

After seeing what happened to the Amorites, Balak, the king of Moab, became fearful and made contact with the elders of the neighboring country to the east, Midian, for the purpose of developing a joint strategy against their common enemy. According to *Chizkuni* (Num. 22:4), Midian was a long-time ally of Moab, while Rashi holds that on the contrary, they were ancient enemies. Rashi bases himself on the verse in Genesis stating that the king of Edom "defeated Midian in the field of Moab" (Gen. 36:35). Rashi *in situ* explains that Midian had attacked Moab, who was allied with Edom, whose help they requested. Together they were able to overcome Midian. In the present situation, after Israel celebrated a string of victories, "because of their mutual fear of Israel, they made peace with each other" (Rashi, Num. 22:3). In the words of the Midrash:

> To what is this comparable? To two dogs who were fighting with each other. A wolf attacked one of them. The other said: "If I do not help him, today he will kill this one and tomorrow he will attack me." Therefore, Moab and Midian collaborated (*Tanchuma Balak* 3).

Balak's fears reflected those of his countrymen (or perhaps vice versa), concerning whom the verse states: "Moab became terrified of the people, for they were numerous, and Moab became disgusted by the Children of Israel" (Num. 22:3).

The First Question: What Was Balak Afraid Of?

The first question to be asked is: Why were the people so scared? Certainly they were aware that Israel had asked to pass through their land, and when they had refused, Israel had silently accepted being spurned, without resorting to violence. Furthermore, from a geographical perspective, the Nation of Israel had passed the Arnon valley, which served as the northern border of Moab, and was already at Kedemot (Deut. 2:26) to the north, which was near Heshbon (which had been annexed by the Amorites from Moab). They had also arrived at Ammon, which was not of interest to them to either capture or even pass through (*Da'at Mikra*, Num., p. 261). Finally, the Moabites may not have been aware of the exhortations from God not to harm the Edomites, Moabites, and Ammonites. However, the opening verse of the present portion states that "Balak the son of Zippor saw all that Israel had done to the Amorites" (Num. 22:2), and he certainly must have realized that although Israel overran the entire Amorite country, including those sections that had previously belonged to either Moab or Bnei Ammon, they were careful not to attack lands which were still possessed by the Moabites and Ammonites.

ANSWERING THE FIRST QUESTION: WHAT BALAK WAS AFRAID OF?

The Talmud actually deals with this question.

> R. Hiyya b. Abba said that R. Yochanan had stated: The Holy One, blessed be He, does not deprive any creature of the reward due to it, even the reward for [using] a becoming expression, for in the case of the [descendants of the] elder [daughter of Lot] who named her son Moab (Gen. 19:37) [meaning "from father"], the Holy One, blessed be He, said to Moses: "Do not distress the Moabites, nor provoke them in battle" (Deut. 2:9), [implying that] it is battle that you should not [engage in with Moab]. However, *requisitioning* [Rashi: food and water from them] *was allowed*, [whereas in the case of] the younger [daughter],

Balak

who called her son Ben Ammi (Gen. 19:38) [meaning "son of my people," thus concealing the identity of the child's father], the Holy One, blessed be He, said to Moses: "And when you approach Bnei Ammon, do not distress them, nor provoke them" (Deut. 2:19) at all, [meaning that] you should *not even* subject them to *requisitioning* (BT *Bava Kamma* 38b).

One might ask why the behavior of the two sisters should affect the way God related to the nations that descended from them hundreds of years later. The Talmud obviously assumes that the personality of each matriarch was imprinted on the nation that emanated from her.

Interestingly, the identical segment appears in two other locations in the Talmud (BT *Nazir* 23b, BT *Horayot* 10b) and once in the Midrash (*Gen. Rabbah*, *Vayera* 51), with one change. In the Talmudic texts, instead of saying "requisitioning was allowed" it states "annoying them was allowed," while in the Midrashic text it replaces that phrase with "obstructing their rivers and burning their grain stacks with fire was allowed."

The *Torah Temimah* (Gen. 19:38) concludes that the version appearing in *Bava Kamma* ("requisitioning was allowed") is the proper one, since "it is impossible that God would have commanded [Israel] to annoy them for no reason." Ramban is apparently of the same opinion as the *Torah Temimah*, for on the words at the beginning of the portion, "Moab became terrified of the people, for they were numerous" (Num. 22:3), he explains that Moab was a small nation in comparison to the Canaanites and the Amorites, so Balak was frightened by the sheer size of the Israelite nation, which had "increased abundantly and multiplied and waxed exceedingly mighty" (Exod. 1:7). Moving on to the next verse, in which Moab tells the elders of Midian: "Now this assembly will lick up everything around us, as the ox licks up the grass of the field," Ramban explains that Moab was not afraid of a military confrontation, for they were probably aware of God's command to Israel not to wage battle with the Moabites. Nevertheless, if Israel captured all of the surrounding territories, just as they had requisitioned food, they could also impose forced labor on the Moabites. It will be recalled that paying tribute and living under subjugation were routine demands made by the Israelites of the nations they conquered.

Rashi, in contrast to Ramban, prefers the alternate version of the Midrash, stating that Israel "frightened them, appearing before them armed for battle" (Rashi, Deut. 2:9). It would seem that according to both Rashi and Ramban, Moab had ample reasons to initially fear the effect that the Israelite presence would have in their region, although more thorough research would have indicated that their trepidation was unjustified.

THE SECOND QUESTION: WHAT STIMULATED THE MOABITES TO BECOME "DISGUSTED BY THE CHILDREN OF ISRAEL?"
As noted, the portion opens by telling how the Moabites were "terrified," but also "disgusted" by the Israelites (Num. 22:3). The latter adjective is also used in the verse stated by Rebecca: "I am disgusted with my life because of the daughters of Heth. If Jacob takes a wife of the daughters of Heth like these, from the daughters of the land, of what use is life to me" (Gen. 27:46). It is clear that the "disgust" being referred to in this case does not relate to fear of physical attack (as does "terrified"), but to the moral and emotional repulsion that Rebecca felt towards the corrupt Hittite women.

The difference between fear and disgust relates to the lasting power of each. Fear exists when there is a justifiable reason to be anxious. As time passes, antipathy develops with regard to the source of distress, and the hatred so engendered eventually generates feelings of disgust. These emotions tend to metastasize and do not evanesce even if the original apprehension proves baseless.

In the present situation, the initial threat was certainly not very great, although Rashi and Ramban try to provide a rational basis. Probably Balak himself was well aware of the truth, but for his own reasons (to be discussed later), he did not reveal the facts to his nation, but reinforced their feelings of anxiety. As time went on, the source of fear dissipated, but nevertheless, the emotionally-based loathing was maintained, leading to desperate efforts to engage the evil prophet Balaam to curse the Jewish nation.

Parallel Situation Regarding Pharaoh and the Children of Israel

The Torah quotes a new Pharaoh, who arose in Egypt and said:

> Behold, the people of Israel are more numerous and stronger than we are. Let us deal wisely with them, lest they increase, and when a war occurs, they will join our enemies and wage war against us and depart from the land (Exod. 1:9-10).

The text appears contradictory. On the one hand, Pharaoh was afraid that the Israelites will fight against Egypt. On the other hand, he said they would escape. If they ran away, then they would have no intention of attacking Egypt. The Talmud notes the incongruity and states: "It is like a man who curses himself and relates the curse to somebody else" (BT *Sotah* 11a). In other words, Pharaoh was spreading a rumor to the effect that the Israelites intended to displace the Egyptians in their own homeland, but such an event would be so calamitous in their eyes that Pharaoh dared not even enunciate it. Instead of saying "we will [be forced to] depart from the land," he said "they… will depart from the land." As in the case of Moab, Pharaoh was fanning the flames of a highly unlikely scenario, apparently for the purpose of arousing dread among the populace.

The Egyptian nation was in no position to verify the facts, and after a long period of time they too developed an emotional repugnance to the supposed enemy. Indeed, the text in Exodus uses the identical expression, noting that the Egyptians "were disgusted by the Children of Israel" (Exod. 1:12).

Enmity led to oppression, as the text states: "So the Egyptians enslaved the Children of Israel with back-breaking labor" (Exod. 1:13). At this point, the Egyptian population did not want to allow the Israelites to leave, so that they could continue to torment them. The words "they… will depart from the land" may then be understood literally. Rashi in fact brings both interpretations, namely: (1) "we will [be forced to] depart from the land," or (2) "they… will depart from the land."

It is possible that both interpretations are valid. The classical pattern of anti-Semitism has always been to initially generate a fictional fear, such as that Jews control all of the world's capital or that they use the blood of Gentile children in baking *matzah* for Passover. The second stage is to inculcate members of the younger generation with these false accusations when they are too young to verify them, so that they develop an emotional repugnance to Jewish people. The third stage is for the local population, when they come of age, to actively persecute Jewish people. Even though they are capable of checking the facts at this stage, after having been brainwashed in their youth, they no longer have an inclination to do so.

Similarly, Pharaoh initially spread the rumor that the Israelites were planning to revolt, displace the locals, and exile the Egyptians, thus generating consternation (explanation 1). After arousing fear and eventually disgust amongst the populace, he stimulated his

Balak

subjects to seek revenge by oppressing and abusing them as slaves and preventing them from emigrating (explanation 2).[70]

THE THIRD QUESTION: DID BALAK MAKE FALSE ACCUSATIONS?

At this point, it is instructive to analyze the request made by Moses to the king of Edom to allow the congregation to pass through his land. The verse states:

> (A) Please let us pass through your land. (B) We will not pass through fields or vineyards, (C) nor will we drink the water of a well. (D) We will walk along the king's road [the public highway made for the king and his armies], and (E) we will turn neither to the right nor to the left until we have passed through your territory (Num. 20:17).

A. The request is made in a polite and respectful manner.
B. Moses clarifies that crops and vegetation will not be trampled upon.
C. The Midrash[71] asks:

> It says "the water of a well." It should have said the "water of cisterns" [stored water, since many cisterns would be required to feed the entire congregation]. The Torah teaches proper behavior; namely, that if one travels to a foreign land and has his own provisions, he should not eat from his own, but he should allow his own to remain untouched and buy from the [local] shopkeeper, in order to benefit him. So, Moses said to them [Edom]: The well [of Miriam] accompanies us and we eat manna. Do not

---

70. Abba Engelberg, *The Ethics of Exodus* (2014), pp. 21-22.
71. *Tanchuma Chukat* 12, *Num. Rabbah* 19:15, cited by Rashi *in situ*.

say we are burdening you [to supply our needs]. [We are allowing you] to make profit for yourselves. Accordingly, God said to Moses: "You should buy food from them with money, so that you may eat [and also you should purchase water from them with money, so that you may drink]" (Deut. 2:6).

D. Even barren land will remain in its pristine state.
E. We will muzzle our animals so they will not turn to either side to eat.

The gist of the analysis is that the official policy, based on the guidelines provided by the Lord to Moses, is one of extraordinary consideration. The relatively strong fighting force does not brandish its muscle to obtain passage, nor does it expect to be granted the right to transverse *gratis*. Rather, its representative presents its request with the utmost respect and courtesy and accepts the denial of its appeal with *sangfroid*.

ANSWERING THE THIRD QUESTION:
DID BALAK MAKE FALSE ACCUSATIONS?
Clearly, Balak's accusations were false. However, it is now possible to understand the source of the Moabites' fear. It was not that they felt physically endangered, as previously elucidated; rather, they feared that they would be unable to achieve the level of morality displayed by Moses the leader of Israel, and to which each and every Israelite aspired, and they were jealous of those who were able to do so. Instead of engaging in catharsis and self-improvement, they took the easy way out and attempted to destroy the offending nation.

A similar situation occurred at the time of the exodus. The Israelites are seen to be extraordinarily moral. When Pharaoh orders the midwives (Jochebed and Miriam [BT *Sotah* 11b]) to

Balak

commit infanticide, they bravely risk their lives and tell Pharaoh that "the Hebrew women are not like the Egyptian women, for they are skilled as midwives; before the midwife comes to them, they have [already] given birth" (Exod. 1:19).

The text proceeds to describe how Moses smote an Egyptian who was beating a Hebrew slave, thereby showing that he not only empathized with the plight of his brethren, but was also willing to be proactive in his resistance to tyranny and brutality (Exod. 2:11-14).

Finally, the masses as well consciously improved themselves. Having been subdued by their suffering, they learned to behave in a highly moral fashion. This is reflected in the verses which state: "The Children of Israel sighed from the labor, and they cried out, and their cry ascended to God from the labor.... God heard their cry... and God knew" (Exod. 2:23-25), from which the Talmud explains that "God knew" because they sincerely repented for their past sins (JT *Ta'anit* 1:1). But what sins could they have performed? It is true that tradition teaches that Abraham fulfilled all 613 commands (BT *Yoma* 28b, based on Gen. 26:5). However, before the Torah was given the general populace was only committed to the seven Noahide laws, as may be understood from God's description of Abraham's rules pertaining to his followers: "For I have known that he commands his sons and his household after him, to keep the way of the Lord to perform righteousness and justice" (Gen. 18:10). Most of the seven commands reflect basic moral values, which became imbued in the nation. Their sin, therefore, stemmed from violating the seven Noahide laws.

Balaam's Strategy and Philosophy

It has been shown how Balak, king of the Moabites, developed an antipathy to the Israelites which led him to search for ways of harming them. Since the Israelites had successfully escaped from Egypt without resorting to physical violence, the Midianites suggested to the Moabites that they too attempt to achieve victory by verbal, non-violent means (*Tanchuma Balak* 3; Rashi, Num. 22:4), and accordingly they secured the services of Balaam, whose curses were thought to be effective, but what issued from his mouth were blessings and not curses. At this point, Balaam devised another plan, as described in the Talmud:

> The God of these hates lewdness, and they are very partial to linen [worn by the wealthy and noble; Pharaoh dressed Joseph in linen vestures (Gen. 41:42) and the priests wore linen tunics (Exod. 28:39)]. Come, and I will advise you [how to anguish them]. Erect for them [tents enclosed by] curtains, and place harlots inside of them—old women outside, young women inside, and let them [offer] to sell them linen garments. So, he erected curtained tents… and placed harlots in them—old women outside, young women inside. And when an Israelite ate, drank, and was merry, and went for a stroll in the market place, the old woman would say to him, "Would you not like [to buy] linen garments?" The old woman offered it at its true value, but the young one offered it for less. This happened two or three times. After that she [the younger woman] would say to him: "You are now like one of the family; sit down and choose [the garment you wish] for yourself." Containers of Ammonite wine lay near her, and at that time Gentile wine had not yet been [rabbinically] forbidden. Said she to him, "Would you like to drink a glass of wine?" Having drunk, [his passion] was inflamed, and he said to her, "Listen to me [to have relations]." She [then] took out her idol from her bosom and said to him, "Worship this!" He protested:

Balak

"But I am a Jew [I am forbidden to worship idols]." She answered: "Do not worry. Nothing is required but that you defecate in front of it [which was the standard form of worship and he did not know that such was its worship]. Furthermore, I will not leave you until you deny the Torah of Moses your teacher," as it is written: "They came to Baal Peor and separated themselves [from God] to a shameful thing, then they were despised [by Me] as much as they had been [initially] loved" (Hos. 9:10).

"And Israel camped in Shittim" (Num. 25:1): R. Eliezer said: Shittim was its name. R. Yehoshua said: They engaged in ways of folly ["Shittim" from *shetut*, "foolishness"]. "And they invited the people to [partake of] the sacrifices of their gods" (Num. 25:2). R. Eliezer said: When they met them, they [the Midianite women] were naked [thus exciting them; Riaf (R. Yoshiyahu Pinto): as that was the mode of worshipping Peor]. R. Yehoshua said: They experienced seminal emissions [based on the similarity of the Hebrew word for "invited" and *keri*, meaning "semen"] (BT *Sanhedrin* 106a).

This passage emphasizes the devious nature of Balaam, who had no moral compunction in taking advantage of the Israelites' healthy sexual drive to mislead them into sinning. On this occasion, the Jewish men were not specifically attracted to worshipping idols, but were duped into doing so. Sforno (Num. 25:1) notes that this scenario had already been predicted when the Torah stated: "and you will take of their daughters for your sons; and their daughters will go astray after their gods and lead your sons astray after their gods" (Exod. 34:16).

It is now possible to better appreciate a seemingly reprehensible statement made by Moses when the Israelites engaged in a war of retribution against the Midianites—Balaam's nation—who forsook their own daughters in order to blemish the Children of Israel. After Israel was victorious in the ensuing war, Moses said:

> Did you allow all the females to live? They were the same ones who were involved with the Children of Israel on Balaam's advice to betray the Lord in the incident of Peor, resulting in a plague among the congregation of the Lord (Num. 31:15-16).

THE WORDING OF THE DONKEY'S QUESTION

It will be recalled that on Balaam's trip to Moab, his donkey stalled three times when its path was blocked by an angel, after each of which it received a severe beating. After the third time, the Bible states (Num. 22:28): "The Lord opened the mouth of the she-donkey, and she said to Balaam, 'What have I done to you that you have struck me these three times?'" The normative way of saying "three times" in Hebrew is *shalosh pe'amim*, but in this verse, as well as in the following verses (Num. 28: 32, 33), the unusual term *shalosh regalim* is used. *Shalosh regalim* generally refers to the three pilgrimage festivals. The Midrash[72] takes note of this irregularity, stating: "He hinted to him: 'You seek to uproot a nation that celebrates three festivals.'" The question that arises is why was this particular commandment chosen to characterize Israel, since Balaam wished to obliterate every vestige of religious commitment. Before suggesting an answer, the proper celebration of the pilgrimage festivals will be discussed.

---

72. *Tanchuma Balak* 9 and *Num. Rabbah* 20:14, cited by Rashi, Num. 22:28.

Balak

The Three Pilgrimage Festivals

The Talmud states: "Three precepts are enjoined upon Israel when they make their pilgrimage at a festival: the pilgrimage offering, the festal offering, and to rejoice" (BT *Chagigah* 6b). The pilgrimage offering is a burnt offering which is brought by a man on the first day of each of the pilgrimage holidays when he arrives at the Temple, together with the festal offering, a peace offering shared by the priest, the pilgrim, and his family. The requirement to rejoice is based on the verse:

> And you should rejoice on your festival: you, and your son, and your daughter, and your man-servant, and your maid-servant, and the Levite, and the stranger, and the fatherless, and the widow that are within your gates (Deut. 16:14).

On the basis of this verse, it is understandable why the Talmud states that the command to rejoice is incumbent on women as well as men. When the Temple stood, rejoicing meant partaking of sacrificial meat, as stated in the Talmud (BT *Pesachim* 109a):

> It was taught, R. Yehuda b. Beteira said: When the Temple was in existence, one could not rejoice without meat, for it says: "And you will sacrifice peace offerings and eat there; and you will rejoice before the Lord your God" (Deut. 27:7).

Tosafot explains that although the verse cited does not refer to the holidays, it does indicate that rejoicing involves indulging in sacrificial meat. Hence, the command to rejoice is understood to require the bringing of a jubilation (*simchah*) offering.

The *mitzvot* of bringing the festal and jubilation offerings have an ethical facet as well, namely that eating their meat is meant

The Ethics of Numbers

to be done together with poor and lonely people who yearn for fellowship and hospitality. Rambam (*Hilchot Chagigah* 2:14) formulates this requirement as follows:

> When a person sacrifices festal and jubilation offerings, he should not eat alone with his wife and children, and imagine that he is fulfilling the command in the utmost sense, but rather he is required to gladden the indigent and forlorn, for it says "and the Levite, and the stranger, and the fatherless, and the widow" (Deut. 16:14). He must feed and give drink to them to the extent of his ability.

After the destruction of the Temple, the command is to be fulfilled by any activity that engenders enjoyment, as Rambam explains:

> Included in God's statement "you should rejoice on your festival" (Deut. 16:14) are the instructions of our Sages: "You should rejoice with all types of joy" (BT *Chagigah* 8b), including eating meat on the festivals, drinking wine, wearing new clothing, giving fruits and sweets to the women and children, and *Simchat Beit ha-Shoevah*, i.e., rejoicing with musical instruments and dancing in the Temple [on Sukkot]. All the above is included in the commandment "you should rejoice on your festival" (*Sefer ha-Mitzvot*, positive command 54).

The pilgrimage festivals are seen to be a time when entire families celebrate as part of the nation, all of which is required to assemble in Jerusalem. Holidays provide an occasion for families to bond internally and with the entire community in the holy city of Jerusalem, implying that warm social relations are themselves an expression of holiness.

Balak

Eli Merzbach[73] has noted that the pilgrimage festivals strengthened and united the Jewish people on three levels: in terms of purpose (worshipping God), in terms of location (the Temple in Jerusalem), and in terms of time (three times a year: Pesach, Shavuot, and Sukkot). The only other opportunity for strengthening the nation's unity was in conjunction with the mitzvah of *hak'hel*, when the entire congregation gathered at the Temple to hear the king read selected portions from the book of Deuteronomy (*Sotah* 7:8); however, that ceremony itself took place on Sukkot (Deut. 31:10-13).

Balaam's Philosophy Negates the Message of the Festivals

The Talmud (BT *Sanhedrin* 105a) states that the name "Balaam" is formed by combining the two Hebrew words *be-lo am*, which Rashi interprets to mean "not being part of any nation." In fact, Balaam was himself from Midian, yet he was recruited to help the Moabites. In the end, he seriously harmed his own nation, since the result of his corrupting influence upon the Israelites was the war of vengeance in which the Midianites were soundly defeated (Num. 31:7-11). He should have used his innate intelligence to inform Balak of the previously listed reasons indicating that Israel had no intention of attacking Moab, so that no action, cursing or otherwise, was called for on the part of Moab.

Balaam identified with no nation, and so he owed allegiance to himself alone. His hedonism led him to weaken the Nation of Israel and ruin the family life of its members by means of sexual adventurism. This approach is diametrically opposed to the unifica-

---

73. "*Birchotav shel Bil'am ve-Am Yisrael*," *Daf Shevui* 922, Bar Ilan (Internet).

tion process engendered by the family and communal gatherings which result from proper observance of the pilgrimage festivals, and accordingly the appellation *shalosh regalim* is interspersed in the story of Balaam. Perhaps for that reason God placed in the mouth of Balaam the descriptive blessing: "How goodly are your tents, O Jacob, your dwelling places, O Israel" (Num. 24:5), a verse which emphasizes the modesty and purity of Israelite society.

Summary

We have attempted to understand the age-old phenomenon of anti-Semitism. With respect to both the ancient Egyptians and the Moabites, the process seems to have started by floating unsubstantiated rumors among the populace to the effect that the Israelite nation is dangerous and should be feared. In such situations, lacking the possibility of checking the validity of the accusations, the masses gradually develop a strong emotional repulsion regarding the object of the calumny. By the time the charges are finally shown to be baseless, the damage has already been done, because large segments of the population have grown to dislike the Jewish nation as a whole, independent of the facts.

The anti-Semitic hatred of Balak and his intended savior Balaam eventually led to the humiliation of the former and the death of the latter (Num. 31:7-11), although not before the annihilation of twenty-four thousand Israelites (Num. 25:9).

Pinchas

The last section in the portion of *Balak* describes the brazenly licentious behavior which took place between many Israelites and the Moabite and Midianite women as part of the rites of worship of Baal Peor. When the zealot Phinehas saw a Simeonite prince publicly fornicating with the daughter of one of the Midianite kings, he launched his spear at the couple, killing them both simultaneously. The present portion opens with God bestowing His adulatory blessing on Phinehas in recognition of his righteous act and commanding the nation to harass and eventually attack the Midianites in revenge for their scheming, duplicitous beguilement of the ingenuous Israelites.

The portion of *Pinchas* describes events which occurred during the fortieth year after the exodus, when the new generation of Israelites, so to say, could see the light at the end of the tunnel. Other than Joshua and Caleb, no man who had been between twenty and sixty at the time of the first census at the beginning of the voyage through the desert (Num. 1:2-3) was still alive, as it had been decreed that in consequence of the rebellion in the aftermath of hearing the evil report of the spies, they would not live to see the Holy Land (Num. 14:28-35). The women, however, who did not revolt, were not included in the verdict (Rashi, Num. 26:64).

The Ethics of Numbers

In preparation for entering the Holy Land, which would have to be divided among the people, a number of steps were taken. First, a new census was initiated to determine exactly who would inherit the land. Interestingly, an additional census of the Levites was taken, even though they would not be receiving plots of land. Ramban (Num. 26:57) explains that the Levites did receive forty-eight cities with surrounding pasture land, and the division of those lands may have been based on the population of Levites at the end of the forty-year journey. Alternately, the census may have been redundant on a technical level, but psychologically important for their self-esteem. Maharsha (BT *Bava Batra* 122a), basing himself on a Talmudic dictum that in the future the Land of Israel will be divided among thirteen tribes (ostensibly including the Levites), says that this census was also necessary. Perhaps Maharsha's reason could be combined with the second explanation offered by Ramban. Although not immediately required, since the Levites would eventually receive their fair share, out of consideration for their feelings, a census of the Levites was undertaken at this early stage.

Second, the text explains that a lottery which takes the census results into account was to be used to apportion the land among the males. The daughters of Zelophehad brought to the attention of Moses that since they had no brothers, the living descendants of their father were not scheduled to receive an inheritance. After consulting with God, a revised priority list was promulgated.

The third step which had to be taken was to prepare for the demise of Moses, who would be allowed to glimpse the Holy Land, but would not be allowed to enter, in punishment for having struck the rock at Mei Merivah (Num. 20:12). Moses immediately beseeched the Lord to appoint a successor, which He did.

Last comes a list of all of the daily, Sabbath, and holiday public sacrifices. It is not immediately clear why this is included in the list of preparatory steps before entering the Land of Israel, since many of these sacrifices were already being brought in the desert. The Midrash relates it to when Moses suggests that God appoint his successor: "Let the Lord, the God of spirits of all flesh, appoint a man over the congregation" (Num. 27:16), concerning which the Midrash (*Sifrei Pinchas* 142) comments:

> To what may this be compared? To a king whose wife was on her deathbed. She was commanding him concerning her sons. She said to him: "Please be very careful with respect to my sons." He said to her: "Instead of commanding me regarding my sons, command my sons regarding me, not to rebel against me and not to act disrespectfully." Similarly did the Lord say to Moses: "Instead of commanding me regarding my sons, command my sons regarding me, not to rebel against me and not to act disrespectfully and that they not replace the honor [I am entitled to] with that of foreign gods, and so it says:
>
> When I bring them to the land which I have sworn [to give to] their forefathers, [a land] flowing with milk and honey, and they will eat and be satisfied and become fat, and they will turn to other gods and serve them and despise Me and violate My covenant (Deut. 31:20).
>
> Instead of commanding Me regarding my sons, command my sons regarding Me, and that is why it says: "Command the Children of Israel" (Num. 28:2).

The commands given to the sons regarding God refers to the regimen of sacrifices which the priests, as messengers of the nation, were required to bring, as described in chs. 28-29 of this portion.

The Ethics of Numbers

Divine Punishment at Baal Peor

In the portion of *Balak*, the evolution of the sin at Baal Peor was discussed. Here, the process of punishment will be examined. The Bible states: "Israel became attached to Baal Peor, and the anger of the Lord flared against Israel" (Num. 25:3). Ibn Ezra explains that the Hebrew word used for "attached" is more accurately translated as "paired off." The Gentile women paired off with Baal Peor, and the Israelite men paired off with the women, making it appear as if the men had paired off with the idol. Once more, the verse demonstrates how the men's initial sexual attraction led them astray. Ramban (Num. 25:1) notes that although it is the women who are singled out in the first verse ("the people began to commit harlotry with the women of Moab"), the initiators of the scheme were the Midianite men, whom the Israelites were accordingly ordered to harass and smite, together with their main advisor, Balaam, whom the Bible (as well as the Talmud in BT *Sanhedrin* 106a) accuses of wishing for the nation's destruction (Deut. 23:6) and whom they made sure to slay (Num. 31:8).

Regarding the second half of verse 3, "the anger of the Lord flared against Israel," Rashi comments that "He struck them with a plague." If that was the case, there was no need to worry about innocent people being stricken, since God knew who was guilty.

The description of the punishment continues:

> **4** The Lord said to Moses: "Take all the leaders of the people and hang them before the Lord, facing the sun, and then the flaring anger of the Lord will be withdrawn from Israel." **5** Moses said to the judges of Israel: "Each of you must kill the men who became attached to Baal Peor" (Num. 25).

Pinchas

Verse 4 states that the Lord's anger would be withdrawn if the leaders were hanged, and this supports Rashi's comment on v. 3 that they had been stricken by a plague; how else would they know that God's anger had subsided? Additionally, v. 8 mentions "*the* plague" without explicitly specifying one previously, so it must be assumed that it is referring to the one hinted at in v. 3. On the other hand, if they were already being punished, what need was there to have the judges execute their brethren? Sforno (Num. 25:4) explains that by not protesting when the sinners were executed, the members of the congregation were able to atone for not rebuking them when they committed the sin. One might also look upon this procedure as part of the transition from the God-oriented mode of functioning in the desert, when miraculous events occurred routinely, to the human-oriented mode of functioning planned for Israel upon arrival in the Promised Land.

Regarding the Lord's request of Moses to take all of the leaders and hang them, the Talmud asks:

> If the people had sinned, what sin had the leaders transgressed? [V. 2 mentions only the "people" as partaking of pagan sacrifices and bowing to idols.] R. Yehudah said in Rav's name: The Holy One, blessed be He, said to Moses: Split them up [as judges] into [many] courts. [The verse is accordingly translated: "Take the leaders (and appoint them as judges) and hang those (whom they condemn)."]
> (BT *Sanhedrin* 35a)

The Midrash (*Tanchuma Balak* 19) cites two answers to the Talmud's query. The first holds that the leaders were indeed hanged, since they shirked their duty by not preventing the occurrence of the desecration in the first place. It interprets the word "them" in the phrase "Take all the leaders of the people and

The Ethics of Numbers

hang *them*" to be referring back to the leaders. The second answer takes the word "them" to refer to the Israelites mentioned in v. 3, thus concurring with the Talmudic view (*Eitz Yosef* on *Tanchuma Balak* 19, adopted by Rashi on 25:4). However, at this point the Midrash asks a question. According to the first opinion, it was quite clear who the leaders were, so they could easily be designated for punishment. According to the second opinion, however, how would the judges know which Israelites were guilty? The Midrash (cited in Rashi 25:4) answers this question by noting that v. 4 includes the seemingly redundant phrase "facing the sun." Its meaning is:

> I [God] will publicize them [the sinners]. With respect to anyone who sinned, the cloud rolled itself up and the sun shone through, focusing upon he [who had sinned] within the congregation, and everyone knew who had sinned and they would [accordingly] hang him (*Tanchuma Balak* 19).

According to the second opinion of the Midrash, the leaders referred to in v. 4 and the judges of v. 5 may be the same people. Since there were approximately 600,000 male Israelites above the age of twenty (Num. 26:51), and according to Exod. 18:21, there were rulers of thousands (600), hundreds (6,000), fifties (12,000), and tens (60,000), this would lead to a total of 78,600 judges (BT *Sanhedrin* 18a). Rashi (25:5), apparently basing himself on the use of the plural form in the phrase "kill the men," concludes that each judge killed two men, leading to 157,200 casualties (substantiated by JT *Sanhedrin* 10:2).

Ramban notes that according to Rashi's calculation, more than a quarter of the entire male population was decimated. According to Ramban, that seems excessive, so he suggests that normal

Pinchas

court procedure, which requires a court of 23 for capital punishment, was to be used. The number of such courts would then be 78,600 divided by 23, or 3,417 courts, and if each court convicted two people, the number of casualties would be 6,834. Even this number is far too great in the eyes of Ramban, since the reduction in the census results between that at the beginning of the desert journey (Num. 2:32) and the one taken at the end (Num. 26:51) is smaller than this. The only way for this to be possible is if there were a very large number of births between the two censuses to counterbalance the great loss of life at Baal Peor. Ramban believes that the judges did not actually perform any executions, noting that there is no verse which states that the judges carried out Moses' orders. Exactly why will be explained shortly. At any rate, one may deduce from Ramban's reference to normal court proceedings that he does not take the approach of the Midrash that the guilty ones would be indicated miraculously, but that a thorough judicial investigation was to be performed.

The story continues:

(A) And behold, one of the Children of Israel came and brought the Midianite woman close to his brethren, before the eyes of Moses and before the eyes of the entire congregation of the Children of Israel, (B) and they were weeping at the entrance of the Tent of Meeting (Num. 25:6).

EXPLANATION OF PART (A):
Upon hearing that the judges were planning to kill the participants in the orgy, the Talmud portrays the reaction of the tribe of Simeon by providing the following exegesis of part (A) of the previously cited verse:

The Ethics of Numbers

The tribe of Simeon approached Zimri b. Salu and said to him: "Behold, capital punishment is being meted out, yet you sit silent." What did he do? He arose and assembled twenty-four thousand Israelites and went to Cozbi and said to her: "Surrender yourself to me [for sexual relations]." She replied, "I am a king's daughter, and this is what my father instructed me: 'You should only yield to the greatest among them.'" He replied: "he too is [meaning "I too am"] the prince of a tribe; moreover, he is [meaning "I am"] greater than him [Moses], for he [Zimri is descended from he who] was second in birth [Simeon being Jacob's second-born], while he [Moses is descended from he who] was third [Levi being Jacob's third-born]." He [Zimri] then seized her [Cozbi] by the forelock and brought her before Moses and said: "Son of Amram, is this woman forbidden or permitted? And should you say that she is forbidden, who permitted the daughter of Jethro [who is also a Midianite] to you?" (BT *Sanhedrin* 82a).

V. 6 refers to the participants in this narrative anonymously. Their names are revealed in the portion of *Pinchas* as Zimri ben Salu (Num. 25:14) and Cozbi bat Zur (Num. 25:15). According to the Talmud (BT *Sanhedrin* 82b), the former is an alternate name for the same prince called Shlumiel b. Zurishadai in Num. 1:6. The *Baal ha-Turim* (Num. 1:16) points out that in the first chapter of Numbers, when referring to the tribal leaders, the word indicating "the chosen ones" has a deformed letter (*vav*), to indicate that one of them was defective, namely Shlumiel, while in the portion of *Korach* (Num. 16:2), the same word is spelled missing the entire letter, since all of the people referred to there were corrupt. The name "Cozbi" is derived from the Hebrew word *cazav*, meaning "falsehood," since she had falsified her father's command to surrender herself only to the greatest of the Israelites (Moses). Her father, Zur, is indeed mentioned as one of the five Midianite kings killed in the Israelite battle against the Midianites (Num. 31:8). The twenty-four thousand Israelites gathered by Zimri, to oppose Moses and the 78,600 judges, supposedly became the twenty-four thousand victims of the God-inspired pestilence (Num. 25:9).

Maharsha (*in situ*) relates to the fact that the verse at the end of the portion of *Balak* (25:6) mentions neither Zimri's nor Cozbi's names. He says that the absence of their names lays the basis for the Talmudic interpretation that the tribe of Simeon approached Zimri, since by saying "one of the Children of Israel came," the implication is that Zimri issued forth (upon being urged) from the Children of Israel as a representative of his tribe, which we know to be Simeon from Num. 25:14. Similarly, by just calling Cozbi a Midianite, the implication is that the text is specifically focusing on her Midianite background, which leaves open the status of Zipporah, who was a Midianite as well, thus laying the basis for Zimri's repartee as expressed in the Talmud.

Regarding Zimri's provocative remark that having relations with Cozbi was no different from Moses marrying Zipporah, it is clear that the comparison is fallacious. First, how can one compare a noncommittal tryst confounded with idolatrous rites to a formal marriage? Second, even if they could be compared, Zipporah assumedly converted (to the extent that the concept existed before the Torah was given). Third, even if she didn't previously convert, "Moses married her before the Torah was given, and when the Torah was given, they were all considered non-Jewish descendants of Noah who [converted and] accepted the *mitzvot* upon themselves, and she [Zipporah] was together with them and the many converts of the mixed multitude" (Rashi, BT *Sanhedrin* 82a, s.v. *bat Yitro*). Fourth, even if she hadn't converted, the Talmud (BT *Shabbat* 87a)

The Ethics of Numbers

states that Moses refrained from cohabiting with her from the time that the Torah was given, since God was liable to appear to him at any moment, and he had to be ritually pure (*Aruch le-Ner, in situ*).

EXPLANATION OF PART (B):
The Talmudic text continues:

> [At that moment] Moses forgot the *halachah* [concerning public intimacy with a heathen woman]. All of the people burst into tears; hence it is written: "and they were weeping at the entrance of the Tent of Meeting" (BT *Sanhedrin* 82a).

The Torah does not explicitly deal with the subject of sexual relations between Jews and Gentiles. Leviticus ch. 20 prohibits incest and adultery within the nation only, but Moses had been taught extra-textually the relevant law as one of many *halachot le-Moshe mi-Sinai* (laws given to Moses orally on Mt. Sinai). One may propose two reasons why Moses might not have known the law in the present situation.

The Talmud (BT *Nedarim* 38a) states:

> At first Moses used to study the Torah and forget it, until it was given to him as a gift, for it says: "And He gave Moses, when He had finished speaking with him [on Mt. Sinai], the two tablets of the testimony—stone tablets, written with the finger of God." (Exod. 31:18).

Rashi in Exodus explains how this is derived. He notes that the word *ke-challoto*, "when he finished," is spelled defectively in Hebrew, and can also be read as *ke-challato*, "as his bride," which the Talmud understands to mean that the Torah was given to him as a gift. Just as a bride is given as a gift to her groom, so was the

Pinchas

Torah miraculously transmitted to Moses, since there was no way that Moses could have mastered the entire Torah in the forty days that he spent on the mountain.

Nevertheless, since the knowledge had indeed been implanted in his head, how is it that he did not recall it? *Targum Yonatan* (Num. 25:6) says that the false accusation (for the previously stated reasons) generated anger in Moses, causing him to forget. Rashi (Num. 31:21), citing the Midrash *(Sifrei Matot* 157), notes three other times when anger caused Moses to err, namely on the eighth day of the inauguration ceremony, when he improperly rebuked Eleazar and Ithamar for not partaking of the sin offering on the day of the demise of their brothers, Nadab and Abihu (Lev. 10:16); at Mei Merivah, where he spoke insolently to the Children of Israel and struck the rock rather than speaking to it (Num. 20:10-11); and in the plains of Moab, after defeating the Midianites and allowing the females to remain alive, where the laws concerning the purification of vessels escaped him (Num. 31:14).

On the other hand, it is possible that because of the highly charged atmosphere, where Moses had basically been accused by Zimri of improper behavior, his sense of embarrassment clouded his mind and prevented clear thinking and absolute recall. The following Midrash would seem to support this thesis:

> To what may the situation be compared? To the daughter of a king who was adorned with jewelry preparatory to sitting in a palanquin under a canopy. It was discovered that she was having an affair with another man, causing her father and relatives to act helpless [in desperation]. Similarly, Israel at the end of forty years camped on the [banks of the] Jordan in order to cross it into the Land of Israel… and there they broke out in prostitution, and Moses and the righteous people who were with him acted helpless, and so they cried (*Tanchuma Balak* 20).

The Ethics of Numbers

That Moses was faulted for letting his emotions get the better of him may be understood from the conclusion of the same Midrash:

> Because he [Moses] was lazy [emotionally], no man knew where he was buried (Deut. 34:6). This comes to teach you that a man should be as bold as a leopard, light as an eagle, fast as a deer, and strong as a lion to do the will of his Maker. And from here you learn that God is punctilious to a hairbreadth with righteous people.

However, the same Midrash also relates skeptically to this explanation, stating:

> At the incident of the golden calf, Moses successfully confronted six hundred thousand [male members of the congregation], as it says: "And he took the calf that they had made, [burned it in fire, ground it to fine powder, scattered it upon the surface of the water, and gave it to the Children of Israel to drink]" (Exod. 32:20). However, this happened so that Phinehas should come and take what he was entitled to.

According to this view in the Midrash, Moses was not upset or angry, conditions which prevented him from being able to recall the *halachah*. On the contrary, he maintained his equanimity in spite of the decadent behavior of the congregation and the vicious accusations of Zimri. The only reason he did not know the law is that while God enabled Moses to grasp and retain the entire corpus of written and oral laws, He deleted this law from his memory, since He wished to give Phinehas the opportunity to distinguish himself. Another indication that this situation was tailored to

Pinchas

give Phinehas the opportunity to act on his righteous impulse is the Midrash which attributes the following words to Phinehas: "Did you not teach me this when you descended from Mt. Sinai" (elaborated on further). But Moses transmitted every law to the entire congregation (BT *Eruvin* 54b), not only to Phinehas. Apparently, this law was singled out from all of the others to be taught privately to Phinehas to be utilized by him alone at the appropriate time (Ben Yehoyada, *Sanhedrin* 82a).

Integrating part (B) of the verse with the Midrash, two items must be explained. First, what is the basis for relating the weeping to the inability of Moses to posit the relevant *halachah*? Second, exactly why were they weeping?

Maharsha *in situ* answers both of these questions. He notes that the verse says that "they were weeping at the entrance of the Tent of Meeting," the place where Moses prophetically received the Law from God. By linking the weeping with the Tent of Meeting, the Rabbis deduced that one had to do with the other. Maharsha continues to explain that the specific connection was their bewilderment at not knowing the proper halachic treatment for such a situation. Whether Moses himself was among those weeping would depend on which view in the Midrash is adopted. If Moses forgot for emotional reasons, then he too must have been upset, but if God specifically singled out this law as one which He would not teach Moses, or as one which would be the object of Divinely-inspired forgetting, then Moses would have had nothing to cry about.

The Intervention of Phinehas

The text continues with the following verse: "Phinehas the son of Eleazar the son of Aaron the priest saw [this], arose from among the congregation, and took a spear in his hand" (Num. 25:7). The Talmud asks the obvious question: The verse says "he saw," but it does not specify what he actually saw that was so powerful that it motivated him to take a spear in his hand and use it. Additionally, why does the verse only mention Phinehas? After all, the previous verse had stated that the public act of fornication took place "before the eyes of Moses and before the eyes of the entire congregation of the Children of Israel."

The Talmud answers that the word "saw" in this case is not referring to visually seeing, since as noted, the entire congregation saw what was occurring. Rather, "saw" is being used in the sense of "understanding" and knowing how to relate what was being seen to how one should react to such an event.

The Talmud suggests three possibilities for exactly what Phinehas understood that the others did not, the first of which is:

> Rav said: He saw what was happening and remembered the *halachah*. He [Phinehas] said to him [Moses]: "Brother of my grandfather [Moses being the brother of Aaron, who was the grandfather of Phinehas], did you not teach me this when you descended from Mt. Sinai: 'He who cohabits with a heathen woman, zealots [may] attack him?'" He [Moses] replied: "He who reads the letter, let him be the agent [to carry out its instructions]" (BT *Sanhedrin* 82a).

The particular teaching which, as noted previously, was forgotten by Moses, is quite strange in that it seems to clash with the ordered civil judiciary legislated by the Torah, which requires a court procedure to convict people, who are then penalized in accordance with the punishment specified in the Torah, as understood by the Sages (see **Appendix IV – Law Enforcement in Judaism**). However, the written law does not deal with the case of Jews having casual sexual relations with non-Jews. Many restrictions in such situations are rabbinic in origin (see **Appendix V – Intimate Relations with Gentiles**). The particular law in question is considered to be a law given to Moses at Sinai (*halachah le-Moshe mi-Sinai*), i.e., a Torah level law transmitted orally, and not in writing, to Moses. Whether Moses simply forgot out of emotion, or did so as a result of Divine intervention, was previously examined.

A second answer supplied by the Talmud, which rests on the first answer, is:

> Shmuel said: He saw that [Phinehas anticipated the meaning of the verse]: "There is neither wisdom nor understanding nor counsel against the Lord" (Prov. 21:30). Wherever the Divine Name is being profaned, one does not pay honor to his teacher.

The simple meaning of the verse is that God's will is insuperable. The Midrashic explanation being proposed is that when God's honor is being degraded, one need not seek advice from his teachers, and more specifically he may issue halachic decisions without getting the approval of his rabbi, even though in general one is forbidden to do so in his presence (*Yoreh De'ah* 242:4, based on BT *Sanhedrin* 5b).

The third answer supplied by the Talmud is: "R. Yitzchak said in the name of R. Elazar: He saw the angel wreaking destruction among the people." In other words, the act of Phinehas was in reaction to the angel's destructive behavior. *Midrash Rabbah* (Num. 20:25) describes this event picturesquely, comparing the situation to the case of a king who passed a gathering of rabble and heard one of them calling out a curse. In his anger, he ordered the liquidation of the entire crowd. Only when his bodyguard killed the lone perpetrator did his wrath subside.

The Ethics of Numbers

Further on (82b), the Talmud describes a miracle that took place on that occasion:

> An angel came and wrought destruction among the people. Then he [Phinehas] came and struck them down before the Almighty, saying. "Sovereign of the universe, will twenty-four thousand perish because of these [two, Zimri and Cozbi]?" For it says: "And those that died in the plague were twenty-four thousand" (Num. 25:9), and that is what is written: "And Phinehas stood up and… argued with his Maker [on the justice of punishing so many]" (Ps. 106:30).

The twenty-four thousand that were killed were the twenty-four thousand mentioned by the Talmud as having been gathered by Zimri. Phinehas's attempt to save them was unsuccessful, but perhaps it prevented the plague from spreading further. Rashi (BT *Sanhedrin* 82b, s.v. *ve-echad*) says that the miracle which occurred was the appearance of the angel, which distracted the sinners from pursuing Phinehas.

This exegesis, however, contradicts the third answer, which claims that Phinehas's seeing the destructive angel was what motivated him to perform his act in the first place. It seems preferable to explain the third answer of the Talmud in accordance with the explanation of *Targum Yonatan* (Num. 25:8), that the appearance of the angel was the provocation which sparked his response, and the miracle referred to was his successful neutralization of the angel.

Another problem must be dealt with. It will be recalled that Rashi and Ramban interpret the words in v. 3, "the anger of the Lord flared against Israel," to mean that a plague spread among the nation

Pinchas

in punishment for their participation in the Moabite idol worship ceremony. But the Talmudic narrative implies that the twenty-four thousand people who died in the plague were those whom Zimri gathered afterwards in consequence of the *ad hoc* courts set up by Moses. Certainly, the total number should have been greater, since many had died earlier. Since v. 3 does not explicitly refer to a plague, and many commentators (e.g., Sforno, Chizkuni, and Saadiah Gaon) do not interpret those words as such, this question does not necessarily arise. However, according to Rashi and Ramban, as well as Rashbam (25:3), how is this to be understood?

Sukkat David (R. Dovid Kviat on Num. 25:3, pp. 161-164) answers that there were two separate plagues. The first, referred to in v. 3, was a consequence of the idol worship mentioned in vv. 2-3 ("They called the people to [join them in] the sacrifices to their gods, and the people ate and prostrated themselves to their gods. And Israel attached themselves to Baal Peor."). At this stage Moses, at God's command, arranged for courts to be set up. Doing so was an act of mercy, since the angel of death, when given free reign, kills people indiscriminately, including those who were guilty of other sins, or had only considered sinning but had not actually done so. Although many had already engaged in forbidden sexual relations, as stated in v. 1 ("and the people began to commit harlotry"), since it was only done in private, vigilantism was not permitted, although, as previously noted, their sin was—according to some views—a Biblical transgression.

The second plague, however, resulted from the public shameful act perpetrated by Zimri, who wished to issue a blanket pass for promiscuity-based idol-worship with Gentiles, by claiming that Moses himself had engaged in such. In addition to exposing Moses as a hypocrite, by undermining his authority he was nullifying the laws of the Torah and their overall message. As Sforno (Num.

25:13) points out, the failure of the nation to resist and protest Zimri's actions made them all equally culpable of a heavenly-administered death penalty, as is clear from the second verse of the portion of *Pinchas*:

> Phinehas the son of Eleazar the son of Aaron the priest has turned My anger away from the Children of Israel by his zealously avenging Me among them, *so that I did not destroy the Children of Israel* in My jealousy (Num. 25:11).

Since the entire nation was guilty, even individually arraigning them in court would not have saved them, as occurred during the first plague, since there were no innocents. The only way to redeem the Israelites was by performing an equally public act of affirmation of the leadership of Moses and the Torah which he represented. The unquestioned acceptance of Phinehas's zealous protection of the Divine law was the only possible means of atonement for such a heinous sin, and that is what saved the majority of the nation from the punishment inflicted on the twenty-four thousand who died in the second plague alone.

Restrictions on Vigilantism

Although the Talmud justifies and highly praises the valorous act of Phinehas, it immediately curtails its use, as is evident from the following text:

> Rabbah b. Bar Hannah said in R. Yochanan's name: If he comes [to court] to take counsel, we do not instruct him to do so [to execute a person who is fornicating in public]. What is more, had Zimri withdrawn and Phinehas slain

him, Phinehas would have been executed on his account [in court, since permission to slay was only granted while the act was in progress]; and had Zimri turned upon Phinehas and slain him, he would not have been executed, since Phinehas was a pursuer [seeking to take his life] (BT *Sanhedrin* 82a).

In other words, a court will never give a person free reign to be a vigilante in such situations. If he initiates action on his own, he is risking his life, since the person attacked has a right to defend himself from the zealot, who is considered a *rodef* (pursuer). There is, however, one difference between the zealot and a typical *rodef*. The latter may be killed by the victim as well as by any bystander. In this case, since the zealot is allowed to kill the cohabiter, others are forbidden from killing the zealot, since in principle they too could (or should, see further) have killed the cohabiter. The cohabiter, on the other hand, is not expected to kill himself—or even allow himself to be killed, so he is permitted to defend himself (*Yad Rama*, BT *Sanhedrin* 82a; *Kitzur Piskei ha-Rosh*, *Sanhedrin* 9:4).

Furthermore, if he attacks him after he has completed the act, he himself is liable to be indicted for murder. Ra'avad (*Hilchot Isurei Bi'ah* 12:4) adds the additional requirement that the perpetrator must be warned that he is liable to the death penalty, and he must answer that he is aware of this fact and is willing to suffer the consequences (Tosefta, *Sanhedrin* 11:1; *Hilchot Sanhedrin* 12:2). *Maggid Mishneh* (*in situ*) maintains that Rambam argues with Ra'avad and does not require a warning here, since the Torah does not indicate that Phinehas warned Zimri. On the other hand, *Maggid Mishneh* says that since the Talmud mentions the possibility of Zimri withdrawing, perhaps it means to say that Phinehas did indeed warn him to do so.

Interestingly, although Jewish courts could not enforce the death penalty once rabbinic ordination ceased (shortly after the destruction of the Temple), *Tur* (*Choshen Mishpat* 425, uncensored version) says that cases which do not require court approval, such as the case of the *rodef* and that of the zealot, where one is allowed to take the law into one's own hands and execute the criminal, may be implemented to this very day, and so posits Rama (*Choshen Mishpat* 425:4).

Even if none of the restrictions are in effect and a zealot wishes to act when public cohabitation is in progress, the Sages still looked askance upon anyone who performs such a deed, as is evident from the following passage (JT *Sanhedrin* 9:7):

> We learned: He [Phinehas] acted against the will of the Sages. Could Phinehas have acted contrary to the will of the Sages? [Indeed,] R. Yehudah b. Pazi said: "They wanted to ostracize him, but the Holy Spirit intervened and stated: 'And upon him and his descendants after him will be bestowed an eternal covenant of priesthood'" (Num. 25:13).

The *Torah Temimah, in situ,* explains that in general such behavior cannot be permitted, because there is no way of knowing if the zealot is righteously motivated or whether he has ulterior motives. Even with regard to Phinehas, this could not have been known had not God Himself produced a heavenly voice (*bat kol*) proclaiming the reward of Phinehas.

The *Torah Temimah* further points out that the Jerusalem Talmud differs with the previously cited view of Rav (BT *Sanhedrin* 82a) that Phinehas asked permission of Moses, because he would not have been in a position to answer, since only God knows one's true level of sincerity. Rather, it concurs with the view of Shmuel that he was permitted to act without first consulting his teacher, or R. Yitzchak that he saw the dimensions of the calamity and performed his act of zealotry, at which point the heavenly voice confirmed that he was in fact on a spiritual level which ensured that his motives were sufficiently pure to justify vigilantism.

THE REWARD OF PHINEHAS

Phinehas was promised by God "an eternal covenant of priesthood" (Num. 25:13). As noted, the very fact that he was rewarded by God showed that his action was viewed positively. But what was the essence of his reward? At first blush, Phinehas was being rewarded with an office to which he was already a party, as indicated in the second verse of the portion: "Phinehas the son of Eleazar the son of Aaron the priest." Priesthood being of a hereditary nature, as a grandson of Aaron he must have already been considered to be a priest.

However, there is reason to believe that Phinehas was not yet a priest. Rashi explains:

> Although the priesthood had already been given to Aaron's descendants, it had been given only to Aaron and those sons who had been anointed with him, and to their children who would be born after their anointment. Phinehas, however, who had been born before that and had not been anointed, had not heretofore been included in the priesthood (Num. 25:13).

Whether Phinehas was or was not yet a priest is perhaps reflected in the interpretation of the phrase "Phinehas the son of Eleazar the son of Aaron the priest." If the word "priest" refers back to Phinehas, then he is considered to be a priest even before God bestows upon him "an eternal covenant of priesthood." On the other hand, the word "priest" may be referring only to the adjacent name "Aaron," implying that Phinehas himself had not yet become a priest.

Assuming Phinehas was not yet a priest, exactly what did the "eternal covenant of priesthood" confer upon Phinehas? The Talmud provides two answers to this question, but before delving into them, one must be familiar with a story from the book of Joshua.

When the tribes of Reuben, Gad, and half of Manasseh returned from helping the other tribes conquer Canaan west of the Jordan, the Bible states that they "built an altar there by the Jordan, a great altar to look upon" (Josh. 22:10). The words "to look upon" stress that their intention was to be reminded of the altar located in the Tabernacle at Shiloh, and not to use it for sacrifices (*Metzudat David*). However, the tribes on the western side feared that that was exactly what they had in mind, and it had been taught that "from the time they came to Shiloh, high places were forbidden [to be used for sacrifices]" (*Sifrei Re'eh* 65:8). A single site for sacrifices emphasizes the singleness and uniqueness of God. The brutal punishment that the nation had suffered at Baal Peor (Num. 24:9) and the less severe but more recent tragedy that had occurred as a result of the sin of Achan (Josh. 7:5) were still fresh in their minds. They therefore prepared to go to war over the sin of building the altar in order to prevent a potentially greater tragedy. However, before doing so, they sent a delegation of tribal princes led by Phinehas. Abravanel explains that the suspicion was that the east-bank tribes wished to be independent religiously (hence the sending of Phinehas) and politically (hence the sending

Pinchas

of the princes). When they finally had a chance to speak, the east-bank tribes explained that the situation was quite different than what had been surmised. Not only did they not wish to use the altar for sacrifices nor to separate from the rest of the nation, but exactly the opposite. They built the altar as a testimonial object to emphasize to future generations that, despite being physically distant, they were part of the same nation, and should be related to as such (Josh. 22:11-29). The Bible continues: "And *Phinehas the priest* and the princes of the congregation, the heads of the thousands of Israel who were with him, heard the words that the members of Reuben and the members of Gad and the members of Manasseh spoke, and it pleased them" (Josh. 22:30). In other words, their reply allayed the fears of Phinehas and the western tribes. Note that this time the designation of Phinehas as a priest is unambiguous.

The Talmud's definition of the "eternal covenant of priesthood" given to Phinehas can now be presented. The Talmud states:

> R. Elazar said in R. Chanina's name: Phinehas did not become a priest until he slew Zimri, for it is written: "And upon him and his descendants after him will be bestowed an eternal covenant of priesthood" (Num. 25:13). R. Ashi said: Until he made peace between the tribes, for it says: "And *Phinehas the priest* and the princes of the congregation, the heads of the thousands of Israel who were with him, [heard the words that the members of Reuben and the members of Gad and the members of Manasseh spoke, and it pleased them]" (Josh. 22:30). And as to the others too, surely it says: "And upon him and his descendants after him [will be bestowed an eternal

covenant of priesthood]." That is written as a blessing [that his descendants would be priests, but it was not yet conferred on him]. As to the other too, surely it is written, "And *Phinehas the priest*... heard." That was to invest his descendants with the prestigious rank [of high priest].

According to R. Elazar, "eternal covenant" refers to Phinehas becoming a priest, while his outstanding leadership in resolving the potential conflict with the east-Jordan tribes led to the high priests during the First Temple period being chosen from his descendants. Indeed, 1 Chron. 5:30-41 lists the descendants of Phinehas, which includes the names of the high priests during the First Temple period and even the beginning of the Second Temple period (Tosafot, BT *Yoma* 9a, s.v. *ve-lo*, lists eight; Rashi, 1 Chron. 5:36, lists twelve). It should be noted that before Solomon's Temple was built, the high priests, such as Eli, were not descended from Phinehas, but from his uncle Ithamar (Rashi, 1 Chron. 24:3).

According to R. Ashi, the "eternal covenant" was that his descendants would be priests, while the actual investiture took place only after he had manifested his leadership qualities in the book of Joshua. The delay could be explained by saying that achieving permanent priesthood represents such a high level that even one audacious act of zealotry which served as a prime example of crisis leadership, as impressive as it was, was not sufficient to allow Phinehas to be endowed as a priest. When he also manifested leadership qualities in precarious, but somewhat less intense situations, it was determined that he met even the most rigorous demands. Just as the Canaanites could not be expelled from the land until their measure was full (Rashi, Gen. 15:16., based on Isa. 27:8), similarly Phinehas could not receive his entire reward until he had accumulated sufficient merit.

Chizkuni (Num. 25:13) goes further than both Talmudic views,

Pinchas

saying that already in the present portion what was being promised to him and his descendants was the high priesthood. *Chizkuni* assumes that in the phrase "Phinehas the son of Eleazar the son of Aaron the priest," the word "priest" refers to Phinehas, and this is certainly the simple meaning of the phrase. Nowhere did the Bible mention that Phinehas was not numbered among the priests. Finally, no reward is mentioned at all in the book of Joshua, where Phinehas is routinely referred to as a priest (Josh. 22:30-32), and here he is being rewarded with "a covenant of peace" (Num. 25:12) and also "an eternal covenant of priesthood." The verse could have simply spoken of a "covenant of priesthood." What is added by mentioning two covenants and "eternal priesthood"? *Chizkuni* assumes that it is referring to a form of priesthood which is more significant, and perhaps more political, than simple priesthood, namely the position of high priest.

Summary

Although the bulk of this portion describes events which are preparatory to the demise of Moses, his replacement by Joshua, and the entry of the tribes to the Promised Land, of particular interest is the opening of the portion, which deals with the conclusion of the story of the zealotry displayed by Phinehas at the end of the previous portion, *Balak*. The entire Torah is dedicated to laws which are adjudicated by a judicial system, and here the Torah seems to be advocating "taking the law into one's own hands." Appendix IV describes the penal system laid out in the written and oral law, and Appendix V relates specifically to the law concerning the sin which aroused the ire of Phinehas, engaging in sexual relations publicly with a heathen woman. It was explained that the vigilante approach adopted by Phinehas is indeed enshrined in Jewish law,

The Ethics of Numbers

but its applicability is severely limited by that same Jewish law. In fact, the sources indicate that it may be considered irrelevant in contemporary times. Nevertheless, its existence in ancient times serves to focus one's attention on the enormity of those sins for which it was once implemented.

Matot

The portion of *Matot* deals mostly with military matters whose origin was described earlier in the book of Numbers. At the end of *Balak* and the beginning of *Pinchas*, the story of how the Israelites were seduced by the Moabite and Midianite women was narrated, leading to a plague in which twenty-four thousand people were killed. After the plague was stopped with the help of Phinehas, Moses had been commanded by God: "Distress the Midianites and smite them" (Num. 25:17). The resulting battle is described in ch. 31 in the portion of *Matot*. The Israelites were victorious and did not lose even one soldier (Num. 31:49).

A second topic discussed is the desire of the tribes of Reuben and Gad (Num. 32), later joined by half of the tribe of Manasseh (32:33), to settle on the eastern side of the Jordan River. After the nation successfully conquered a large swath of land to the east of the Jordan (Num. 21:21-35), these tribes—who engaged in husbandry—realized that the conquered land was highly suitable for raising cattle, and accordingly desired to appropriate it. Moses was initially unwilling to acquiesce to their request, since it would be unfair of them to abandon the fighting force after the other tribes had helped them conquer the land which they now desired to possess. However, Moses was convinced when they clarified that they did not mean to shirk their responsibility to remain a part of

The Ethics of Numbers

the armed forces. They merely wished to be allowed to leave their families, children, and livestock on the eastern side while they fought, together with the other soldiers, until the land of Canaan was conquered, and only then to return home.

Vows and Oaths

Two Types of Vows

Matot opens with a non-military-oriented section dealing with vows. Vows in Jewish law are of two types: dedicatory and prohibitive. Vows of dedication to the Temple (*nidrei hekdesh*) relate to vows that a person makes to bring a sacrifice or donate money or possessions of his to the Temple. The main Biblical source regarding such vows is found in the following verse:

> When you make a vow to the Lord your God, you may not delay fulfilling it, for the Lord your God will demand it of you, and it will be [counted as] a sin for you [if not fulfilled] (Deut. 23:22).

The Talmud (BT *Rosh Hashanah* 4a-b) explains that if three holidays (Pesach, Shavuot, and Sukkot) pass and the person has not honored his promise, he transgresses the sin to "not delay fulfilling it" (*bal te'acher*). Rif (BT *Rosh Hashanah* 1a) requires the three holidays to be in order (i.e., starting from Pesach), while Rambam starts the count from the nearest holiday (*Hilchot Ma'aseh ha-Korbanot* 14:13).

The Torah refers to such vows incidentally in two locations: in Lev. 22:18 and in the second last verse of the portion of *Pinchas*, where it states:

Matot

These you should offer to the Lord on your festivals, in addition to your vows and voluntary offerings, whether they be your burnt offerings, your meal offerings, your libations, or your peace offerings (Num. 29:39).

The verse relates to two different types of sacrifices. The first is the set of communal sacrifices offered in the Tabernacle, and later the Temple, on the three pilgrimage holidays, as enumerated in the preceding verses in *Pinchas*, ch. 29. The second refers to sacrifices which a person chooses to give voluntarily. The end of the verse refers to the fact that sacrificial animals donated as the result of a *neder* (a vow) or *nedavah* (voluntary offering) must be given either as burnt or peace offerings, and they must be accompanied by meal offerings and libations (Num. 15:3-11;[74] *Menachot* 9:6).

The second type of vows are prohibitive vows (*nidrei issur*). When a person makes such a vow, he prohibits himself from deriving enjoyment from otherwise permissible items owned by himself or by others, or from performing specific actions associated with certain items. Alternatively, he can vow that specific people not derive enjoyment from items owned by him or actions performed by him. For example, if a person says that figs are forbidden to him for a month, or forever, he has made a vow. If one vows not to derive benefit from a specific person, he may not borrow money from him, nor sell him merchandise (*Nedarim* 4:6).

The proper way of making a vow is to say: "An item is prohibited to me as if it were a sacrifice." However, since it is sufficient if the intention is clear, it is enough to merely say that the item is prohibited (called *yadot nedarim*, BT *Nedarim* 2b), and, for the same reason, it can be said in any language (*Hilchot Nedarim* 1:1,

---

74. Num. 15:3 speaks of a burnt offering or a sacrifice (*zevach*). The same word is used in Lev. 3:1, where it is expanded to "a sacrifice of peace offerings."

Beit Yosef, Yoreh De'ah, s.v. *ve-ha-Rambam*). However, if one says that the item is prohibited like pig, the vow is invalid, since pig is prohibited not because it is in his power to make it so (like a sacrifice), but because the Torah made it so (*Nedarim* 2:1).

FULFILLING VOWS

The source of the requirement to fulfill vows is one of the 248 positive commands (Rambam's *Sefer ha-Mitzvot*, Positive #94), and it appears in two places in the Torah:

1. In the portion of *Matot*, the verse states: "If a man makes a vow to the Lord or makes an oath to prohibit himself [from some item or activity], *he may not violate his word; he must do all that came out of his mouth*" (Num. 30:3).
2. In the portion of *Ki Teitzei*, the verse states: "Observe and do what emanates from your lips in accordance with what you have pledged to the Lord your God as a donation, that which you have spoken with your mouth" (Deut. 23:24).

Although the Rambam considers these to be one mitzvah, the verse from *Matot* describes a prohibitive vow, while that from *Ki Teitzei* describes a vow of dedication. Ramban (gloss on *Sefer ha-Mitzvot*, Positive #94), on the other hand, counts these as two separate commands exactly for this reason. It has been suggested that *Matot* opens with a section on vows as a continuation of the end of *Pinchas*, which—it will be recalled—spoke of "vows and voluntary offerings" (Num. 29:39). According to Rambam, who holds that both types of vows are lumped together in one command, this is a natural progression, while according to Ramban, who distinguishes between them, this explanation is less convincing.

Matot

One who fails to fulfill a vow transgresses the negative command (Rambam's *Sefer ha-Mitzvot*, Negative #157) which appears in the verse cited above together with the positive commandment (Num. 30:3). The punishment is lashes, as is the case for every uncorrectable negative command actively transgressed (*Sifrei Devarim* 286, *Makkot* 3:4, *Hilchot Sanhedrin* 18:1-2).

There exists a distinction between *nidrei issur* (prohibitive vows), which must be pronounced out loud and which must be synchronized with what the person had in mind, and *nidrei hekdesh* (vows of dedication), for which even a mental decision is sufficient to create an obligation (BT *Shavuot* 26b, *Hilchot Nedarim* 2:2, *Hilchot Ma'aseh Korbanot* 14:12).

OATHS

The difference between a prohibitive vow (*neder*) and an oath (*shevu'ah*) is that by making a vow, one makes an object into a prohibited item for himself or others. A *neder* thus creates an *issur cheftza*, an object-oriented prohibition. By making an oath, on the other hand, one either creates an obligation on himself (to do or not do some act), or formulates a statement with regard to past behavior, i.e., that he did or did not perform some act (*Hilchot Shavuot* 1:2). An oath can thus create either a *chovat gavra*, a person-oriented obligation, when one swears to perform a given act, or an *issur gavra*, a person-oriented prohibition, when one swears to refrain from performing a given act. In either case, the requirement focuses on the person who makes the oath, e.g., one may swear that he will buy figs tomorrow. The distinction between a vow and an oath was first formulated by Rambam, who wrote:

> When a person takes an oath he forbids himself from [doing or partaking of] the entity mentioned in the oath.

The Ethics of Numbers

> When one takes a vow, he causes the entity mentioned in the vow to be forbidden to him (*Hilchot Nedarim* 3:7).

Rambam (ibid.) utilizes this logic to explain why an oath cannot override a Torah-given law, but a vow may do so:

> When a person takes an oath to nullify a mitzvah, he is placing a prohibition upon himself and he is already bound by an oath [to observe that mitzvah] from Mt. Sinai, and one oath does not take effect if another is already in effect. When [by contrast] a person causes an entity to be forbidden through a vow, the entity itself becomes prohibited, and that entity is not under oath from Mt. Sinai.

As an example, suppose a person makes an oath that he will not sit in a *sukkah* on the holiday of Tabernacles. The oath does not exempt him from the duty to perform the mitzvah because, as a member of the Jewish nation, he had already sworn at Sinai to perform that mitzvah. On the other hand, had he said "sitting in the *sukkah* is forbidden to me" rather than "I will not sit in the *sukkah*," the vow would take effect.

The technical explanation for this is that whereas breaking a vow violates both the negative commandment of "*he may not violate his word*" (Num. 30:3) and the positive commandment of "*he must do all that came out of his mouth*" (Num. 30:3), not sitting in the *sukkah* violates only a positive commandment, and is thus the lesser of the two evils. The philosophical explanation may be that the Torah wishes to stress the significance and centrality of honesty and integrity, which overrides the importance of fulfilling any specific mitzvah.

Matot

One who violates an oath transgresses the negative command: "You may not swear falsely using My Name, thereby profaning the Name of your God" (Lev. 19:12). The implication of this verse is that if the person swore falsely using God's name (or any reference to His name), he is actively transgressing and is punished with lashes (*Hilchot Shavuot* 1:7; *Sefer ha-Mitzvot*, Negative #61), unless the oath was to perform a future act which he neglected to do (i.e., no act was performed), which is prohibited but not punishable by lashes (*Hilchot Shavuot* 4:20-21).

Rambam describes how one could accidentally swear falsely:

> For example, if one took an oath that he did not eat and then remembered that he did in fact eat, or he took an oath that he would not eat and then forgot and ate, or that he would not benefit his wife because she stole his wallet or beat his son and afterwards he found out that she did not steal it or beat him (*Hilchot Shavuot* 3:6).

In such a case, one is not punished with lashes. Rather, he brings a guilt offering, the value of which is proportionate to the person's financial status (Lev. 5:4-13).

If the formulation includes words indicating that an oath is being made, but without reference to God, since this is not the literal intent of the verse, Rambam says that neither lashes, when transgressed intentionally, nor sacrifices, when transgressed inadvertently, are applicable. Nevertheless, Rambam says that one who violates such an oath transgresses a Torah-level law (*Hilchot Shavuot* 2:4). Ran (on Rif, BT *Shavuot* 16a) bases Rambam's view on the occasion when King Saul adjured the nation not to slack off in their pursuit of the Philistines, saying: "Cursed is the man who will eat food until evening, until I am avenged of my enemies" (1 Sam. 14:24), where no reference to God is mentioned, yet his words were taken as a stereotypical oath. Ra'avad (*Hilchot Shavuot* 2:3) goes further than Rambam, saying that even a sacrifice (for inadvertent commission) would be brought in such a case, while Ran quotes others who say that even lashes would be given. However, if neither God's name is mentioned, nor a word indicative of an oath, nor aliases of either, then the laws of oaths and vows do not apply (*Sefer ha-Chinuch* 407). For example, if a person says: "I will go to the store," and he does not do so, he is not in violation of the Biblical command.

Like vows, oaths must be vocalized and intent-driven (BT *Shavuot* 26b, *Hilchot Shavuot* 2:10-12). The source for this requirement is based on the verse regarding the procedure when one inadvertently violates an oath, which states: "Or if a person swears, *expressing with [his] lips* to do harm or to do good, whatever a man may express in an oath, and it is hidden from [forgotten by] him and [later] he knows" (Lev. 5:4).

The age of culpability for both vows and oaths is eleven for girls and twelve for boys, a year earlier than for most other laws of the Torah. An in-depth study of this matter appears in **Appendix VI – Age of Culpability**.

If a person who made a vow or an oath is not willing or able to abide by it, it may be cancelled. There are two methods of cancellation: revocation and annulment. The first, which is of limited application, is dealt with explicitly in the portion of *Matot*. The second is known only from the oral law.

Revocation

Although Rambam stresses the undesirability of losing one's temper (see **Appendix III – Anger Management**), it does happen, and in anger, someone might make a vow which he will eventually regret. Although a man's vows are irrevocable, in certain circumstances a woman's may be revoked by her father, her husband, or both.

Matot

REVOCATION BY THE FATHER

In the portion of *Matot* it states: "If her father impedes her on the day he hears it, all the vows and prohibitions that she has imposed upon herself will not stand" (Num. 30:6). The Midrash (*Sifrei*, Num. 153), wondering what is meant by "impeding," derives the answer from verse 9 ("And if her husband impedes her on the day he hears it, then he has revoked the vow that she had taken upon herself and the utterance which she had imposed upon herself"), where the result of impeding is described as revocation, which according to the Talmud means to say out loud (BT *Nedarim* 79a) that her vow is revoked or cancelled, or to use any other synonym (BT *Nedarim* 77b; *Hilchot Nedarim* 13:2). A parallel method is for the father to force his daughter to disobey her vow, or alternately to explicitly tell her to do so, in which case he need not mention that he is revoking it (BT *Nedarim* 77b; *Hilchot Nedarim* 13:2).

Regarding girls, until what age does the verse apply? Certainly not to a minor under the age of eleven, since the Mishnah (see **Appendix VI – Age of Culpability**) clearly states that such a child's vows are invalid. A hint may be obtained by analyzing the last verse of this chapter, which summarizes these laws as follows: "These are the statutes which the Lord commanded Moses concerning... a father and his daughter, in her damselhood, while in her father's house" (Num. 30:17). In the appendix, it is noted that damselhood is between the ages of twelve and twelve and a half. This verse thus teaches that throughout her damselhood her father can revoke her vows. Rashi (BT *Ketubot* 47a, s.v. *bi-ne'ureha*) explains that if only the previous verse had been written, one would have thought that a father can only revoke the vows of a child nearing maturity, i.e., a girl between the ages of eleven and twelve. The present verse extends the period of revocation to twelve and a half. Beyond that, the girl is an adult and her father has no authority over her (*Nedarim* 11:10).

As far as a married woman is concerned, her husband may revoke her vows, as stated in this portion:

> If she vowed in her husband's house, or imposed a prohibition upon herself with an oath… If her husband revokes them on the day he hears them, anything issuing from her lips regarding her vows or self-imposed prohibitions will not stand (Num. 30:11-13).

Sifrei (*Matot* 154, JT *Nedarim* 10:1) relates this verse to a married (as opposed to betrothed) woman. Since the power of the husband to cancel his wife's vows is explicitly stated in the verse, it may be looked upon as a Divine decree (*gezeirat ha-katuv*). Nevertheless, the Talmud in a number of locations rationalizes the law by explaining that "any woman who vows, does so on condition that her husband agrees [that she be permitted to fulfill it]."[75] Ran (*Chidushei ha-Ran, Gittin* 83b) explains that the justification is merely motivational. In any specific case, even if the woman says explicitly that she is vowing whether her husband agrees or not, he still has the right to revoke it, in conformity with the Biblical command.

WHICH VOWS ARE REVOCABLE?
Regarding the vows which a father may revoke, the verse states: "all the vows and prohibitions that she has imposed upon herself will not stand" (Num. 30:6). Similarly, in conjunction with vows which the husband cancels, the verse states: "anything issuing from her lips regarding her vows or self-imposed prohibitions will not stand" (Num. 30:13). However, the latter verse is qualified by that which follows: "Any vow or any binding oath of self-affliction, her husband can either uphold it or revoke it." Based on this verse, the Mishnah states: "These are the vows which he can revoke: vows which involve self-affliction" (*Nedarim* 11:1).

---

75. BT *Gittin* 83b, *Yevamot* 29b, *Niddah* 46b, *Nedarim* 73b, *Shabbat* 46b.

Matot

Vows of self-affliction are vows that the wife makes which may cause her pain, discomfort, inconvenience, or even denial of pleasure, such as if she vows that she will not bathe herself, adorn herself with jewelry, eat fruit, or accept gifts. Malbim *in situ* explains that "her pain is his pain." In other words, the marital relationship is meant to be so binding that each feels a pin-prick to the other. Ran (BT *Nedarim* 82b), on the other hand, sees revocation as part of the responsibility of a husband to protect his wife by extracting her from unpleasant circumstances which she encounters. Combining the two reasons, it may be assumed that if either partner feels discomfort, both members will not be able to achieve the highest level of interaction, empathy, and couplehood.

The Midrash (*Sifrei Matot* 155) and Talmud (BT *Nedarim* 79b) describe another type of vow which a husband can revoke, namely one that pertains to personal relations between the husband and wife (*beino le-veinah*). Rosh (*Peirush ha-Rosh, Nedarim* 79b, s.v. *melammed*) provides the following example: "if she vowed not to serve him, or other things which might cause strife between him and her." The vow may be very specific, for example if she vowed not to cook a particular food of which he is fond. In distinguishing between vows of affliction and those pertaining to their relationship, one might say that in the former the focus is on the wife—what she vowed concerning herself, while in the latter it is on the husband—what she vowed concerning him. The previous citations derive the ability of the husband to revoke vows *beino le-veinah* from the summary verse at the end of the section dealing with vows, which states: "These are the statutes which the Lord commanded Moses *concerning a man and his wife*" (Num. 30:17), where the marital relationship is emphasized.

There is one difference between revocation of vows of affliction and those pertaining to their relationship. With regard to the former, revocation leads to permanent cancellation. However, regarding those pertaining to their relationship, if she gets divorced and remarries, her first husband's revocation lapses, and the original vow is re-instated until the second husband revokes it. The Talmud uses this distinction to explain why the Mishnah only lists "vows which involve self-affliction" as being in the realm of those which the husband can revoke, and not vows *beino le-veinah*. It is because the Mishnah confines itself to vows that can be permanently removed, as opposed to those which will be revived if she marries another man (BT *Nedarim* 79b) or if her husband dies (*Hilchot Nedarim* 12:3).

The limitation of revocation to the two categories enumerated would seem to apply only to a husband, and not to a father, for two reasons. First, regarding a father the verse states "all the vows and prohibitions" (Num. 30:6), while only with respect to a husband does it say "any vow or any binding oath *of self-affliction*" (Num. 30:14). Furthermore, it is not clear what *beino le-veinah* would mean in the context of a father and daughter. Rambam (*Hilchot Nedarim* 12:1) concisely summarizes these points:

> A father may nullify any vows and oaths [taken by his daughter] on the day he hears of them, for it says: "all of her vows and prohibitions [… will not stand]" (Num. 30:6). A husband, by contrast, may nullify only those vows and oaths that involve self-affliction or pertain to personal relations between the husband and wife… for it says "between a man and his wife" (Num. 30:17).

In spite of logic being on the side of Rambam, the Midrash says that the same restrictions which limit a husband relate to a father, based on the concluding verse of the section dealing with vows: "These are the statutes which the Lord commanded Moses concerning a man and his wife, a father and his daughter" (Num. 30:17), and the Midrash continues:

> Perforce you must liken the father to the husband. Just as a husband can only revoke vows pertaining to their relationship and vows of affliction, so a father can only revoke vows pertaining to their relationship and vows of affliction *(Sifrei Matot* 155).

With regard to the question of the meaning of vows pertaining to their relationship in the case of a father and daughter, perhaps this is why Rosh explains *beino le-veinah* to include "things which might cause strife between him and her," which can apply to a father-daughter as well as a husband-wife relationship (R. Yehuda Rock, VBM, *Parshat Matot*). At any rate, Rosh (*Peirush ha-Rosh, Nedarim* 79b, s.v. *melammed*) accepts the view of *Sifrei* as opposed to that of Rambam.

The wise men of Lunel wrote to Rambam and asked him how he could contradict the *Sifrei* (Rambam, responsum 326), a Tannaitic source. Rambam answered that the *Sifrei* represents the minority opinion of R. Shimon only (BT *Sanhedrin* 86a). Furthermore, he says the comparison between a father and a husband cited in the Midrash does not appear in either of the two Talmuds (Jerusalem and Babylonian), nor in the Tannaitic collection called Tosefta, nor in the Amoraic discussion in the Talmud. Finally, as previously noted, this distinction appears in the Torah only with regard to the husband, while the verse says explicitly that the father can revoke all vows. In the *Kessef Mishneh* (*Hilchot Nedarim* 12:1), however, R. Yosef Karo points out that the Jerusalem Talmud (*Nedarim* 11:1) does indeed cite the scriptural basis for the equivalence between the father and the husband. In his *Shulchan Aruch* (*Yoreh De'ah*

234:58), R. Karo mentions both views without stating which one should be followed.

REVOKING THE VOW OF AN ENGAGED DAMSEL
It has been noted that between the ages of twelve and twelve and a half, a young woman is termed a damsel (*na'arah*), older than a child but not yet an adult. and there are special laws with respect to vows that apply specifically to this period. The Mishnah states:

> A betrothed damsel—her father and her husband revoke her vows. If the father revoked and the husband did not revoke, or if the husband revoked and the father did not revoke, it is not revoked (*Nedarim* 10:1).

The implication of the Mishnah is that if a damsel is married, her husband alone may revoke her vow, as he may do for his wife of any age. If she is unmarried, her father may do so, since she is still under his authority. Only if she is engaged, during which time she still resides in the house of her father but has a commitment to her future husband, is revocation shared by both.

The Talmud derives this law from the following verses:

> And if she is attached to a man, with her vows upon her or with an utterance of her lips which she has imposed upon herself.... And if her husband impedes her on the day he hears it, then he has revoked the vow that she had taken upon herself and the utterance which she had imposed upon herself (Num. 30:7-9).

These verses appear between the reference to vows made by an unmarried damsel (i.e., "in her youth," Num. 30:4) and those made by a married woman ("If she vowed in her husband's house," Num.

30:11), so the Talmud (BT *Nedarim* 67a-b) understands them to be referring to a damsel who is engaged (and that is the attachment referred to in the verse). It is explicitly stated that her fiancé can revoke her vows (Num. 30:7-9). However, if he alone could do so, there would be no need to single out this particular case. It thus follows that he can do so only in conjunction with the father, and likewise the father can do so only in conjunction with the fiancé.

The school of R. Yishmael found a second way to derive the partnership of the damsel's father and fiancé, based on the verse "These are the statutes which the Lord commanded Moses *concerning a man and his wife, a father and his daughter* in her damselhood while in her father's house" (Num. 30:17). While the verse speaks of a damsel who is still living in her father's house, a husband is also mentioned, implying that at this stage she must be betrothed. Furthermore, since the verse explicates the involvement of both the future husband and the father in all facets of vowing, including revocation, it thereby reinforces the previous derivation.

It was noted earlier that Rambam says that a father may revoke all of his daughter's vows, while *Sifrei* implies that he can only revoke vows of affliction and those pertaining to their relationship, i.e., those which a husband can revoke. *Mirkevet ha-Mishneh* (*Hilchot Nedarim* 12:1) reconciles these sources by explaining that Rambam is referring to vows of an unmarried daughter, which the father can revoke independent of their content, while *Sifrei* is referring to those of a betrothed damsel, regarding which the limitations imposed on the fiancé apply to the father as well.

Annulment of Vows

Any person capable of making a vow or an oath may be released from fulfilling it by a scholar or any three laymen (BT *Nedarim* 78a), providing the person regrets making it. The procedure is

The Ethics of Numbers

identical for vows and oaths (*Kessef Mishneh, Hilchot Nedarim* 4:5), since the Torah itself deals with them jointly in the present portion, when it says: "If a man makes a *vow* to the Lord or makes an *oath*" (Num. 30:3).

Generally, a vow is annulled by finding an opening (*petach*), i.e., grounds which did not exist or which the person did not appreciate at the time it was made, which allows the individual to assert that had he been aware of the opening when he made the vow, he would not have done so. Since he was misinformed, the vow is invalid. The Talmud presents the following example of finding an opening:

> A certain woman made a vow with regard to her daughter [that the daughter may not benefit from her]. She came before R. Yochanan to dissolve the vow. He said to her: "Had you known that your neighbors would say about your daughter: 'Had her mother not seen inappropriate matters in her [she would not have vowed]. She would not have taken a vow with regard to her for no reason,' would you have taken a vow with regard to her?" She said to him: "No," and he annulled [the vow] (BT *Nedarim* 21b-22a).

The Talmud (according to Ran, *Nedarim* 21b) discusses whether it is a valid opening for one to say that he made a vow in anger or impatience and regrets it now, even though no circumstance was found which would have dissuaded him from vowing in the first place had he known of it. The Talmud concludes that it is sufficient to do so (BT *Nedarim* 22b), as indicated by a number of stories cited on the preceding Talmudic page (21b), such as when R. Huna asked a person who approached him to annul a vow: "Was your mind with you [i.e., settled and not in a state of anger when you made the vow]?" and R. Assi who asked: "Have you already

236

Matot

regretted [making the vow]?" and R. Elazar who asked: "Did you want your vow [from the very start]?" The Talmud is making the point that even though he desires annulment from the time of the request, he must regret ever having made the vow originally.

Rambam (as well as pseudo-Rashi) understands the discussion differently. In his opinion, regretting making the vow in the first place is the essence of annulment, and unknown facts or events are not an integral part of the process. Typically, the one who vowed says:

> I took an oath concerning so-and-so, and I have changed my mind. If I had known that I would feel such discomfort concerning this, or that some given event would occur, I would not have taken the oath. If, at the time of the oath, my understanding was as it is now, I would not have taken the oath (*Hilchot Shavuot* 6:5).

The question dealt with by the Talmud, according to Rambam, is whether the one who vowed must initiate the discussion by expressing regret, or whether the panel is permitted to coax him until he does so, the fear being that in the latter case he may not be sincere. Reflecting the fact that the Talmud takes the more lenient approach, Rambam states:

> Regarding a person who took an oath, did not regret it, and came to the court intending to fulfill his oath, if the judges saw that releasing this oath would be a mitzvah and lead to peace between a husband and his wife or between a man and his compatriot, and carrying it out will lead to transgression and strife, they create an opening for him and discuss the matter with him, pointing out the consequences of his oath until he regrets [having taken it].

> If he changes his mind because of their words, we release his oath. If he does not change his mind and persists in his rebelliousness, he must carry out his oath (*Hilchot Shavuot* 6:10).

It would seem that, according to Rambam, unforeseen consequences are not so much intrinsic to the annulment process as they are a catalyst to stimulate the one who vowed to regret his words.

After approving the vower's "opening" (whether according to the view of Ran or Rambam), the conclusion of the procedure is described in Rambam's *Peirush ha-Mishnayot* (*Nedarim* 10:8, based on BT *Sanhedrin* 68a):

> The foremost of the three [judges] addresses him with this wording: "It is permitted for you, it is permitted for you, it is permitted for you. It is absolved for you in the heavenly academy and the earthly academy, as it is written: 'And it will be forgiven for the entire congregation of Israel and the stranger who dwells among them, for the entire nation has acted inadvertently'" (Num. 15:26).

THE BIBLICAL SOURCE OF ANNULMENT

Throughout the discussion of annulment, no Biblical verses have been cited. Unlike revocation, which is presented in *Matot* ch. 30, whose text is closely analyzed in Midrash and Talmud, there is no explicit Biblical source that permits the annulment of vows. The Mishnah is the first to admit this when it says:

> [The laws concerning] the annulment of vows float in the air and have nothing to support them [Rashi: rather, they have been transmitted by the Sages as part of the oral tradition] (*Chagigah* 1:8).

Matot

The Talmud points out that although not dealt with explicitly, there are numerous phrases which at least hint at the possibility of annulment and might be considered *asmachtot* (supportive verses). The most convincing is the verse in the present portion which states: "he may not nullify his word" (Num. 30:3), from which Shmuel inferred: "He [himself] may not nullify his word; however, others [i.e., a Sage or a court of three laymen] may nullify it for him" (BT *Chagigah* 10a).

The Talmud proceeds to bring another potential *asmachta* from the repeated use of the Hebrew word *le-hafli* (Lev. 27:2; Num. 6:2), meaning "to utter clearly," with one relating to proper formulation of the vow (from which one may derive that all kinds of vows must be clearly expressed), and the second (which is redundant if it too relates to proper formulation) to its annulment (which also requires a lucid description of why the vower regrets making it). A third *asmachta* relates to a Tannaitic argument as to whether those Hebrews who were not permitted to enter the Land of Israel after the spying incident will have a portion in the world to come (BT *Sanhedrin* 110b). R. Akiva cites the following verse in support of his view that they would be denied entry into the next world: "For I swore in My anger: 'They [the generation of the desert] will never come to My resting-place [the world to come]'" (Ps. 95:11), whereupon R. Yishmael replied that the words "in My anger," which apply to God, are redundant, and may provide an opening for God to annul His vow by saying that it was made, so to say, under extreme circumstances (Rashi, *in situ*). A fourth *asmachta* is from the verse concerning donations to the Tabernacle: "Let every generous-hearted person bring it, [namely] the Lord's offering: gold, silver, and copper" (Exod. 35:5), the implication being that he is forced to make donations which he vowed to bring only as long as his heart is willing to do so. If he regrets his initial vow, he may arrange annulment (Rashi). Finally, the Talmud cites the verse: "I swore and I fulfilled, to keep Your righteous judgments" (Ps. 119:106). Rashi points out that the words "and I fulfilled" are redundant, and imply that not everything that is sworn must be kept, which occurs if one seeks annulment of his oath.

ETHICAL CONCLUSIONS

Why is so much attention devoted to the subject of vows and oaths? As previously enumerated, a number of positive and negative *mitzvot* relate to the requirement to fulfill vows and oaths and the prohibition against violating them. In addition, entire tractates in both the Babylonian and Jerusalem Talmuds are devoted to these subjects. The answer is that being truthful is a very pervasive motif in Judaism. By insisting that one fulfill any promise that he makes, the Torah reinforces the all-inclusive importance of always telling the truth. By defining two separate commands, one requiring fulfillment of vows and oaths, and a second prohibiting their violation, the Torah at once stresses the beauty of adhering to the truth and the repugnance of deviating from it.

However, if one does not use the specified language for making vows (e.g., the word "prohibited," *Hilchot Nedarim* 1:1) and oaths (e.g., oath, curse, etc., *Hilchot Shavuot* 2:4) he has not transgressed these commandments. This was noted by the author of *Sefer ha-Chinuch* (command 407), who wrote:

> One who says "I will do something" or "I will not do something" and does not use the specific formulation of vows, prohibitions, or sacrifices—even though it is ugly, and it is only small-souled people who do it—he does not transgress the prohibition of "he may not violate his word"

Matot

.... However, with respect to every formulation it is stated in the Torah: "Keep far from a false thing" (Exod. 23:7).

Interestingly enough, neither Rambam nor *Sefer ha-Chinuch* count "Keep far from a false thing" as one of the 613 commandments (*Minchat Chinuch* # 37).

It could be that the cluster of different behaviors associated with honesty—namely sincerity, integrity, transparency, rectitude, and uprightness—plays such a central role in so many aspects of Judaism that it would be limiting and even misleading to enumerate it as a single mitzvah. It is in the category of a *mitzvah kollelet* (all-inclusive command) and is not counted among the 613 *mitzvot*, which is described by Rambam as the fourth root (*shoresh*) in his *Sefer ha-Mitzvot*. R. Ovadiah Yosef (*Yechaveh Daʾat* 5:57, s.v. *ve-nodah*) cites R. Chayim Palaji, who uses a similar approach to explain why Rambam does not count *yishuv Eretz Yisrael* (living in the Land of Israel) as one of the 613 commands, since it is a prerequisite for the fulfillment of many *mitzvot*, and essential as an enabler to achieve the ultimate goal of Judaism, which is the creation of a model society.[76] In a similar vein, Ramban (*Sefer ha-Mitzvot*, positive command 1) explains the view of the *Behag*, who does not count belief in God as one of the commands, since this belief is implicit in all of the *mitzvot*. After all, if one believes in God, he will obey His commands, and if he does not believe in God, he will not observe any of the laws cited in His name, including the one that requires one to believe in His existence.

Reservations about Making Vows

Already in the Torah itself, the text seems to express reservations about making vows, as may be understood from the phrase: "But if

---

76. Yehuda Levi, *Mul Etgarei ha-Tekufah* (1993), pp. 13, 48.

you refrain from making vows, you will have no sin" (Deut. 23:23). In relation to this verse, the Talmud states:

> Anyone who vows, even though he fulfills it, is designated a sinner. R. Zevid said: What verse [teaches this]? "But if you refrain from making vows, you will have no sin." This implies that if you do not refrain, there is a sin (BT *Nedarim* 77b).

Why would the Torah devote an entire section to the laws of oaths and vows if, in principle, the Torah deprecates making them in the first place? The Talmud apparently believes that the Torah does not wish to encourage vows, but to supply a means of extracting oneself from vows made in a state of rage. In another location (BT *Nedarim* 22a) the Talmud derives that one who vows is considered to be a wicked person (even worse than a sinner) by noting that the word "refrain" appears both in the verse from Deuteronomy: "But if you refrain from making vows," as well as in the book of Job, which states: "There [in the grave] the wicked refrain from anger" (Job 3:16). The Talmud proceeds to deplore the evils of anger, thus implying that one who angers easily and vows in his anger is a wicked person.

A Biblical verse from the later writings reinforces this approach. In Ecclesiastes, it says: "When you make a [monetary] vow to God, do not delay payment, for He has no desire for fools; [1] that which you vow, pay" (Ecc. 5:3). Rashi *in situ* says that the word "fools" is a euphemism for "the wicked who vow and do not pay." The next verse states: "[2] It is better that you not vow than that you [3] vow and do not pay for it [fulfill it]." These verses delineate three cases: [1] fulfilling one's vows, [2] not vowing at all, and [3] vowing and not fulfilling. Although the second verse seems to be saying that [2] is better than [3], R. Meir (BT *Nedarim* 91, BT *Chullin*

Matot

2a) understands it to be saying that [2] is better than [1], i.e., not vowing is even better than vowing and paying. Ran explains that it is better not to vow, because even if one generally vows and pays, there is always the chance that one time he will forget to pay. R. Meir considers keeping one's word so essential that he is willing to dissuade one from ever vowing just to avoid the rare occasion when he might violate his vow.

The Mishnah itself terms those who make vows and oaths wicked people. Three cases are enumerated:

> [If one says]: "As the vows of the wicked," he has vowed with respect to being a Nazirite [if one happens to be passing by], [bringing] a sacrifice [the default assumption is that he is taking upon himself to bring a sacrifice (BT *Nedarim* 6a)], and an oath [if a food item happens to be in front of him]. [If one says]: "As the vows of the righteous," he has said nothing [i.e., his words are of no effect] (*Nedarim* 1:1).[77]

The implication of the Mishnah is that wicked people tend to vow, so that one is being accurate when he ties his vow to those of wicked people. If he compares his vow to that of righteous people, it is assumed that he did not wish to make a vow, since the righteous do not vow altogether.

The fear that getting in the habit of making vows might lead to eventually taking them lightly and possibly breaking them is reflected in such Talmudic statements as:

1. "Never make a practice of vowing, for ultimately you will trespass in the matter of vows" (BT *Nedarim* 20a). Tosafot

---

77. Ran says that in the case of a sacrifice there was an animal in front of him, but *Kessef Mishneh* (*Hilchot Ma'aseh ha-Korbanot* 14:11) says that Rambam in *Hilchot Nedarim* 1:26 does not require that, since "I take upon myself" implies a sacrifice.

explain that some versions replace the word "vows" with "oaths," as if to say that eventually not only will you transgress vows, which is a relatively minor sin, but even oaths, which are considered more serious, since regarding them the Bible states: "the Lord will *not cleanse* anyone who takes His name in vain" (Exod. 20:7).

2. "One who vows is as if he built a *bamah* (high place), and he who fulfills it is as if he brought a sacrifice on it" (BT *Nedarim* 22a). During the time of the holy Temple, sacrifices were permitted to be brought (i.e., slaughtered and sacrificed) only on its premises. Slaughtering an animal intended to be a sacrifice on a *bamah* off of the Temple grounds was considered to be a serious transgression, based on the following verses:

> Any man of the House of Israel who slaughters an ox, a lamb, or a goat inside the camp [but outside of the courtyard where the slaughtering should take place — *Torat Kohanim* 17:89; BT *Zevachim* 107b], or who slaughters outside the camp and does not bring it to the entrance of the Tent of Meeting to offer as a sacrifice to the Lord before the Tabernacle of the Lord, this [act] will be counted for that man as blood. He has shed blood, and that man will be cut off from among his people (Lev. 17:3-4).

Ran explains the similarity between sacrificing outside of the Temple and making vows. In both cases, the individual is extending the God-given laws unnecessarily. In the former case, God only required sacrifices within the Temple, not in every location where an Israelite finds himself. In the latter case, God has forbidden certain foods and activities, and one who vows wishes to add to the list. As the Jerusalem Talmud (*Nedarim* 9:1) states: "Is what the Torah prohibits not sufficient, that you must go and prohibit

Matot

additional items to yourself?" The initial sin is thus making a vow in the first place. The second is fulfilling it after having made it, rather than seeking its annulment.

In spite of the serious reservations expressed regarding the making of vows and oaths, or perhaps specifically because of them, there are two situations in which the *halachah* looks positively upon doing so.

First Exception

The first exception occurs when a vow of dedication is considered to be a *nedavah* and not a *neder* (to be explained). In fact, the same Mishnah which speaks of vows as being made by *resha'im* (wicked people), and also says that righteous people do not make vows, finishes by saying that if one mentions the voluntary obligations (*nedavot*) of the righteous, this is a valid way of becoming a Nazirite or sanctifying a sacrificial animal. The Mishnah explains the meaning of *nedavot*:

> What constitutes a vow (*neder*)? When one says: "It is incumbent upon me to bring a burnt offering." And what constitutes a voluntary obligation (*nedavah*)? When one says: "Behold, this [animal standing before me] will be a burnt offering." What is the [practical] difference between vows and voluntary obligations? In the case of vows, one is responsible to replace them if they die or are stolen, and with respect to voluntary obligations, one is not responsible to replace them if they die or are stolen (*Kinnim* 1:1).

Righteous people do not make vows because they fear that for one reason or another they may not fulfill them. On the other hand, they make *nedavot* because, since the animal is present and the

245

obligation applies to that animal alone, there is almost no way that they will end up not keeping their word, as illustrated by the behavior of Hillel:

> It was said of Hillel the Elder that no man ever unlawfully derived benefit from [an animal which he had designated to be] his burnt offering; he would bring it to the Temple court before it was consecrated, then sanctify it, and lay [his hands] upon it and slaughter it (BT *Nedarim* 9b).

By minimizing the time between the consecration of his offering and its slaughter, and donating it as a *nedavah* so that in case of a mishap no further obligation devolves upon him, Hillel ensured that his vow would be fulfilled, and this is why the virtuous limit themselves to *nedavot* rather than *nedarim*.

The distinction outlined in the Mishnah between voluntary obligations, where a specific animal is consecrated, as opposed to vows, where the obligation is on the person to bring an animal, is clear. How does this distinction come into play with regard to a Nazirite? Ran (BT *Nedarim* 9a) concludes that since these concepts relate to Nazirites as well, there must be a more intrinsic distinction between *neder* and *nedavah*. He characterizes the difference between the two by the degree of sincerity and enthusiasm manifested. The very fact that one points to the specific animal to be sacrificed without hesitation shows the depth of his desire to donate. The parallel situation with regard to Nazirism is when it is not taken upon oneself haphazardly or randomly, but after much forethought and with a very specific benefit in mind, as indicated by the following extract from which it may be seen that Ran's explanation follows from the Talmudic text:

Matot

That is well with respect to a voluntary offering of sacrifices, but what can be said regarding a voluntary vow of Nazirism [since the danger of transgressing one of the Nazirite restrictions is ever present]?—It is as [in such cases as] that dealt with by Shimon ha-Tzaddik (BT *Nedarim* 9b).

At this point, the Talmud tells the previously cited story of how Shimon ha-Tzaddik, who was a priest, never partook of the guilt offering of a Nazirite who had inadvertently defiled himself and had to extend his period of Nazirism. Shimon felt that when the typical Nazirite realized that his period of asceticism was to be lengthened, he probably regretted his initial vow, which would eliminate the requirement to bring sacrifices altogether, in which case Shimon would be eating unconsecrated meat which should not have been brought to the Temple. The exception, when Shimon did eat of the guilt offering, was the case of a very sincere young man who became a Nazirite to overcome his vanity. This type of occurrence exemplifies the concept of *nedavah* with regard to a Nazirite.

Second Exception

The second exception relates to a case when an oath is not even valid. A Mishnah in *Shavuot* states: "If a person swore to annul a mitzvah but did not annul it, he is exempt; to fulfill, and he did not fulfill it, he is exempt [from punishment if he violates the oath; i.e., in both cases the oath is invalid]" (*Shavuot* 3:6). This teaching is based on the accepted interpretation of a verse regarding oaths: "If a person swears, expressing with [his] lips to do harm or to do good" (Lev. 5:4), which the Talmud (BT *Shavuot* 27a) understands to be referring to an optional act which can be either harmful or beneficial for oneself, and not to a required act (mitzvah). In spite of this restriction, the Talmud states:

The Ethics of Numbers

> R. Giddal also said in the name of Rav: From where do we know that one may swear that he will fulfill a mitzvah? From the verse: "I swore and I fulfilled to observe the laws of Your righteousness" (Ps. 119:106). But is he not already under oath to do so from the time of Mt. Sinai?—But what it [R. Giddal] teaches us is that one may [swear in order to] stimulate himself [to obey a specific command] (BT *Nedarim* 8a).

The verse quoted cites King David in Psalms saying that he swore that he would fulfill the commands of the Torah. The Midrash (*Num. Rabbah, Naso* 9:54) says that the Israelites made an oath to accept upon themselves the 613 *mitzvot*. The Talmud accordingly asks: Since it has been noted that an oath to fulfill a given command is invalid (as well as an oath to fulfill an oath), how can R. Giddal say that it is a valid oath? The Talmud answers that of course it does not actually take effect as a normative oath,[78] for the reason stated, i.e. that David was already commanded to observe the Law. However, R. Giddal is teaching that one may swear in order to urge himself not to be lax in the observance of *mitzvot*, and even if God's name is mentioned, it is not considered to be in vain.

The Talmudic text continues:

> R. Giddal also said in the name of Rav: One who says, "I will rise early to study this chapter or this tractate," has vowed a great vow [Ritva on Rif: "actually, an oath"] to the God of Israel.... What does he teach us—that a person may

---

78. The reason it doesn't take effect is debated. Ramban (*in situ*) and Rambam (*Hilchot Shavuot* 5:11, 16, 11:3) say it doesn't take effect at all. Ran (*in situ*) says while it does not mean he has to bring a sacrifice on a Biblical level if broken inadvertently, he still does violate the prohibition of not violating his word.

Matot

thus stimulate himself? That is identical with R. Giddal's first [statement]. This is what R. Giddal teaches: The oath is binding [in this case], since one can free himself [i.e., satisfy the requirement] by reading the *Shema* [prayer in the] morning and evening [and the oath is valid because it requires him to study more than he is Biblically required].

First, it must be noted that studying Torah is a Biblical commandment. The Torah states: "And you must teach them [the laws of the Torah] to your sons" (Deut. 6:7). This verse appears in the previously mentioned *Shema* prayer. In connection with this very phrase, the Talmud comments:

> Our Rabbis taught: *ve-shinantam* ["And you must teach them," means] that the words of the Torah must be clear-cut in your mouth [*shanun* in Hebrew means "sharp"], so that if anyone asks you something, you should not hesitate and then answer him, but [be able to] answer him immediately (BT *Kiddushin* 30a).

Since it is impossible to attain the level of competence described by merely reciting the *Shema* prayer in the morning and evening, it follows that more intense study is required in order to fulfill the Torah-level requirement. A second source from the prophetic writings describes Torah study as a full-time pursuit:

> This book of the Torah should not leave your mouth; you must meditate upon it day and night, in order that you will be able to observe and to do all that is written in it, for then will you succeed in your ways and then will you prosper (Josh. 1:8).

The Ethics of Numbers

The word used in the latter source is "meditate," which implies that even in one's secular pursuits, he should be aware of the Jewish approach and maintain it in his consciousness.

It is now possible to explain the additional lesson of the second teaching of R. Giddal. According to Ran, the oath in this case is valid. Even though learning Torah is a Biblical-level command, since to fulfill the explicit command it suffices to recite the *Shema* in the morning and evening, the oath is valid because it surpasses the requirement of the written law. Ritva on Rif says that even if the oral law (which demands much more study than what derives from the mere recital of the *Shema*) is considered to be on the same level as the written law, he may fulfill the requirement to study Torah by learning any chapter. By specifying a particular chapter, he has gone beyond the Biblical requirement, thus creating virgin territory upon which the oath may operate.

Summary

The introductory portion of *Matot* deals exhaustively with the subject of vows. Two types of vows have been described, those of dedication and those of prohibition. The similarities and differences between vows and oaths have been discussed, as well as the means of their cancellation by revocation or annulment.

The general viewpoint of the Sages is that being truthful is such a central and major aspect of Judaism that one should shy away from ever making a vow or an oath, since having made one introduces the possibility of lying if, for whatever reason, even inadvertently, one does not fulfill his vow or oath. The rabbinical view is that the system of laws and the associated judicial branch which the Torah presents can only be implemented on the basis of absolute honesty.

Matot

Only because a high standard of truthfulness is universally adhered to is it possible to permit vows in two exceptional cases: when one wishes to make sincere improvements of his personal traits, and when one wants to stimulate himself to obey religious law with alacrity and integrity.

Massei

As a fitting conclusion to the book of Numbers, *Bamidbar* in Hebrew (which means "in the desert"), this portion begins with a list of the forty-two stages of the Israelites' journey from Egypt to the plains of Moab. Rashi immediately asks the obvious question: what is the benefit of presenting this long and tedious litany? He supplies two answers. The first, which he attributes to R. Moshe ha-Darshan ("the Preacher"), is that upon close examination, it will be noted that twenty-two of the forty-two stops occurred in the first and last of their forty years in the desert. The remaining twenty encampments were thus spread over thirty-eight years, so that on the average, they spent two years at each site. In other words, it would be incorrect to say that they were in constant turmoil. In the words of Rashi (Num. 33:1):

> Why were these journeys recorded? To inform us of the kind deeds of the Omnipresent, for although He issued a decree to move them around [from place to place] and make them wander in the desert, do not say that they were moving about and wandering from station to station for all forty years, and they had no rest.

Rashi's second answer is based on the Midrash (*Tanchuma Massei* 3, *Num. Rabbah* 23), which states:

Massei

To what is this analogous? To a king whose son was sick. He took him to another place to have him healed. On the way back, the father began recounting all the stages of their journey, saying to him: "This is where we sat, here we were cold, here you had a headache." Similarly, the Holy One said to Moses: "Recount to them all of the places where they provoked me." It is therefore stated: "These are the stages" (Num. 33:1).

There appears to be a dissonance between the parable and its object. The parable highlights the king's love for his son. Its object seems to stress the rebellious nature of the Israelites. However, one may also interpret the Midrash to be demonstrating God's deep-seated compassion and love for the Children of Israel, as if He is telling them that in spite of their initial immaturity and the hard times they experienced together, He now forgives them and can look back at those years with tolerance and understanding.

Upon further examination, the parallel becomes clearer. Having a headache is not a positive occurrence, but it is also not the prince's fault. Later, he is cured and does not suffer any more. God is telling His people: "Your misbehavior is certainly far from desirable. But similar to a headache, it may not have been your fault, because you were young (intellectually), inexperienced (religiously), and uneducated. You have now been cured by receiving the Torah, educated by the teachings transmitted by Moses your teacher, and have become experienced by undergoing the trials and tribulations of your journey through the desert."

The remainder of the portion presents a number of topics dealing with the subdivision of the land when the nation will arrive in Israel. Initial discussion of two of these topics, the method of allocation (Num. 34) and the inheritance rights of women (Num. 36), were first broached in the portion of *Pinchas* (Num. 26:52-56,

The Ethics of Numbers

27:1-11). A third topic is the setting aside of forty-eight Levitical cities, six of which were to serve as cities of refuge for accidental killers, and the relevant laws with respect to the perpetrators of such deeds.

Allocating the Land

After counting the males between the ages of twenty and sixty in the portion of *Pinchas* (Num. 26:1-51), the method of land apportionment is introduced in the following verses from the same chapter:

> **52** The Lord spoke to Moses, saying: **53** Among these the land will be divided as an inheritance, in accordance with the number of names. **54** To the large [tribe] you will give a larger inheritance and to the smaller you will give a smaller inheritance, each [Saadiah Gaon: tribe] will be given an inheritance according to its number. **55** Only by a lottery will the land be divided; they will inherit it according to the names of their fathers' tribes. **56** The inheritance will be divided between the numerous and the few, by lottery.

Who was entitled to a portion of the land? The text is contradictory. V. 53 uses the term "among these." Since the previous section reports the results of a census taken just before the nation entered the Land of Israel, the simple meaning is that the land would be divided among those entering it. However, v. 55 speaks of the division being "according to the names of their fathers' tribes." The latter phrase is itself ambiguous. Which fathers does it mean? Does it mean the fathers who established the tribes, meaning that the

Massei

land would be divided into twelve equal segments, or does it mean some other fathers, e.g., the fathers who left Egypt? The Talmud (BT *Bava Batra* 117b) concludes that the second option is correct, based on the words addressed by Moses (in the name of the Lord) to those people who subsequently left Egypt: "I will bring you to the land, concerning which I raised My hand [i.e., swore] to give to Abraham, to Isaac, and to Jacob, and I will give it to you as a heritage" (Exod. 6:8).

At any rate, the original contradiction is still unanswered. Was it divided equally among those who arrived in Israel, or among those who left Egypt, who were represented by their descendants? For example, according to the second option, if two brothers left Egypt, one of whom had fifty descendants and the other of whom had only five, the fifty would have to split among themselves the same amount of land that was apportioned to the five.

There is a Mishnah that seems to supply the answer:

> The daughters of Zelophehad took shares in the inheritance [after the conquest led by Joshua]: the share of their father, who was one of those who came out of Egypt, and his share [which was double, i.e., two shares] among his brothers in the possessions of Chefer [who also came out of Egypt], since he was a first-born son who takes two shares (*Bava Batra* 8:3).

This Mishnah refers to the story of the daughters of the deceased Zelophehad (Num. 27:1-11), the son of Chefer of the tribe of Manasseh. Zelophehad had no sons, and until that point it was thought to be that only sons could inherit. The daughters complained to Moses that their father's share in the land would pass over to his brothers and nothing would be registered under his name. Moses referred the question to God, who replied that in such a case the daughters were entitled to inherit their father's property. The Mishnah explains that the five daughters were entitled to three shares. One was from Zelophehad himself, since he was above twenty when the Israelites left Egypt. But Zelophehad's father Chefer was also among those who left Egypt. Since Zelophehad was the first-born, by the laws of primogeniture (Deut. 21:17), he was entitled to a double portion of the land of his deceased father Chefer, which in turn would pass over to Zelophehad's daughters, leaving them overall with three shares, one from their father and two from their grandfather.

This Mishnah clearly relates the division of the land to those who left Egypt. The question previously posed would seem to be answered, except for the fact that the Talmud notes that the Tanna of the Mishnah is R. Yoshiya. Another Tanna, however, R. Yonatan, takes the alternate view that the shares were based on those who entered Canaan,[79] while a third Tanna combines both approaches.

UNDERSTANDING THE LOTTERY

With regard to the allocation of land to the various tribes, the verses also seem to be contradictory. Verse 54 says that the larger tribes would be allocated more land, which seems only fair. On the other hand, vv. 55-56 say that a lottery will be used. A lottery would imply that the land areas being raffled are equal in size. However, even if some of the allocations were larger than others, there is no guarantee

---

79. It is a bit more complicated than saying that each person arriving in Israel who was above the age of twenty received a share. For example, if a father who left Egypt had two sons, one with one child and the other with three, then the grandchildren got four shares which related back to the grandfather. Each of his two sons got two of the four shares, which each set of grandsons inherited, so that the single grandson got two shares, and the three grandsons through the other son had to split the other two shares. In this sense, the dead grandfather actually inherited from the living grandchildren, leading to the anomaly of the dead inheriting from the living (BT *Bava Batra* 117a).

that those plots would end up in the possession of the larger tribes. The Talmud answers the apparent contradiction as follows:

> Eleazar was wearing the *Urim ve-Tumim*, while Joshua and all Israel stood before him. An urn [containing the names] of the [twelve] tribes and an urn [containing descriptions] of the boundaries were placed before him. Infused with the Holy Spirit, he would say: "Zebulun is coming up. The borders of Acco will come up with it." He shook the urn of the tribes and Zebulun came up in his hand. He shook the urn of the borders and the borders of Acco came up in his hand. Infused again with the Holy Spirit, he would say: "Naphtali is coming up, and the borders of Gennesar will come up with it. He shook the urn of the tribes and Naphtali came up in his hand. He shook the urn of the borders, and the borders of Gennesar came up in his hand. And so [was the procedure] with every [other] tribe (BT *Bava Batra* 122a).

The Talmud is saying that the allocations were of different sizes. If the raffle was random, this would be grossly unfair. What happened, instead, is that God intervened to make sure that each tribe was paired with its proper land allocation, and by means of the *Urim ve-Tumim* the priest was able to announce the results of the drawing before it happened. A phrase in v. 56 translates literally as "by the mouth of the lottery." The Talmud sees this as a hint that the lottery was given a mouth by means of the announcements of Eleazar the High Priest.

CONCLUDING DETAILS IN THE PORTION OF *MASSEI*

The portion of *Massei* completes the picture with regard to the division of the land. Three additional aspects are contained in this portion: the exact boundaries, the tribal princes who will help administer the subdivision, and the Levitical cities.

FIRST ASPECT: BOUNDARIES OF THE LAND

First, the exact boundaries of the Land of Israel west of the Jordan are presented in detail (Num. 34:1-12). In many cases these are natural boundaries, such as the Sea of Galilee, Jordan River, and Dead Sea on the east; the Mediterranean Sea on the west; and the brook of Egypt on the south. These boundaries are theoretical more than actual, having only really been attained during the reigns of David and Solomon.[80] Clearly, it would have been impossible to divide up the land among the tribes if its exact delineation was not provided. It is further stressed that the entire area was to be divided up among only nine and a half of the tribes, since two and a half had already been given land to the east of the Jordan (34:13-15).

There are three stages in the division of the land. The first is to define the overall boundaries of the Land of Israel, which appears at the beginning of ch. 34. The second is to divide up the land enclosed by these boundaries among the remaining tribes, excluding Levi. As noted, the method for doing so is described in the portion of *Pinchas* and clarified in the Talmud, while the actual subdivision takes place in the book of Joshua, chs. 14-19. Finally, each tribe's land would have to be divided up among those who were entitled to receive shares. Although all shares were to be equal, the equality would have to be expressed in overall value. A small piece of very fertile land is equal in value to a larger plot of arid land. Furthermore, personal preferences may enter. Some may prefer their land on a mountain, others in a valley, and yet others on a plain. Many prefer close relatives as neighbors, others do not, and some are indifferent. In order to implement such decisions among a crowd known to be fractious, it was imperative

---

80. J.H. Hertz, *The Pentateuch* (1938), p. 717.

Massei

to secure administrators who were considerate on the one hand and authoritative on the other. The tribal princes were chosen for this task.

Second Aspect: The Tribal Princes

The second aspect is the listing of the princes of the tribes in the remainder of ch. 34. This is the fourth time that the names of the princes appear in the book of Numbers. The first time was when the census was taken upon entering the desert (Num. 1:5-16), and the second was when the princes brought sacrifices at the inauguration of the Tabernacle (Num. 7:12-83), which actually took place before the census. The names appearing in those lists were identical. However, the third list, which contains the names of the spies sent by the various tribes (Num. 13:1-17), is different. Although the Bible says "every one a prince among them" (Num. 13:2), many commentators (e.g., Rashbam, *Chizkuni*, and Sforno) explain that they were actually only messengers of the princes, so understandably they differ from the names in the previous lists. The fourth list is also different, and this is clearly because the princes of forty years earlier had all died as a result of the sin of the spies (Num. 14:29). Accordingly, in reporting the results of the census taken at the end of their forty-year trek, the Bible states: "Among these there was no man [Rashi: but the women were not included in the decree (resulting from the sin) of the spies, for they cherished the land] who had been [included] in the census of Moses and Aaron the priest when they counted the Children of Israel in the Sinai desert [forty years earlier]" (Num. 26:64).

The present list starts with the following introductory verse: "You will take one prince, one prince from each tribe to [help you to] acquire the land" (Num. 34:18), after which the name of each appears, preceded by the title *nasi* (prince), with the exception of those of the first three tribes mentioned—Judah, Simeon, and

Benjamin, whose names appear without a title. The question that arises is whether these three were indeed princes, or perhaps just administrative leaders. *Or ha-Chaim* and *Chizkuni* assume that they too were princes. *Or ha-Chaim* explains simply that since the introductory phrase says explicitly "one prince, one prince" it was not necessary to repeat the appellation for the earlier members of the list. *Midrash ha-Gadol* says that Caleb was already called a "prince" (which he takes literally) when he was chosen to be one of the spies (Num. 13:2). Other reasons advanced are that it was already well known that Caleb had become a prince (even if the spies were not so initially), having shone in the story of the spies (Num. 13:30), when he was even called God's servant (Num. 14:24). On the other hand, being termed a prince may have been an affront to him, as the future leader of the tribe of Judah was destined for something greater—kingship.

The person chosen from Benjamin is named Elidad, which these commentators assume is identical to Eldad, one of the pair of prophets (Num. 11:26). As in the case of Caleb, a prince perhaps ranked lower than a prophet, and his tribe too was associated with the kingship, which was to be initiated by Saul of the tribe of Benjamin (1 Sam. 9:16). Finally, with regard to Simeon, these commentators adopt the opposite approach. Since this tribe was intimately connected with the atrocity which took place at Baal Peor (Num. 25:14; Rashi, Num. 25:6), it was punished by not having its leader referred to by the sobriquet to which he was entitled. *Midrash ha-Gadol* proposes a similar possibility with regard to Benjamin, the tribe which perpetrated the outrage at Gibeah (*pilegesh be-Givah*, Judg. 19:14). It suggests that Moses chose not to honor Benjamin, being prophetically aware of that future event.

Shadal *in situ* holds that the princely title was not bestowed on the leaders of Judah, Simeon, and Benjamin because they were actually not the tribal princes. In the case of the other tribes, the prince was chosen by popular vote, while in the case of Judah, God wished to honor Caleb for his good works even though he was not the tribal prince. He further surmises that Caleb might have been very close with the leaders of Simeon and Benjamin, whom he considered to be righteous people, and he might have insisted on them joining him if he were to accept the administrative appointment offered by God. His sensitivity might have stemmed from his bitter experience in coping with the ten corrupt spies many years before. Shadal cites the willingness of the tribe of Judah to cede land to the tribe of Simeon (Josh. 19:9) as evidence of the close-knit relationship between their leaders.

These explanations may lay a basis for understanding the strange order of enumeration of the tribes on this occasion. Obviously, the complete traditional order was irrelevant, since Reuben and Gad were not to be included, having already received their inheritance on the eastern side of the Jordan. Nevertheless, the remaining tribes could have been listed in order of their birth, their flags, or their mothers. One may suggest that the tribes listed first were those whose leaders were either not princes or not referred to as princes, for whatever reason, even though they actually were.

THIRD ASPECT: THE LEVITICAL CITIES

The third aspect, which was noted previously—namely the setting aside of forty-eight Levitical cities, six of which were to serve as cities of refuge for accidental killers—is first introduced in *Massei* (Num. 35:1-15), although additional details are provided in the book of Deuteronomy (4:41-43, 19:1-10). In conjunction with accidental deaths, rules concerning premeditated murder are included both here (Num. 35:16-34) and in later references (Deut. 19:11-13), since in all cases the perpetrator would escape to one of the cities of refuge in order to save himself from the wrath of relatives of the deceased wishing to avenge their kin's blood. If the murder was intentional, the court would remove him from the city of refuge and pass judgment on him.

Eleazar and Joshua

Eleazar the High Priest and Joshua were named as the overall administrators (Num. 34:17)—the superiors of the enumerated princes, available to answer difficult queries, as recorded again at the time of the plan's implementation (Josh. 14:1). Joshua, as one of the righteous spies and Moses' successor, obviously survived the passage through the desert, as did Caleb, the princely representative of Judah (Num. 14:30; Ramban 26:65). They were included in the earlier census, but not the later one, because they were already over the age of sixty. However, one might ask: should not Eleazar the priest have died in the desert together with all of the other male Israelites who were above the age of twenty at the time of the spying fiasco? The answer is that just as the tribe of Levi did not sin with respect to the golden calf (Exod. 32:26), similarly they did not sin in conjunction with the evil report brought by the spies. The list of spies (Num. 13:4-15) does not include a representative of the tribe of Levi, hence no representative of their tribe slandered the Land of Israel, and it may thus be assumed that they were not among the crowd that murmured against Moses, Aaron, and ultimately God (Num. 14:1-4). Only those who participated in the congregational complaint were to be punished, as it says: "all of those who despised Me will not see it [the Land of Israel]" (Num. 14:23). This conjecture may be confirmed by once more examining the verse which states: "Among these there was no man who had been [included] in the census of Moses and Aaron when they counted the Children of Israel in the Sinai desert" (Num. 26:64).

Massei

Those who were included in the earlier census were punished; however, the Levites were not counted in that census, as the verse states: "But the Levites, according to their father's tribe, were not numbered among them" (Num. 1:47).

THE DAUGHTERS OF ZELOPHEHAD

The case of the daughters of Zelophehad, who asked to be apportioned the land which would have been given to their father had he still been alive, has already been mentioned. Two questions may be asked. First, on what basis did the daughters deduce that they would not inherit the land allotted to their father? Second, if their deduction was indeed correct, on what basis did they think that this law was susceptible to being overturned any more than any of the other 613 *mitzvot* commanded by Moses?

In answer to the first question, it may be noted that the daughters' request follows the census and the description of the land apportionment among the tribes. Regarding the census, the Bible states: "Count all of the congregation of the Children of Israel from twenty years old and upwards, by their fathers' houses, all that are fit to go out to war in Israel" (Num. 26:2). The implication of this verse is that only men (who are fit to go out to war) above the age of twenty are to be counted. With regard to land apportionment, the Bible states: "each tribe will be given an inheritance according to its number" (Num. 26:54). However, since only the males were counted, the implication is that the land would only be apportioned to them. These inferences were the source of the daughters' knowledge.

As regards the second question, the Midrash (*Sifrei Pinchas* 133) explains that the daughters were convinced that God's law must make allowance for situations such as theirs:

The Ethics of Numbers

> "And the daughters of Zelophehad *drew near*" (Num. 27:1): When the daughters of Zelophehad heard that the land would be divided amongst the tribes, but not to the females, they gathered together to take advice [from each other]. They said: "The mercy of the Omnipresent is not like that of humans. Humans are more merciful to males than females. However, He who created the world by His word is not so, but rather His mercy is on all creatures— male and female, as it says: 'The Lord is good to all, and His mercy is on all His creations'" (Ps. 145:9).

The Midrash apparently took note of the words "drew near." Although the simple meaning is that they approached Moses, "drew near" implies a closeness more appropriately used with regard to sisters, and so the Midrash understands the verse to be saying that both occurred. The Midrash seems to imply that the daughters considered the possibility that God had not explicitly legislated a law relating to their specific circumstance. Perhaps He had left it to Moses or the Sanhedrin to deal with such a situation. In that case, they feared that the ruling would be in favor of the males. However, if the case could be referred to God Himself, they were quite confident that His ruling would be balanced and take into consideration their needs as well. The import of this Midrash is that when Israel was a young and as yet culturally unenlightened nation, perhaps even its greatest Sages had not yet achieved the intellectual maturity necessary to enable them to anticipate Divine justice, which would become perceptible only as Jewish tradition developed and progressed (Rashi, Num. 27:7, s.v. *ken*). Of course, it must be realized that this approach is not necessarily mainstream in early and even more so later rabbinical literature.

Massei

THE QUALITIES OF THE DAUGHTERS

The Talmud lavishes praise on the daughters of Zelophehad:

> It was taught: The daughters of Zelophehad were wise women, they were scholarly, they were righteous. They were wise [in worldly ways, i.e. adept and efficient], since they spoke at an appropriate time [when an associated topic was under discussion]; for R. Shmuel son of R. Yitzchak said: [Scripture] teaches that Moses our master was sitting and holding forth an exposition on the section of levirate marriages, for it says: "If brothers dwell together, [and one of them dies having no son, the dead man's wife may not marry an outsider. (Rather,) her husband's brother should be intimate with her, and take her as a wife and carry out levirate marriage with her]" (Deut. 25:5).
>
> They said to him: "If we are like a son, give us an inheritance like a son; if not, let our mother undergo levirate marriage!" Immediately [after this occurred, the verse states]: "And Moses brought their case before the Lord" (Num. 27:5). They [must] have been scholarly, for they said: "If he had a son we would not have spoken" [they knew that where there are sons, only they inherit, as indeed Moses said later (Num. 27:8)]. They were righteous, since they only married men who were worthy of them. R. Eliezer b. Ya'akov taught: Even the youngest among them did not marry when she was under forty years of age [until she found a meritorious man] (BT *Bava Batra* 119b).

What hint is there from the words of the daughters that Moses was teaching the subject of levirate marriage? The daughters justified their request by saying: "Why should our father's *name* be missing from his family because he had no son?" (Num. 27:4).

265

The Ethics of Numbers

When discussing levirate marriage, the Bible states that the son who will be born "will rise up in the *name* of his [father's] deceased brother" (Deut. 25:6). The similarity in language, which was also noted by the Midrash (*Sifrei Pinchas* 133), implies that the daughters listened attentively to Moses' lesson, and formulated their question using subject-appropriate language. The daughters understood that "having no son" (Deut. 25:5) means also having no daughter, which implies that if one did have a daughter, she would adequately represent her deceased father's name. If that is the case, the daughters claimed, then also in the case of inheritance, the existence of daughters should suffice to maintain their father's name by inheriting his birthright.

Furthermore, the Talmud stresses that the wonderful traits of being wise, scholarly, and righteous were shared equally among all of the sisters, who were said to be "equal" (BT *Bava Batra* 120a). This is derived from the fact that the list of the sisters' names appears three times. In the portion of *Pinchas*, where they are mentioned twice (Num. 26:33, 27:1), the order is: "Machlah, Noah, Choglah, Milcah, and Tirzah;" in the portion of *Massei*, the order is changed, with the verse stating "Machlah, Tirzah, Choglah, Milcah, and Noah married their cousins" (Num. 36:11). In the latter case, it would certainly have sufficed to say, "They married their cousins." Why was it necessary to repeat their names for the third time? Rashbam (*in situ*) understands that by recording the names in a different order, the Bible wishes to indicate that since items are frequently mentioned in order of importance, in this case it was impossible to do so because they were all equally distinguished. It is unusual for one person to possess all of these qualities, but it is

Massei

highly extraordinary for five sisters to be equally blessed with the entire complement of positive traits.

In fact, the following Talmudic text claims that the story of Zelophehad's daughters could have been omitted entirely had Moses presented the laws of inheritance in detail in the same manner that he introduced so many other Scriptural laws, since case studies are quite rare in Scripture. It was cited in their name only to honor them in light of their superb characters:

> It was fitting that the section containing the laws of inheritance be written [in the Torah] by Moses, but the daughters of Zelophehad merited that it be written in connection with them (BT *Bava Batra* 119a).

Moses' Apparent Lack of Knowledge

The question that arises is whether these laws were actually known to Moses, just that their public declaration occurred only as a result of the daughters' query, or whether it was upon this occasion that God transmitted the laws of inheritance for the first time.

On the one hand, according to R. Akiva (BT *Zevachim* 115b, BT *Chagigah* 6a), Moses became acquainted with all of the written and oral law during the forty days that he spent on Mt. Sinai (Exod. 24:18). Even according to R. Yishmael—who says that the limited time which Moses spent on Mt. Sinai only sufficed to present him with an outline of general principles—Moses could have derived the relevant law from the basic definition of levirate marriage in the same way that the daughters of Zelophehad did. Additionally, it is possible that these laws were among the social laws which had already been given at Marah (Rashi, Exod. 15:25), although if this were the case, the daughters would have already been acquainted with them, since the common perception is that those laws were publicized by Moses immediately upon receiving them.[81]

On the other hand, when confronted with the daughters' request to receive a plot, the verse states that Moses "brought their case before the Lord" (Num. 27:5), implying that he did not know if they were in fact entitled to an inheritance.

One possibility expressed in the Talmud is that Moses knew that daughters in such a situation would receive an inheritance. His question was only with regard to a minor detail. Since Zelophehad was his father's first-born, he was entitled to two shares, as opposed to each of his brothers, who would each receive one share. Moses was unclear as to whether his entitlement to a double portion was also passed on to his daughters. In the words of the Talmud:

> R. Chidka said: "Shimon of Shikmona was my friend among the disciples of R. Akiva. And thus did R. Shimon of Shikmona say: 'Moses our Master knew that the daughters of Zelophehad were to be heiresses, but he did not know whether or not they were to take the [added] portion of the birthright'" (BT *Bava Batra* 119a).

According to R. Shimon of Shikmona, then, Moses was taught almost all Torah knowledge with the exception of just one or a few minor details, but the subject of inheritance was presented to the entire Israelite congregation only in response to the daughters' query in honor and recognition of their outstanding character.

R. Chanina (BT *Sanhedrin* 8a), however, saw Moses' lack of knowledge of the laws of inheritance as a punishment for his conceit when he stated: "and the case that is too difficult for you,

---

81. For a more extensive discussion, see Abba Engelberg, *The Ethics of Exodus* (2014), pp. 292-305.

Massei

bring to me" (Deut. 1:17). Although the simple meaning would indicate that God did not enlighten Moses with respect to the entire subject of lone female inheritance, one may still maintain the view of Shimon of Shikmona that his punishment only consisted of him not being informed of one minor detail.

Rashi, in his typically concise fashion, summarizes and clarifies the two possible options. He states:

> The law eluded him, and here he was punished for crowning himself [with authority] by saying, "and the case that is too difficult for you, bring to me" (Deut. 1:17). Another interpretation: It would have been fitting that this section be written by Moses, but Zelophehad's daughters were meritorious, so it was written in connection with them (Num. 27:5).

Rashi has clarified three points:

1. According to the view that Moses was being punished, he may still have been taught all details of the Torah at Mt. Sinai, in accordance with the view of R. Akiva, just that God caused him to forget them upon being asked, in punishment for the vain statement which he made to the Children of Israel.

2. The two options—that Moses was being punished and that God wanted to honor the daughters—are in conflict with each other and not meant to be harmonized. In fact, the Talmud in *Sanhedrin* (8a) rejects the possibility that Moses was being punished by noting that the entire statement uttered by Moses was: "and the case that is too difficult for you, bring to me *and I will hear it*," meaning that if I have been taught the answer to your question, I will answer you immediately, and if not, I will pass on the question to the Lord and hear it (the answer)

from Him. Moses' behavior was thus impeccable, and the Talmud accordingly concludes that there was no basis for him to be punished.

3. Since the main motivation for presenting these laws in conjunction with the daughters of Zelophehad was to honor them, no disrespect of Moses was intended and he certainly was not being punished. Alternatively, it may be suggested that he was not culturally ready to deal with such aspects of societal functioning, as indicated by a previously cited Rashi (Num. 27:7, s.v. *ken*).

THE COMPLAINT OF THE TRIBE OF MANASSEH

In the portion of *Pinchas*, in response to an appeal by the daughters of Zelophehad, it was determined that in the absence of sons, daughters would inherit their father's property. In the present portion, members of the tribe of Manasseh presented the following grievance to Moses:

> If they marry a member of another tribe of the Children of Israel, their inheritance will be diminished from the inheritance of our fathers, and it will be added to the inheritance of the tribe into which they marry, and thus, it will be diminished from the lot of our inheritance. And when the Children of Israel will have a Jubilee, [their plot will not return to our tribe, but] their inheritance will be added to the inheritance of the [family of the] tribe into which they marry, and their inheritance will be diminished from the inheritance of our father's tribe (Num. 36:3-4).

In short, the tribal leaders of Manasseh feared that by passing ownership of land to women, the land would eventually be

Massei

inherited by their husbands, if their wives pre-decease them, or by their sons, who are members of their husbands' tribes and not their own, thus reducing the size of the tribal allocation.

Once more Moses was apparently stymied, since the verse states: "And Moses commanded the Children of Israel *according to the words of the Lord*, saying, '*The tribe of Joseph's descendants speak justly*'" (Num. 36:5). Note that the language used parallels that of Moses when he could not answer the daughters' query in the portion of *Pinchas*, where the Lord is quoted as saying: "*Zelophehad's daughters speak justly*" (Num. 27:7). On the other hand, Moses' lack of knowledge is made into quite an issue in the first case, where it says: "And Moses brought their case before the Lord" (Num. 27:5), while here it glibly states that Moses answered "according to the words of the Lord." It is of course possible to say that the phrase does not mean to imply that he asked God at that moment. Perhaps this information was included in God's earlier conversation with Moses back in the portion of *Pinchas*, but only revealed at this point in answer to the just fears of the daughters' tribe.

God's answer is explicit: "Let them marry whomever they please, but they must marry only into the family of their father's tribe" (Num. 36:6). Does this apply to all women who find themselves in this situation, or only to the daughters of Zelophehad? Regarding this, Scripture is equally explicit: "And every daughter from the tribes of the Children of Israel who inherits property must marry a member of her father's tribe" (Num. 36:8). The rationale behind this policy is also clearly stated: "And no inheritance will be transferred from one tribe to another tribe" (Num. 36:9).

Three points follow from the above verses. First, the daughters of Zelophehad were required to marry members of their own tribe (36:6). Second, the same rule applies to all women who have no brothers and are accordingly destined to be benefactors of their fathers' property (36:8). Third, since the rationale of this law is to prevent the transfer of land between tribes, clearly it applies for all generations.

Although these three points follow from a simple reading of the text, surprisingly the Talmud rejects two of the three, as will be seen.

The Daughters of Zelophehad Were Not Required to Marry Members of Their Own Tribe

> R. Yehuda said in the name of Shmuel: The daughters of Zelophehad were given permission to be married into any of the tribes, for it says: "Let them marry whomever they please." How, then, may one explain [the continuation of 36:6]: "But they must marry only into the family of their father's tribe?" [The answer is that] Scripture gave them good advice [Rashbam: but not a positive commandment], that they should marry only [men who are] appropriate for them [*Ha'amek Davar* (36:6): by being from their father's tribe] (BT *Bava Batra* 120a).

Why are men from their father's tribe more appropriate for them? One might answer that although on a personal level there may be no difference, on a national level such behavior would prevent confusion as to the exact land allocated to each tribe. In addition, one might say that in general, marriages are most successful when the inherent differences between the couple are kept to a minimum, and their backgrounds are as similar as possible.[82]

On the other hand, the second point, namely that women in the same situation as the daughters of Zelophehad would be required to

---

82. Robert Emery, *Cultural Sociology of Divorce: An Encyclopedia* (2013), vol. 1, p. 1040.

Massei

marry members of their own tribe, was accepted and implemented as written. Two questions follow. First, on what Scriptural basis did the Talmud make this distinction? Second, what was the reasoning behind it? Although one must obey Torah law even when its rationale escapes him, great luminaries, including Rambam, have written works which provide enlightenment with respect to the motivation underlying many of the commands.

Sources for Special Treatment for the Daughters of Zelophehad

The *Torah Temimah* (Num. 36:7) suggests two possible sources for singling out the daughters. First, the verse relating to them states: "Let them marry whomever they please, but they must marry only into the family of their father's tribe" (Num. 36:6). He says that the first phrase is redundant. Had the verse contained only the last phrase, which confines their marital options to their own tribe, since no further limitation is recorded, it would have been obvious that within their tribe they are permitted to marry whomever they choose. Since the first phrase is included, it must mean that they are each allowed to pick any man whom they so desire as their husband, with the second phrase merely intended to offer a beneficial suggestion.

The *Torah Temimah*'s second proposal relates to a distinction the Talmud (BT *Bava Batra* 9b) makes between Biblical usage of the word "giving" and "transferring." The former is used with respect to male inheritance, where the bequeathed receives land which maintains its tribal status. The latter refers to female inheritance, where the land will eventually be absorbed by the husband's tribe. In answer to the query of the daughters of Zelophehad, God tells Moses:

> **7** Zelophehad's daughters speak justly. You should certainly *give* them a portion of inheritance along with their father's brothers, and you should *transfer* their father's inheritance to them. **8** Speak to the Children of Israel, saying: If a man dies and has no son, you should *transfer* his inheritance to his daughter (Num. 27).

The *Torah Temimah* notes that since "transfer" is used in v. 7 with regard to the daughters, it must be that they were to be permitted to marry outside of their tribe, because otherwise no "transfer" would occur.

The only weakness with this theory is that in v. 8, which supposedly relates to all cases of female inheritance, the word "transfer" is also used, yet it has been noted that women other than Zelophehad's daughters were indeed restricted to marry only within the tribe. A possible resolution is that eventually the plan was that women inheritors could marry out, and only as a result of the complaint of the tribe of Manasseh was this limitation temporarily enacted. Accordingly, in the above citation from the portion of *Pinchas*, which was stated before the complaint, transferring was still a possibility both for the daughters as well as for other women, and this option may have been temporarily suspended at a later stage for the latter group. One may say that v. 8 could indeed be interpreted as referring to a later period, when inter-tribal marriage was permitted, while v. 7 was said specifically with regard to the daughters of Zelophehad. In fact, v. 7 must be meant to impart something distinctive concerning the daughters, for otherwise it is extraneous, as their case is covered by the rubric of v. 8.

Perhaps *Ha'amek Davar* (Num. 27:7) was also bothered by this conundrum. He notes that in v. 7, with regard to the daughters, both "giving" and "transferring" are written. Interestingly, in connection with "giving," the pronoun used is masculine (*lahem*), and only with respect to the "transferring" is a female pronoun (*lahen*) used. *Ha'amek Davar* understands this to mean that the daughters were worthy of entitlement on a par with the males, who are of course entitled to marry whomever they wish, since marriage could never lead to the "transferring" of male property, as their land always remains within their own tribe and is hence "given" to them.

As a result of the grievance of the tribe of Manasseh, it was decreed that unmarried women who had inherited or who could potentially inherit were required to marry within their tribe. How about those who disobeyed this command or those who were already married before the command was issued? Ramban (Num. 36:7) says that in that situation, the law introduced as a result of the daughters' request would be suspended, and their fathers' portion would not go to them, but to their fathers' brothers.

REASONS FOR SPECIAL TREATMENT OF ZELOPHEHAD'S DAUGHTERS

Both the *Torah Temimah* (Num. 36: 7) and *Ha'amek Davar* (Num. 36:6) trace the special treatment to their being distinguished women. *Ha'amek Davar* feels that as such they were placed on the same level as males who were born into their husbands' tribes, so inheriting in their case is not considered to be transferring. A simpler explanation would be that being very outstanding, it was naturally harder for them to find appropriate husbands, and it would thus be unfair to limit their options, as opposed to less exceptional women, who could easily choose a husband from among the many average men in their own tribe.

The *Or ha-Chaim* (Num. 36:10) proposes an original reason. He says that God purposely allowed them total freedom of choice, as opposed to other women in similar circumstances, specifically to highlight their righteousness if and when they would choose not to benefit from the special privileges afforded them. He explained the following verse based on his approach: "As the Lord had commanded Moses, so did Zelophehad's daughters do" (Num. 36:10). This verse does not follow the normal sequence—placing the action before the command—which would have led to: "Zelophehad's daughters did as the Lord had commanded Moses." The reversal indicates that the true meaning is: "As the Lord had commanded Moses [regarding other women], so did Zelophehad's daughters do [regarding themselves]." Their behavior emphasized that in spite of their intellectual ability and attainments, they maintained their modest demeanor and did not seek special treatment.

Women Inheritors Would Eventually Be Allowed to Marry Out of Their Tribes

With regard to the previously mentioned third point, namely that the rules given in relation to the daughters of Zelophehad were permanent, the Talmud (BT *Bava Batra* 120a) states otherwise. It says that the verse: "Every daughter from the tribes of the Children of Israel who inherits property must marry a member of her father's tribe" (Num. 36:8) was valid only during the generation preceding the final allotment of lands to the various tribes, based on the preceding verse:

> *This is the thing* that the Lord has commanded regarding Zelophehad's daughters. Let them marry whomever they please, but they must marry only into the family of their father's tribe" (Num. 36:6).

Massei

The expression "This is the thing" is generally stated in connection with a one-time commandment rather than a permanent law. Some examples are:

1. Regarding manna: "*This is the thing* that the Lord has commanded. Gather of it each one according to his eating [amount], an *omer* for each person" (Exod. 16:16).
2. Regarding the consecration of the priests: "And *this is the thing* that you must do for them to sanctify them to serve Me [as priests]" (Exod. 29:1, Lev. 8:5).
3. Regarding donations for building the Tabernacle:

And Moses spoke to the entire community of the Children of Israel, saying: "*This is the thing* that the Lord has commanded to say: 'Take from yourselves an offering for the Lord; every generous-hearted person may bring it, [namely] the Lord's offering: gold, silver, and copper'" (Exod. 35:4-5).

One might ask that even after the initial allocation of the land, women who inherit from their tribal affiliation by marriage would diminish the land allocated to their original tribe. If so, why was the command to marry within the tribe limited in scope? The answer is that the Torah strives to create a democratic society, and in such a community people must have freedom of choice as much as possible with respect to whom they are permitted to marry. Of course, there are certain restrictions as to marital partners for priests (Lev. 21:7, 14) and even laymen (Deut. 23:3-4), but they should be kept to a minimum. Furthermore, according to a previously cited Ramban, in certain circumstances the laws permitting female inheritance were suspended during the period of land allocation. Certainly, that ruling could not be permanent, since it contradicts the specific Torah law allowing such inheritance (Num. 27:8), where the word *leimor* (saying) is used, indicating that this is a permanent law (*Mechilta, Beshallach, parsha* A). Why, then, was it so important to breach that law even temporarily?

Ramban (Num. 36:7) explains that it was critical that the land originally allocated to each tribe be clearly delineated, so that each tribe could be associated with a specific district. Clearly, this would be impossible if the inaugural pattern was checkered. *Yad Rama* (BT *Bava Batra* 120a) points out that if properties were not initially kept within well-defined tribal regions, it would be impossible to fulfill the guidelines established for the Biblical subdivision of the land in the book of Joshua, chs. 14-19. Malbim (Num. 27:8) suggests that if land transfer were possible at the time of the conquest, this might negatively affect the motivation of each tribe's soldiers, since they might conjecture that the land which they were risking their lives to capture would not even remain part of their own tribe's portion.

After the conquest and subdivision of the land by tribal boundaries, Malbim explains that even if a woman intermarries and inherits a plot far from her own marital dwelling, when her son eventually inherits that land, he would probably sell it as fast and cheaply as possible to a member of his mother's native tribe, since it would be grossly inconvenient to possess land so distant from home.

Summary

The Torah aims to create a democratic society with equal opportunity for all citizens to optimize their self-achievement. On the other hand, as an agrarian society, it was mainly the men who would work the fields. Accordingly, land was generally inherited

Massei

by a man's sons, who would take it upon themselves to support any single daughters. Married women would of course be supported by their husbands. In the case of men who had no sons, consequential to the request of the daughters of Zelophehad, daughters could also inherit land. When such women married, this policy would potentially lead to the transfer of property between tribes. It was estimated that such transfers would not create insuperable problems, and furthermore, it was highly desirable for the tribes to be closely bound to each other both socially and family-wise, in order to strengthen the unity of the nation.

In the portion of *Matot,* the tribes of Reuben and Gad requested to settle on the eastern side of the Jordan River (Num. 32). Moses was very hesitant to allow them to do so. According to *Ha'amek Davar* (Deut. 3:16), he feared that the distance between them and the main region would lead them to be detached from the community. It may be noted that the original request was made by the tribes of Reuben and Gad (Num. 32:5), and only later was the tribe of Manasseh added (Num. 32:33). According to *Ha'amek Davar,* that was because they were great scholars, and Moses tasked them with keeping the other two tribes synchronized with the rest of the nation intellectually and religiously. According to Yehuda Eisenberg (*Iyunim be-Sefer Yehoshua,* ch. 22, Internet), this same apprehension stimulated Joshua, after Reuben and Gad fulfilled their commitment to fight along with their brethren and were about to depart and return eastward to their homelands, to issue the following warning:

> Just be very careful to do the commandment and the Torah, which Moses the servant of the Lord commanded you, to love the Lord your God, and to walk in all His ways, and to keep His commandments, and to cling to

Him, and to serve Him with all your heart and with all your soul (Josh. 22:5).

In observing the Torah, the nation not only obeys the Lord, but also maintains itself as a tightly-knit and united community.

Appendix I: Zipporah

The woman who played a very central role in the life of Moses, and hence in the history of the Jewish nation, is Zipporah. Her name appears in the Torah three times, and she is referred to anonymously twice. The Midrash contains numerous stories which shed light on her personality, although sometimes these stories contradict one another.

Zipporah's name is mentioned when her father gives her hand in marriage to Moses (Exod. 2:21), when she saves her husband's life in connection with his failure to circumcise their son (Exod. 4:24-26), and when she returns from Midian with her father Jethro in order to re-unite with her husband (Exod. 18:2). She is referred to anonymously when Moses meets and assists the seven daughters of Jethro by the well (Exod. 2:16), and when Miriam and Aaron disparage Moses because of the Cushite woman whom he had married (*Beha'alotcha*, ch. 12). Most commentators[83] consider the Cushite woman to be Zipporah.

---

83. Midrashim (*Tanchuma Tzav* 13, *Midrash Tehillim* Psalm 7, *Lekach Tov Beha'alotcha*, *Midrash Aggadah Beha'alotcha*, *Pirkei de-Rabbi Eliezer* 52, *Avot de-Rabbi Natan* A:9; B:43), Rashi, Ibn Ezra, Abravanel, but not Rashbam.

The Ethics of Numbers

The First Meeting

The introduction to Zipporah is not very auspicious. After all, when Jacob met Rachel at the well, he fell in love with her instantly (Gen. 29:11), and apparently the love never abated, as indicated by the uniquely direct and explicit phrase which appears soon after: "and Jacob loved Rachel" (Gen. 29:18). Contrast this with Moses' meeting Zipporah at the well. She is not even mentioned by name, but is just one of the seven daughters of Jethro (Exod. 2:16). Ramban explains that Moses had been wandering in the desert for upwards of fifty years, having left Egypt as an adolescent and being in his seventies at this point (Exod. 2:23). It must have been very difficult for Moses to support himself, so when Jethro offered him a steady job, he undoubtedly jumped at the offer. But Jethro explained that there is a string attached: his youngest daughter Zipporah is still single, and Moses must marry her. And so it says: "And he [Jethro] gave Zipporah his daughter to Moses" (Exod. 2:21). There is no indication of physical or intellectual attraction on the part of Moses. However, this is not to say that under the positive influence of her great husband, she could not have eventually become a righteous and deserving woman in her own right.

Zipporah's Personality

The question that arises is whether Zipporah was an outstandingly wonderful woman, on the same level as the matriarchs, and a worthy counterpart to her husband, or whether she was renowned mainly for being "the wife of," an average woman who just happened to be the wife of one of the greatest men that ever lived.

Zipporah

The answer to this question might be found in three slight variations of a story from the Midrash. In the first version, Miriam meets Zipporah one day and asks her why she doesn't adorn herself with jewelry. Zipporah answers that her husband is so engrossed in his spiritual life that he barely notices what she wears (*Sifrei Bamidbar*, par. 99). Miriam concludes that Zipporah is no longer having relations with her husband (this conclusion does not necessarily follow but, as it turns out, Miriam was on target), and she promptly reports the news to her brother Aaron. In this version, Zipporah gives a simple, modest reply, while Miriam is depicted as a gossiper.

R. Natan, in the same Midrash, presents a different scenario. Joshua hears Eldad and Medad prophesying, and becomes jealous for his master Moses, fearing that the two have usurped Moses' monopoly on prophecy. Under her breath, Zipporah sighs, "I pity their wives." Here, it is Zipporah who initiates the comment, although it is not explicit, nor is it meant for public consumption. Miriam, nevertheless, who apparently has perfect hearing, overhears it and passes it on. According to R. Natan, Zipporah is a bit less righteous and Miriam is a bit less of a gossip.

A third version formulates the story as follows: Seventy elders have just been appointed to assist Moses. Miriam expresses her heartfelt joy at the honor bestowed upon the elders and their wives, whereupon Zipporah says: "Woe unto their wives, for from the first day that God spoke to my husband Moses, he ceased having a sexual relationship with me" (*Sifrei Zuta, Bamidbar* 12). Here, Zipporah has become the gossiper, while Miriam is sincerely empathetic. Miriam was punished only on account of her single slanderous misstep.

283

The Ethics of Numbers

In the View of the Commentators

The Biblical commentators align themselves with one or another of the versions of the Midrash. Abravanel describes Zipporah as being completely aware and accepting of the necessity for Moses to be at the highest level of purity continually, since God could appear to him at any time without warning (Abravanel, Exod. 4:24). It was she who realized that the life of Moses was in danger when he dealt with the lodging arrangements for his family and did not give priority to his son's circumcision (Exod. 4:25). By being the protector of Moses, she played an essential role in the transmission of God's word to the Hebrews, and she was highly gratified by the opportunity provided her. Abravanel's Zipporah is in alignment with the first version of the Midrash.

On the other hand, *Targum Yonatan* (Exod. 4:24), based on the *Mechilta*,[84] says that the life of Moses' and Zipporah's eldest child was in danger because of a second string which Jethro had attached to his offer of employment to Moses (Ibn Ezra on Exod. 4:25 says this was in collusion with Zipporah), namely that the first-born son would become a priest for idolatry. Zipporah saved her son's life when she realized the deleterious effect of the imposed condition, and perhaps gave up idol-worship, but did not necessarily appreciate Moses' Divine mission, nor did she necessarily perfect her character. This approach would be in accordance with the third version of the Midrash discussed above.

Now, one might say, it is understandable that Zipporah was not yet weaned from idolatry, but how could Moses acquiesce to Jethro's condition? In fact, *Ba'al ha-Turim* (on Exod. 18:3) says that Moses was punished for accepting this condition. It is stated in Judg. 18:30 that Micah hired a priest named Jonathan, the son of Gershom, the son of Manasseh, to serve in his idolatrous Temple. According

---

84. *Mechilta de-Rabbi Yishmael, Yitro*, tractate Amalek, portion Aleph.

Zipporah

to many commentaries, Manasseh is in fact Moses, with the name altered by the insertion of a small, raised Hebrew letter *nun*, in order to diminish the embarrassment to Moses. In other words, the grandson of Moses ministered in a place of idol-worship.

A second commentator, *Siftei Kohen*,[85] justifies Moses' behavior by noting that Moses felt that Jethro was not committed to any particular idol, but was a wavering seeker of the Divine. Moses had enough confidence in the validity of his own belief in the true God to be convinced that Jethro would eventually make the right choice, just as the King of Khazar described by Judah Halevi did.[86]

Modern Application

Two contrasting views of Zipporah have been presented. In addition to a historical analysis, a topic which is quite relevant today has been broached, namely, whether Moses could have only been married to a righteous woman of his own stature and, by extension, whether one should limit his own contacts as much as possible to people who are as religious and righteous as he is. Alternatively, by his marriage to a woman who was, at least initially, mediocre, perhaps one is being told that it is proper to have open communication channels to co-religionists, as well as to members of other faiths. There exist cogent reasons to support either approach. By maintaining contact with people who have questionable views, one may be negatively affected. Rashi apparently accepted this view when he ascribed the death of Aaron as punishment for the fact that the Children of Israel in their passage to the Holy Land considered the possibility of passing through the territory of Esau, thus exposing themselves to the negative influence of the descendants of Esau (Rashi, Num. 20:23). On the other hand, if

---

85. *Siftei Kohen, Shemot*, p. 18.
86. *Kuzari*, pt. 1, Introduction.

one maintains a cloistered existence, he foregoes the possibility of cross-pollination. Our Sages have said: "If someone tells you that there is wisdom among the Gentiles, believe him; there is Torah among the Gentiles, do not believe him" (*Lam. Rabbah* 2:13).

By living in isolation, one loses the possibility of being a positive influence on others. Rashi comments that the unpleasant incident experienced by Dinah was in retribution for Jacob's enclosing her in a box in order to prevent Esau from seeing her.[87] Perhaps Dinah could have stimulated Esau to improve his behavior. Apparently, Rashi himself realized that there was no single answer to the previously outlined dilemma. The right approach is a function of the stability and intellectual maturity of the people involved.

Rabbi Naftali Zvi Yehuda Berlin (the Netziv) writes that during the time of the Second Temple, most Jews were religious, yet the Temple was destroyed because of superfluous hate. The Netziv elucidates this concept as follows: "They accused anyone whose behavior deviated from their way of fearing God as being a Sadducee or a heretic."[88]

A Modern Example

A modern example of this dilemma occurred in 1956, when the question arose as to whether Orthodox rabbis and congregations should join organizations composed of rabbis and synagogues from all streams of Judaism. Two halachic bodies worked on the subject simultaneously, the Rabbinical Council of America (RCA) Halachah Committee, and the rabbinic advisory board of the Rabbinical Alliance, consisting of prominent *roshei yeshiva*

---

87. *Gen. Rabbah* 76:9 says Dinah was hidden in a box, without making a value judgment. Rashi, Gen. 32:23, relates Jacob's behavior to the rape of Dinah.
88. *Ha'amek Davar*, Introduction to Genesis.

(heads of Yeshivas). Five days before the former was to meet, the latter group issued a prohibition on such participation. However, the head of the Rabbinical Alliance advisory committee, R. Aharon Kotler, requested that the decision be kept secret until he had a chance to discuss it with R. Joseph B. Soloveitchik, the head of the RCA Halachah Committee. Unfortunately, the decision was leaked before R. Kotler had a chance to meet with R. Soloveitchik, whereupon R. Kotler remarked: "This day is a tragic day in the history of Judaism in America."[89] What would R. Soloveitchik have decided? Although there were many within the RCA who agreed with the decision of the Rabbinical Alliance, he might have suggested joining these organizations and working jointly on neutral matters of interest to all Jews, and refraining from discussing or participating in topics related to *halachah*, *hashkafah*, or ritual.[90]

The Ethical Approach

The lesson to be learned from Moses' willingness to engage with people of different viewpoints, and the stress which the Netziv places on his approach, is that tolerance of others and deference to their opinions is an essential part of a Jew's *Weltanschauung*. The Mishnah states that every person should be judged in a favorable light (*Avot* 1:6). Doing so means that people are required to hear out everyone's opinion respectfully, and even if they differ, their own perspective must be presented in a manner which does not denigrate the views or the persona of their interlocutor.

---

89. See the blog: *Hirhurim – Musings*, Sept. 8, 2006.
90. George E. Johnson, *We Have Found the Enemy, and the Enemy is Us: Rethinking Rav Soloveitchik's Views on Orthodox – Non-Orthodox Relations.* "Jewish Ideas Daily," Jan. 20, 2013.

The Ethics of Numbers

Why Did Moses Intermarry?

Understanding the Question

Although the benefits of a broad-minded approach have been presented, it is also true that marrying a heathen is prohibited by Jewish law. Certainly, God's future messenger for the purpose of transmitting Jewish law to the Hebrews should have been sensitive to such an issue. How then did it come about that Moses made no effort to marry within the fold? In addition, if he already chose a non-Jew to be his wife, did she convert at any stage?

In fact, his intermarriage proved to be the source of future problems for Moses. Zimri, son of Salu, who publicly committed harlotry as part of a pagan rite with the Midianite woman Cozbi, daughter of Zur (Num. 25:14-15), is said to have presented Moses with the following query: "Son of Amram, is this woman permitted or forbidden to me? And if you claim she is forbidden, who permitted you to marry the daughter of Jethro?" (BT *Sanhedrin* 82a). The background of this event is examined in the portion of *Pinchas*.

Before answering the question at hand, two more basic questions must be dealt with. First, did Moses know at the time of his marriage, before he encountered the burning bush, that he was destined for greatness and would be expected to serve as a role model? Second, was the concept of conversion applicable or even meaningful before the Torah was given?

With regard to the first question, it may be assumed that Moses was aware of his great potential. His mother had brought him up in the king's palace (Exod. 2:8), and she undoubtedly told him of the miraculous events which accompanied his birth and rescue from danger. But even without the mystical facet, he was certainly educated to believe that there lay in store a common fate to be shared by him with the Children of Israel, as indicated by his empathy with the Hebrew who was being beaten by the Egyptian taskmaster (Exod. 2:11). Furthermore, he certainly realized that he was living in a palace while his brethren were enslaved in the fields, and that must have caused him to wonder. As previously noted, Ramban claimed that Moses wandered in the desert for many years before experiencing Divine revelation at the burning bush. Had he been unaware of his intimate connection to the Children of Israel, one could not even ask why he did not marry an Israelite. After all, why should he? But if he saw himself as an integral member of the nation, the question is very much in place.

With regard to the second question, it must be pointed out that before the Torah was given, there were no Jews. The first conversion occurred at the time of the giving of the Torah, as Rashi states: "Our ancestors entered into the Covenant [converted] by means of circumcision, immersion, and sprinkling of blood [since in Temple times a sacrifice was required as well]" (Exod. 24:6, based on BT *Krietot* 9a).

On the other hand, with respect to the phrase in Genesis, "and the souls that they had made in Haran" (Gen. 12:5), Rashi attempts to explain how it is possible to attribute the making of a soul to Abraham and Sarah: "Abraham converted the men, and Sarah converted the women, and Scripture considers it as if they had made them." Apparently, the conversion referred to is of the type described by Rashi on a later verse in Genesis: "Thus he commands his children: Keep the way of the Lord, to do righteousness and justice" (Gen. 18:19).

The following Midrash specifies additional elements that pre-Torah conversion might have entailed: "Three good measures were in the hands of the Israelites in Egypt, and in their merit they were redeemed: they did not change their names, they did not change their language, and they guarded themselves against incest" (*Num. Rabbah* 13:20).

In short, pre-revelational conversion quite possibly required one to accept a code consisting of both moral and nationalistic elements. Apparently, even before the Torah was given, Judaism was both a religion and a nationality.

ANSWERING THE QUESTIONS

The aforementioned Ramban (Exod. 2:23) provides a practical answer to the first question concerning Moses' intermarriage. He had wandered for forty to sixty years in a desert devoid of descendants of Jacob, before arriving in Midian. Tosafot states clearly: "Moses did not take a wife from among the Children of Israel… he was fleeing Pharaoh and was forced by circumstances."[91]

Regarding the question of Zipporah's conversion, the answer would depend on whether one accepts the view of Abravanel that she had outstanding traits from the very beginning—in which case she certainly would have acquiesced to all of the aforementioned elements of pre-Torah conversion, or whether one accepts the view of *Targum Yonatan* and *Siftei Kohen* that initially she was an idolater of unrefined character, and only improved gradually under the guidance of Moses. If the latter approach is taken, her conversion would have been of the pre-Torah variety only if it happened before the giving of the Torah, or of the post-Torah variety if it occurred afterwards.

SUMMARIZING ZIPPORAH'S PERSONALITY

It is possible to identify two narratives in the Biblical and Midrashic stories which relate to Zipporah.

---

91. *Da'at Zekenim mi-Ba'alei Tosafot*, Num. 12:1.

Zipporah

According to the first narrative,[92] Moses noticed from the start that Zipporah was endowed with outstanding traits. She, like her father, arrived independently at belief in the one and only God, possibly employing philosophical analysis coupled with logical deduction, just as the patriarch Abraham had done. She revered her husband Moses, appreciated his mission, and fully understood the necessity of his withdrawal from the family in order to achieve his predetermined goals. She possessed both wisdom and initiative, and knew how to operate in case of emergency, e.g., when her husband and son were threatened, and she was even able to defiantly cast the foreskin back at the angel and inform him that he had accomplished his mission. In fact, the Midrash derives the name Zipporah from her behavior on that occasion, which showed her to be as agile as a bird—*tzippor* in Hebrew (*Midrash Lekach Tov*, Exod. 4).

Zipporah is thus depicted as the rare individual whose character merges grace and benevolence with the ability to be proactive when the situation calls for it—a combination which depicts her as a worthy successor of the matriarchs described in the book of Genesis, and Jochebed and Miriam, who are portrayed at the beginning of the book of Exodus. She serves as a prototype for women of Israel in the future, who will be involved at the highest echelon of leadership and Torah learning, and so the Midrash notes with regard to the circumcision which Zipporah performed: "From here we derive that a woman may circumcise" (*Midrash Lekach Tov*, Exod. 4).

Sefer ha-Chinuch follows this approach in its discussion of the law forbidding entry to the Temple or making halachic decisions while intoxicated:

---

92. A more thorough treatment may be found in Sharon Rimon, "Zipporah," VBM.

The Ethics of Numbers

> The prohibition of entering the Temple while intoxicated applies to both males and females, when the Temple is standing, and the prohibition of serving as a halachic decisor [while intoxicated] applies in all places and at all times to males, *as well as to a wise woman who is fit to issue decisions*. Anyone who is a wise person, whose decisions people trust, is prohibited to teach his students when intoxicated, since his teaching is tantamount to issuing halachic decisions (command 152).

The tendency is to utilize the outstanding talents of the women of Israel to the fullest extent in studying and teaching Torah, halachic decision-making, and Jewish leadership, and Zipporah was among the first to demonstrate these abilities.

The second narrative depicts Zipporah as a mediocre woman, fully immersed in idolatry at the time she entered into a marriage of convenience with Moses, which allowed him to subsist as a shepherd, a profession which availed him of much free time to ponder the Almighty and deepen his faith. Moses was willing to consider such an arrangement because he relied on his ability to serve as a positive influence on Zipporah and to nudge her in the direction of true religious belief, and there is no question that he eventually succeeded in this task.

The implication of this approach is that in the early years of his marriage, Moses had to deal with a wife and father-in-law who were pagans. According to one view in the Talmud (JT *Nedarim* ch. 3), Zipporah's behavior toward Moses during the incident at the lodging, when she impatiently said: "Here is the foreskin which *you* were actually supposed to remove," was grossly disrespectful, and even the circumcision she performed for their son did not indicate an emotional attachment to Moses as much as the

Zipporah

instinctive reaction of a mother to save her son.[93] Confirmation of this approach may be seen in the portion of *Va'era*, where the descendants of Kohath are enumerated, including Moses and Aaron, as well as Aaron's wife and children, while Zipporah and her children are not listed (full disclosure: Miriam is also not included; Exod. 6:20-25).

Although according to most opinions, Moses separated from Zipporah, this behavior was a result of the requirements of his occupation, and not in disgust at her beliefs and activities, which indicates that Zipporah developed into a righteous woman who was an appropriate consort for Moses. The development of their relationship provides another instance of the greatness of Moses, who was willing to endanger himself and his future, and to nurture a relationship with a woman who was not yet at the right level, hoping that he would be able to influence her to progress in the desired direction. As was quoted in the name of the *Siftei Kohen*, Moses relied on his intuition that Jethro and Zipporah had open minds, and he relied on his personal influence and the example which he set, an approach epitomized by the Talmudic dictum: "Let the left hand repulse, but the right hand always draw back" (BT *Sanhedrin* 107b). One of Moses' greatest, but least recognized, achievements may have been the positive outcome of his efforts in transforming Jethro and Zipporah into moral, God-fearing individuals.

---

93. For an alternative view, see Abba Engelberg, *The Ethics of Exodus* (2014), p. 45.

Appendix II: R. Akiva's Opinion Regarding the Oral Law

The first two verses of the portion of *Behar* in the book of Leviticus state:

> And the Lord spoke to Moses on Mt. Sinai, saying: "Speak to the Children of Israel and say to them: 'When you come to the land that I am giving you, then the land will keep a Sabbath for the Lord'" (Lev. 25:1-2).

In regard to this verse, the Midrash asks:

> What [special relevance] does the subject of *shemittah* [the "release" of fields in the Sabbatical year] have to do with Mt. Sinai? Were not all the *mitzvot* given at Sinai? However, [this teaches us that] just as with *shemitta*h, its general principles and details were all stated at Sinai, likewise, all of them [the other laws] - their general principles and details - were given at Sinai (*Sifra Behar, parshata* A)

The Midrash is quite surprised by the unexpected mention of Mt. Sinai, being that in principle all of the laws were given there,

R. Akiva's Opinion Regarding the Oral Law

not only these particular ones, giving way to the much quoted exclamation: "What does the subject of *shemittah* have to do with Mt. Sinai?" — meaning why is Mt. Sinai mentioned in conjunction with this particular commandment? And it continues: "Were not all the *mitzvot* given at Sinai?" In other words, the transmission of this command occurred in the same place as all of the others, so why is it specifically singled out by mentioning its location of origin. The Midrash somehow derives that what is being taught is that not only were the general rules concerning each command given at Sinai, but the fine details as well. Rashi and Ramban differ as to how exactly this conclusion is derived. What is clear is that this Midrash accepts the view of R. Akiva that both generalities and specifics of each mitzvah were given at Sinai.

Rashi explains that with regard to other *mitzvot*, which were expanded in the book of Deuteronomy on the plains of Moab (from Num. 22:1 until Deut. 34:1), it would be possible to say that the general rules were given at Sinai, but the details were given later in Moab. The law forbidding agricultural work during the Sabbatical year, however, is not mentioned in the book of Deuteronomy (as opposed to the cancellation of debts, which is mentioned in Deut. 15:1-2), so the details must have also originated at Mt. Sinai. That being the case, there should be no need to specify Mt. Sinai in regard to *shemittah*, since it is known that the origin of the Torah is at Sinai (Exod. 24:12). Since Mt. Sinai is in fact mentioned, it must be for the purpose of informing the reader that in addition to the general rules, all of the details were transmitted at Sinai, even regarding those laws which are elucidated a second time in the book of Deuteronomy.

Ramban finds fault with Rashi's logic. He notes that there are numerous laws which were not repeated on the plains of Moab,[94]

---

94. Such as the requirement to leave the corners of a field for the poor (Lev. 19:9, 23:22) or not to shave the corners of one's beard (Lev. 19:27, 21:5).

but do appear in other locations. Perhaps the extraneous mention of Mt. Sinai in connection with the Sabbatical year teaches that only the details of those laws were taught at Mt. Sinai, while the details of many others were indeed taught either on the plains of Moab or in other places.

Ramban therefore reaches the same conclusion in a different way. He says that the basic law of *shemittah* appears first in the portion of *Mishpatim* (Exod. 23:11). There it is taught that the details were also transmitted at Sinai. At the end of the book of Leviticus it says: "These are the commandments which the Lord commanded Moses concerning the Children of Israel on Mt. Sinai" (Lev. 27:34). The latter verse indicates that the details of all of the laws were taught at Sinai, just like the details of the Sabbatical laws.

Additional Sources Supporting the View of R. Akiva

There are a number of additional Talmudic sources for the transmission of both the written and the oral law to Moses at Sinai. Consider the verse:

> And the Lord said to Moses: "Come up to Me on the mountain and remain there; and I will give you the *tablets of stone, and the law and the commandment, which I have written for you to teach*" (Exod. 24:12).

Commenting on the tautology at the end of the verse, the Talmud states:

> "Tablets of stone": these are the Ten Commandments; "the law": this is the Pentateuch; "the commandment": this is the Mishnah; "which I have written": these are the Prophets and the Hagiographa; "for you to teach": this is the Talmud. It teaches [us] that all of these were given to Moses on Sinai (BT *Berachot* 5a).

R. Akiva's Opinion Regarding the Oral Law

From the verse presented below, it is derived that God even taught Moses the exegesis that Rabbis and Sages of the future would develop:

> And the Lord gave me the two tablets of stone written with the finger of God; and on them was written *according to all the words which the Lord spoke with you* on the mountain from inside the fire on the day of the assembly (Deut. 9:10).

The Talmud understands the verse to imply that the tablets contained a synopsis of "all the words which the Lord spoke with you." It then proceeds to explain what "all the words" refers to:

> It teaches us that the Holy One, blessed be He, showed Moses the minutiae of the Torah, and the minutiae of the Scribes, and the innovations which would be introduced by the Scribes (BT *Megillah* 19b).[95]

Alternatively, Maharsha explains that the words "according to" are superfluous and are utilized to extend the scope of the material received at Sinai.

A Contradictory Source

The following Talmudic passage seems to contradict the view of R. Akiva (but not R. Yishmael, who says the details were not yet known to Moses at Mt. Sinai):

---

95. A parallel derivation based on the same verse appears in *Lev. Rabbah* 22:1, JT *Pe'ah* 2:4, and JT *Megillah* 4:1.

The Ethics of Numbers

When Moses ascended to heaven, he found the Holy One, blessed be He, sitting and attaching *tagim*[96] to the letters. He [Moses] said before Him: "Lord of the Universe, who forces Your hand [Rashi: to make crowns, after having written the letters]." He [God] answered: "There is one person, who will live at the end of many generations, and Akiva b. Yosef is his name, who will derive in the future from each and every *tag* heaps and heaps of laws."[97] He [Moses] said before him: "Lord of the Universe, show him to me. He replied: "Turn around." He [Moses] went and sat down behind eight rows [of students, and listened to the discussion] and he did not understand what they were talking about. He felt faint [not being able to follow their arguments]. When they came to a certain subject, his disciples said: "Master, from where do you know it?" He [R. Akiva] said to them: "It is a law [given] to Moses at Sinai [*halachah le-Moshe mi-Sinai*]." His mind was put at ease [Rashi: since it was quoted in his name, even though he had not yet received it]. He turned to the Holy One, blessed be He, and said before Him: "Lord of the Universe, You have such a man and You give the Torah through my hands?" He said to him: "Be silent: that is what I had in mind." He [Moses] said before Him: "Lord of the Universe, You showed me his Torah, [now] show me his reward." He said to him: "Turn around." He [Moses] turned around. He saw that they were weighing his flesh at

---

96. Three small marks, forming a crown, written on top of the Hebrew letters שעטנזגץ.
97. According to *Yalkut Gershuni*, the Torah is composed of 600,000 letters, one for each adult male who left Egypt (actually there are 305,000). R. Akiva was descended from converts, who did not leave Egypt and did not have letters assigned to them. Instead, they had *tagim* assigned to them, and so he concentrated on them.

R. Akiva's Opinion Regarding the Oral Law

the weighing station.[98] He [Moses] said before Him: "Lord of the Universe, is this Torah, and is this its reward?" He said to him: "Be silent: that is what I had in mind" (BT *Menachot* 29b).

The question posed by this text is how could Moses have been confounded by R. Akiva's lecture and the resulting discourse, if he knew the entire Torah, and even the extrapolations which emerged throughout the generations (including those initiated by R. Akiva)? Rashi skirts the issue by saying that the story occurred before God transmitted the entire written and oral law to Moses. Had he completed the forty days of study, he would have been familiar with anything that R. Akiva had to say.

Tosafot Yom Tov (*Avot* 1:1) notes that the previously cited text states that God "showed Moses the minutiae of the Torah, and the minutiae of the Scribes" (*Megillah* 19b), i.e. God fast-forwarded it, but did not elucidate it. Moses did not learn it on a level that implied complete comprehension or that allowed him to teach others, hence his failure to follow the class given by R. Akiva.

Torah Temimah (Exod. 24:12) says that even after receiving the general rules as well as the details, it does not mean that he was aware of all of the technicalities that would be developed in the future. What he was taught was only the entire set of axiomatic laws, the thirteen hermeneutical rules for extrapolating, and those laws which could not be derived logically and were thus termed *halachah le-Moshe mi-Sinai*. It is accordingly clear why Moses could not comprehend R. Akiva's lecture, being that it was based on generations of derived laws to which he had never been exposed.

Torah Temimah proves his point from a Midrash on the following verse which describes the receipt by Moses of the first set

---
98. R. Akiva died a martyr's death at the hands of the Romans during the Hadrianic persecution (BT *Berachot* 61b).

of tablets: "And He gave Moses, when He finished speaking with him on Mt. Sinai, the two tablets of the testimony, tablets of stone, written with the finger of God" (Exod. 31:18).

The Midrash (*Exod. Rabbah* 41:6) comments:

> The entire forty days that Moses spent in heaven, he learned Torah, but soon forgot it. He said: "Lord of the Universe, I have but forty days and I do not know anything." What did the Lord do? When he completed the forty days, the Lord granted him the Torah [knowledge] as a gift, for it says "and He gave Moses." Did Moses learn the entire Torah? But it says concerning the Torah: "Its measure is longer than the earth, and broader than the sea" (Job 11:9), and in forty days Moses learned it? Rather *the principles* the Almighty taught Moses, and that is [what it says]: "when He finished speaking with him" (Exod. 31:18).[99]

The Midrash says that Moses was taught "the principles," meaning the tools necessary to make deductions, but not all of the extrapolations.

The Importance of Torah Study

The previously cited Midrash makes two points. The first is that Moses forgot what he learned. The second is that the Torah (written and oral) is vast and cannot possibly be mastered in forty days. *Torah Temimah* (Exod. 31:18) questions the first point, since Moses was certainly of above average and even superior

---

99. The Hebrew word for "finished" is ככלתו, which is close to the Hebrew word כלל, which means "general rule." In another location (BT *Nedarim* 38a), the Talmud says that Torah knowledge was given by God to Moses as a gift, since the word ככלתו is also close to the Hebrew word כלה, meaning "bride." Rashi (Exod. 31:18) explains this to mean that it was a gift just as a bride is a gift to her groom.

R. Akiva's Opinion Regarding the Oral Law

intelligence, and hence capable of accumulating a lot of knowledge. He therefore says that God purposely caused Moses to forget, in order to encourage people of inferior ability to pursue their studies diligently, with the hope that in the end they too, just as Moses, would be miraculously endowed with Torah knowledge as a gift from God. This idea appears in the following Talmudic excerpt:

> And Rabbah said: One should always learn, even though he will forget, and even if he does not understand what he studies, for it says: "My soul breaks because of the longing that it has for Your ordinances at all times" (Ps. 119:20). "Breaks" is what Scripture says, it does not say "grinds" [i.e., it is worth studying even if one only gets the main idea and does not fully understand, which is comparable to breaking up grain, even though it cannot be ground into flour; grinding implies dissecting to the utmost degree] (BT *Avodah Zarah* 19a).

The concept which the text wishes to convey is that knowledge is not the ultimate goal, but rather the pursuit of knowledge. Accordingly, even if one does not achieve outstanding heights in his study of Jewish sources, he is still commanded to live a life devoted to study, since by doing so he is behaving in the manner prescribed by the Torah. This approach is taken by the following Talmudic text which describes the birth of a Jewish baby: "And it is taught the entire Torah.... As soon as it comes to the light of the world [i.e., is born], an angel comes, slaps it on its mouth, and causes it to forget the entire Torah" (BT *Niddah* 30b). If knowledge were the goal, what would be the point of (unnecessarily) entering the world as an ignoramus? But if greater importance is associated with the process of attaining that knowledge, the fetus is taught the Torah to stress the value of the ultimate goal toward which his

The Ethics of Numbers

efforts should be directed, and his slate is wiped clean at birth so that he can start the process of moving in that direction.

Appendix III: Anger Management

The Talmud states: "The Torah is like two paths (which one must walk between), one of fire and one of snow. If he leans too close to one, he will be burnt to death. If he leans too close to the other, he will freeze to death" (JT *Chagigah* 2:1). Although meant initially to warn the layman to be very circumspect in dealing with philosophical issues, it may also be applied to the performance of *mitzvot*, and its implication would be that one should not be obsessive about any particular one (because doing so might degrade his performance of others), but he must certainly not neglect it. Rambam applies this concept to traits rather than *mitzvot*, and it becomes the basis for his golden mean (*shvil ha-zahav*). He says: "The straight path: this is the midpoint of every trait that man possesses; this refers to the trait which is equidistant from either of the extremes, without being close to either of them" (*Hilchot De'ot* 1:4).

Rambam goes on to say: "Therefore, the early Sages instructed a man to continually evaluate his traits, to estimate them [their quality] and to direct them toward the middle path, so that he will be of sound body" (ibid.), based on the following Talmudic text:

> And R. Yehoshua b. Levi said: He who evaluates [the quality of] his ways in this world will be worthy to behold the salvation of the Holy One, blessed be He, as it says:

The Ethics of Numbers

"For he who notices his way [*Metzudat David* on Psalms: notes whether his path is good or bad] I will show the salvation of God" (Ps. 50:23)—do not read "notices [his way]," but "evaluates his way" (BT *Sotah* 5b).[100]

Rashi defines the evaluation which a person is urged to make as determining how much he loses (financially) by doing a mitzvah as compared to how much he has to gain—in this world and the next. This idea is formulated explicitly in *Avot* (2:1), where one is also told to compare the amount of pleasure he will have in performing a sin to the great spiritual loss which he will incur in this world and the next (R. Yonah). Rambam, however, generalizes this idea to evaluating the level of one's positive traits. There is no Torah law which legislates a person's attributes, but there are many laws concerning interpersonal behavior, such as not hating or even taking revenge on one's compatriot, but cherishing him, and even rebuking him in a loving manner, when the situation demands it (Lev. 19:17-19). Rambam, based on Talmudic sources, takes these laws one step further by recommending personal traits which will ensure that one's behavior is in harmony with the Biblical requirements.

Having established that one should choose the middle path and frequently evaluate his progress, Rambam continues:

> For example: he should not be wrathful, easily angered, nor be like the dead without feeling; rather, [he should adopt an] intermediate [course]; i.e., he should display anger only when the matter is serious enough to warrant it, in order to prevent the matter from recurring.... He should

---

100. The Hebrew word used in the verse is *sam*, meaning "to notice or put." It is Midrashically interpreted as *sham*, meaning "to estimate or evaluate."

Anger Management

not be overly stingy nor spread his money [irresponsibly], but he should give charity according to his capacity and lend to the needy as is fitting. He should not be overly elated and laugh [excessively], nor be sad and depressed in spirit. Rather, he should be quietly happy all his days, with a friendly countenance. The same applies with regard to his other traits.

However, after exhorting one to always adhere to the middle path, and even describing how to do so with regard to anger, Rambam in the following extract seems to contradict himself by singling out anger as an attribute which should be totally subdued:

> There are traits with regard to which a man is forbidden to follow the middle path. He should rather distance himself from one extreme until [he reaches] the other. Among these is arrogance…. Anger is also an exceptionally bad quality. It is proper for one to distance himself from one extreme until [he reaches] the other. He should teach himself not to become angry even when it is fitting to be angry…. The early Sages said: *Anyone who becomes angry is like one who worships idols*, and they [also] said: *Anyone who gets angry—if he is a wise man, his wisdom leaves him; and if he is a prophet, his prophecy leaves him. The life of the irate is not true life.* Therefore, they have commanded that one distance himself from anger and accustom himself not to be sensitive, even to things which [should rightfully] provoke anger. This is the good path (*Hilchot De'ot* 2:3).

The contradiction may be resolved by noting that anger has three aspects: the emotional effect that evil behavior has on the aggrieved person; the vituperative language which the affronted person (who

The Ethics of Numbers

then gets angry) may use to express himself; and the awareness by the aggressor of the effect of his actions, which is conveyed by the words of the recipient, who lost his temper. The citation lauding the middle path allows the victim of malign actions to make the instigator aware of his ill-advised behavior (the first and third aspect). The citation prohibiting anger declares that the victim should attempt to achieve a level of complete emotional detachment, so that he is in total control both of himself and of his mode of expression, thus avoiding the second aspect.

General Approach

Rambam had ample Talmudic sources for his strict approach. The Talmud (BT *Pesachim* 113b) lists those who do not lose their temper among the three types of people whose character God loves. Of course, such people are more popular socially as well, and hence Maharsha explains that the saying is meant to inculcate that he who is beloved below (among mankind) is beloved above (by God) as well. In the same Talmudic section, the hot-tempered are included among those who have a miserable life, and Rashbam explains that this stems from their constant irritability, from which there is no surcease.

According to the *Zohar* (*Zohar Chadash*, *Noach*), the model of serenity is the non-Jew Noah (in Hebrew, *Noach*), who was said to be difficult to anger and easy to pacify. The *Zohar* cites R. Shimon, who says that placidity is the greatest of all attributes, and it is in fact the meaning of Noah's name in Hebrew. R. Shimon proceeds to elucidate the first verse in the portion of *Noach*, which states: "These are the descendants of Noah. Noah was a righteous man. He was blameless in his generation. Noah walked with God" (Gen. 6:9). He homiletically interprets each phrase as follows:

Anger Management

1. **These are the descendants of Noah**: His descendants are his good deeds: his mild temperament in terms of his opinions, his speech, and his actions.
2. **Noah was a righteous man**: A person who behaves in this manner is a righteous person.
3. **He was blameless in his generation**: When he passes away, his good deeds will be remembered by the next generation and he will be recalled as a wonderful human being. It is because of their lasting influence and inspiration that "righteous people even after death are called living" (BT *Berachot* 18a).
4. **Noah walked with God**: As a reward for his impressive behavior, he merited to be accompanied by God throughout his lifetime.

Specific Sources

The specific descriptive phrases employed by Rambam in the above citation (*Hilchot De'ot* 2:3) are gleaned from Talmudic sources:

1. **"Anyone who becomes angry is like one who worships idols."** This is based on the following Talmudic segment:

   R. Shimon b. Elazar said… He who rends his garments in his anger, and he who breaks his vessels in his anger, and he who scatters his money in his anger may be regarded as an idolater, because such is the skill of the evil inclination: Today he says to him "do this," tomorrow he tells him "do that," until he bids him "serve idols" and he goes and serves [them]. R. Abin observed: What is the verse [that intimates this]? "There should not be a strange god within you; neither may you worship any strange god" (Ps. 81:10).[101] Who is the strange god that resides in man himself? Say, that is the evil inclination (BT *Shabbat* 105b).

---

101. On the simplest level, the clauses are repetitive.

The Ethics of Numbers

R. Shimon is saying that one who allows his actions to be dictated by his evil inclination (i.e., he doesn't practice self-restraint), may eventually lose control to the point that he transgresses much more serious commands such as worshipping idols. Lest one object that this text only refers to one who actually commits wanton acts, rather than just "becomes angry," as Rambam wrote, it should be noted that in the *Zohar*, R. Elazar says explicitly: "He who loses his temper [even if no act is performed], it is as if he worshipped idols" (*Zohar Chadash, Noach*).

Having related anger to idol worship, the Talmud (BT *Nedarim* 22a) foretells a very severe punishment for those who do not overcome this evil trait:

He who loses his temper is exposed to all the torments of Gehenna, as is written: "And remove anger from your heart, [and you will thus] remove evil [of Gehenna] from your flesh" (Ecc. 11:10).

In other words, if one continues to be short-tempered, he will suffer. Rosh *in situ* gives two explanations. First, he explains that the reference is either to physical suffering in this world (the Talmud mentions hemorrhoids, and Maharsha presciently speaks of ulcers). The Rosh's second view is that he will endure spiritual suffering in Gehenna.

2. "And they [also] said: *Anyone who gets angry—if he is a wise man, his wisdom leaves him, and if he is a prophet, his prophecy leaves him.*" This is actually a direct quote from the Talmud, which proceeds to provide Biblical derivations:

If he is a wise man, his wisdom leaves him: [we learn this] from [a story involving] Moses. For it is written: "And

Moses became angry with the officers of the army" (Num. 31:14), and it is written: "And Eleazar the priest said to the soldiers coming [back] from battle: 'And this is the statute that the Lord commanded Moses'" (Num. 31:21), from which it follows that it had become hidden from Moses (BT *Pesachim* 66b).

Moses had become angry with the officers because they had not slain the Midianite women and young boys. Ramban (Num. 31:6) explains that the women were culpable because they had taken part in the war by serving as sexual decoys; their young sons were killed in revenge for the devious behavior of the adult Midianites, and perhaps because they had also participated in the war effort. Although Moses had not given the soldiers explicit orders, he expected them to be cognizant of the rules of war in those days, and he was upset when they were not. The Talmud finds fault with the reaction of Moses and explains that his anger caused him to forget the laws of purification of vessels, and it is for that reason that these laws were presented by Eleazar. Had Moses maintained his tranquility, he would have retained his knowledge and transmitted these laws as well, just as he conveyed all of the others.

The text continues to also demonstrate that a prophet loses his power of prophecy if he manifests anger:

If he is a prophet, his prophecy leaves him: [we learn this] from Elisha, for it is written: "Were it not that I respect the presence of Jehoshaphat the king of Judah, I would neither look at you nor would I see you" (2 Kings 3:14), and it is written [in the next verse]: "'And now bring me a musician.' And it was that when the musician played, the hand of the Lord [i.e., the spirit of prophecy] came upon him."

The Ethics of Numbers

When the evil King Ahab of the kingdom of Israel died, King Mesha of Moab, who had formerly paid tribute to Ahab, decided to rebel against Ahab's son Jehoram, who consequently decided to go to war against Mesha. Jehoram asked the righteous King Jehoshaphat of Judah to join him, which he did, together with his own vassal, the king of Edom. Soon they found themselves without water. Jehoshaphat, on the basis of his religious upbringing, suggested that they turn to a prophet, and they were referred to Elisha, who of course was aware of the personalities involved. Elisha had harsh words for the idol-worshipping Jehoram, who accepted them respectfully. Elisha's discourteous demeanor, which had resulted from his indignation, apparently caused him to lose his prophetic abilities, which were only restored when his serenity returned after being calmed by the minstrel's music.

Not only does anger impair one's intellectual and prophetic faculties, it can also disqualify one initially destined for greatness. The continuation of the Talmudic extract infers this from the story of Eliab, the older brother of David, who had been slated to become king:

> R. Mani b. Pattish said: Whoever becomes angry, even if greatness has been decreed for him in Heaven, is eliminated [from attaining it]. From where do we know it? From Eliab, for it says: "... and Eliab's wrath was kindled against David [for coming to see the fight against Goliath] and he said, 'Why have you come down? With whom have you left those few sheep in the desert? I know your impetuousness, and the evil of your heart, for you have come down in order to see the war'" (1 Sam. 17:28). And when Samuel went to anoint [one of] them [the sons of Jesse], regarding all of them [David's brothers] it is

written: "Neither has the Lord chosen this one" (1 Sam. 16:8-10), whereas with respect to Eliab it is written: "And the Lord said to Samuel, 'Do not look at his appearance, or the height of his stature, for I have rejected him [for it is not as man sees, for man sees the outward appearance, while the Lord sees into the heart]'" (1 Sam. 16:7), hence it follows that He had favored him until then.

Eliab was David's oldest brother. In choosing the son of Jesse who was to be the king, Samuel started with the oldest and eliminated the brothers one by one until he reached the eighth and youngest, David. Regarding the remaining brothers, Samuel merely said "neither has the Lord chosen this one," but upon seeing the first, Eliab, Samuel had seemed intent on choosing him. In Samuel's words: "Surely, His anointed is [standing] before the Lord" (1 Sam. 16:6). It was to this comment that God replied that Eliab may look like a king, but because of his mean temper, he is not fitting to be one. Since God is quoted as saying that He "rejected" him, the implication is that until that point he was under consideration, but was eliminated because God recalled his acrimonious behavior.

Rashi *in situ* asks a very obvious question. The Talmudic text first cites Eliab's unacceptable censure of David, and then notes how Eliab was consequently rejected in the selection process. But in reality, Eliab was rejected (ch. 16) before his confrontation with David even took place (ch. 17). Rashi answers that Eliab was rejected because of his personality defect, which was presumably there even before his quarrel with David, which the text only brings to justify his earlier disqualification. Maharsha strengthens this argument by noting that the important part of the verse was omitted in the Talmudic text, namely "the Lord sees into the heart." In other words, the confrontation had not yet occurred, but God realized that the potential existed because of a character flaw which Eliab possessed. One might add that had their clash already occurred, the Bible would not have had to mention that "the Lord sees into the heart," since Eliab's imperfection would be out there for everyone to see. Rashash *in situ* argues with the approach of Rashi, since he believes that a person may be judged only by his actions, not by his potential, even if it is negative. He therefore claims that Eliab must have acted similarly before the selection process, just that it is not recorded in the Bible, which does not publicize the personal behavior of all of its actors.

R. Yoshiyah Pinto (*Ein Ya'akov, Pesachim* 66b) asks why Eliab was deprived of the kingship, while Moses and Elisha, who also got angry, were allowed to retain their positions. He answers that the standard when vetting may rightfully be higher than the demands once a person is already serving, since there is a justifiable fear that weaknesses displayed before assuming a job will become exacerbated after the person is installed. This rule provides a reasonable guideline for worker-employee relations in modern times as well.

Another distinction can be drawn. In the case of Moses, the text mentions that he got angry. In the cases of Elisha and Eliab, their words may be portrayed as mean and sarcastic, but there is no reason to assume that they shouted or even raised their voices. From here, one may understand that when the Talmud and legal codes denigrate anger, they do not limit their ruling to people who completely lose control of their emotions. On the contrary, they apparently include any form of rude, insulting, or discourteous behavior. Even if a rebuke is in order, it must be done in the most gentle and ingratiating manner in order to ensure that a positive relationship is maintained. In fact, that is probably the only way that it will have the desired effect. Perhaps this is the intention of the Mishnah, which states: "In the footsteps of the Messiah, there will be nobody to offer reproof [appropriately]" (*Sotah* 9:15). Since almost everyone is far from perfect and has his own faults, in order not to be hypocritical, people must be very careful and sensitive when reproving others for their misdeeds.

3. **"The life of the irate is not true life."** The Talmud (BT *Pesachim* 113b) includes the hot-tempered among those who have a miserable life, and Rashbam explains that this derives from their constant irritability.

Is It Ever Permitted to Get Angry?

Although he seriously denigrates anger and considers it to be the most reprehensible of traits, Rambam does permit it in the following instance:

> If he wishes to arouse fear in his children and household—or in the community, if he is a communal leader—and wishes to be angry at them to motivate them to return to the proper path, he should present himself to them as if he is angry, in order to punish them, but he should be inwardly calm. He should be like one who acts out the part of an angry man in his wrath, but is not really angry (*Hilchot De'ot* 2:3).

Rambam bases this guideline on a Talmudic extract which states that one may display anger:

The Ethics of Numbers

> ... in order to instill fear in his household, R. Yehuda tore the edges [of his garment], R. Acha b. Ya'akov broke partially broken vessels [Shottenstein: in a way that the members of the household thought he was breaking an undamaged vessel], R. Sheshet threw brine on his maidservant's head, R. Abba broke a lid (BT *Shabbat* 105b).

A second source (BT *Ta'anit* 4a) seems to indicate that actual anger may be permitted in certain cases:

> Rabbah further said: If a young scholar gets into a rage, it is because the Torah inflames him [Rashi: his breadth (of knowledge) is increased by his Torah expertise, and he takes it (deviation from *halachah*) to heart more than other people; we are being taught that he must be given the benefit of the doubt], as it says: "Is not my word like a fire, said the Lord" (Jer. 23:29). R. Ashi said: A scholar who is not as hard as iron [Rashi: particular and intransigent; Rabbeinu Gershom: difficult to appease (after getting angry)] is no scholar, as it says: "And like a hammer that shatters a rock" (ibid.)... Ravina said: Despite this, a man should train himself to be gentle, for it says: "And remove anger from your heart [and take evil away from your flesh]" (Ecc. 11:10).

Me'iri *in situ* explains Ravina to be saying that although it may be understandable that scholars are intolerant of fools, they should still control themselves, since in the long run the chance of influencing the uneducated and directing them to the proper path is considerably greater if they are treated with love and respect. It would seem that Rashi also tends to accept this approach, since he does not justify Rabbah's view that a scholar may lose his temper on an absolute level. He merely implies that such a person's motivation should be understood and he should therefore be given the benefit of the doubt. R. Ya'akov Emden *in situ* explains that Ravina does not argue with R. Ashi, since the latter simply says that a scholar should be insistent on acting properly and not succumb to pressure. Ravina just clarifies that he should do so in a courteous manner without losing his temper, in keeping with the words of Kohelet: "The words of the wise are heard [when spoken] softly" (Ecc. 9:17).

Rabbeinu Gershom's interpretation of R. Ashi seems to be that a scholar is not only permitted to get angry, but he should not even allow his anger to readily subside, in which case Ravina is in disagreement with R. Ashi. Based on this interpretation of R. Ashi, R. Ephraim Greenblatt asked his teacher R. Moshe Feinstein (*Igrot Moshe, Orach Chaim* 1:54) how to reconcile this view with the Mishnah which states that: "[One who is] slow to get angry and easy to be pacified is a pious man [a *chassid*]" (*Avot* 5:11).

R. Feinstein answered that the two situations differ. R. Ashi deals with a case where a rabbi got angry at those who disobeyed his decision, after he had ruled in a certain case. If he immediately reconciles with them, people will say that he did so because he was not confident that his initial ruling was correct. It is for this reason that the Talmud uses the phrase "is no scholar." If he accepts their behavior hastily, he weakens his own stature as a scholar, and his decisions will not be taken seriously in the future. On the other hand, the Mishnah speaks of a case where a scholar got angry after hearing that people acted in a manner which is universally known as being sinful. Since everyone is aware that they had acted wrongly, by easily reconciling afterwards, he sets an outstanding example of a scholarly person's refinement.

R. Feinstein proceeds to say that, based on his distinction, it is possible that R. Ashi and Ravina do not argue, since the former speaks of a case where one already got angry, in which case he should not reconcile easily, while the latter suggests that he avoid losing his temper in the first place. Rather, he should find more gentle ways of influencing his congregants to behave in accordance with *halachah*.

R. Feinstein cites Rabbeinu Yonah, who asks the following question: If we accept Ravina's view, why does the Mishnah say that one should be slow to anger (*Avot* 2:10)? It should say that one should never get angry, since R. Ashi's statement has been relegated to refer to the situation where he inappropriately got angry. R. Yonah answers that there are certain highly exceptional situations where even Ravina requires one to get angry, such as the case of Phinehas (Num. 25:8), who killed a man and woman who were publicly engaging in fornication.

With respect to Phinehas's behavior, the *Torah Temimah* notes that the Jerusalem Talmud (*Sanhedrin* 9:6) states that Phinehas did not act in accordance with the opinion of the Sages, who were actually about to ostracize him when the Holy Spirit intervened and said: "The priesthood will be an eternal covenant for him and for his descendants" (Num. 25:13). This seems contradictory. If the Sages criticized his behavior, why did God make a permanent covenant with him? The answer is that the Sages frowned upon zealous acts, because there is always the fear that one is acting for his own personal aggrandizement, and not for purely spiritual reasons. When God intervened, He was essentially testifying that Phinehas' motives were absolutely pure.

In conclusion, it would seem that neither the Talmudic text in *Shabbat* nor Rambam agree with Rabbah, who permitted scholars to lose their temper in the heat of halachic discourse. R. Ashi, who encourages strict behavior on the part of scholars, may agree with both Rabbah, who permits anger, and Ravina, who says it should be displayed in a controlled fashion and only external, while internally maintaining one's composure. On the other hand, it would seem from R. Feinstein's interpretation of Ravina that it is preferable to avoid even superficial displays of anger as much as possible, and to favor warm and friendly sympathetic guidance and instruction, and accordingly R. Feinstein himself says that Rambam is in agreement with Ravina, and not R. Ashi. Exceptions should not be made even for religious matters, for there is no way of knowing whether it is being done with the proper motivation. Only if the anger is to discipline the members of his household does Rambam (and supposedly also R. Feinstein) allow one to "put on a show" by displaying signs of anger, but only while he is inwardly calm.

On the other hand, the *Zohar* (*Tetzaveh* 182b; *Zohar Chadash, Noach*) seems to lean towards the view of Rabbah that rabbinical anger (*rugza de-rabbanan*) is a positive act and should be used to enforce religious edicts and stimulate respect for the Torah, as well as respect for Torah scholars on the part of their students and congregants. The *Zohar* also justifies angry or belittling language on the part of scholars when delving into the intricacies of Talmudic logic and dealing with uncomprehending students, such as when the same Rabbah called R. Amram a *tarda* (BT *Bava Metzia* 20b; Rashi, BT *Zevachim* 25b: a confused fool), or when Rebbi said of Levi: "It seems to me that this man has no brains in his head" (BT *Yevamot* 9a). The *Zohar*'s view may be based on the many prophetic exhortations which were not short on intemperate and sarcastic language.[102] The *Zohar* adds, however, that the scholar is forbidden to lose his temper with respect to non-Torah issues.

---

102. See, for example, Isa. 5:7, 9:15, 59:3-16; Jer. 6:13, 9:3-7; Ezek. 22:6-12; Hos. 4:1-2; Amos 3:10, 4:1.

Appendix IV:
Law Enforcement in Judaism

Sins Punishable in Court

From the time of Adam, the Noahide laws included a requirement to establish a court system—either to enforce the other Noahide commandments, according to Rambam (*Hilchot Melachim* 9:14), or even to develop an entire legal code and corresponding court system, according to Ramban (Gen. 34:13). When Moses became leader, he initially took upon himself the power of judgment, until his father-in-law Jethro suggested that he divest himself of much of his legal authority and delegate it to lower courts (Exod. 18:14–26). Finally, the systematic establishment of a judicial system was incorporated in the Torah, when it stated: "You are to set up judges and law enforcement officials… and they should judge the people with righteous judgment" (Deut. 16:18). Furthermore, the Torah mentions explicitly that some cases must be brought before a court. One verse (Exod. 22:8) serves as the source for requiring a court composed of three judges for monetary matters (*Sanhedrin* 1:1; BT *Sanhedrin* 3b), while another text (Num. 35:24-25) serves as the source for requiring a twenty-three-member court, called a small Sanhedrin, to decree capital punishment (*Sanhedrin* 1:4, 1:6). Major or national judgments, such as whether to declare war, destroy an idolatrous city (*Sanhedrin* 1:6), sanctify a new month, or intercalate the year (*Mechilta Bo* 2, BT *Sanhedrin* 11b, *Hilchot Kiddush ha-Chodesh* 5:1-2), were to be carried out by the Great Sanhedrin having seventy-one members. The Great Sanhedrin also appointed judges to the lower courts (*Sanhedrin* 1:5) and handled cases that were too difficult for them (Deut. 17:8-11). The word *sanhedrin* is based on a Greek word meaning "sitting together," hence council or assembly. Small Sanhedrins could exist in every sufficiently populated city (*Sanhedrin* 1:6), but there was only one Great Sanhedrin, located in the office of hewn stone in the Temple in Jerusalem.

SINS PUNISHED BY GOD

However, not all sins mentioned in the Torah are punishable in court. Many—especially, but not exclusively, those between man and God—were left to God Himself to chastise in one of two ways, through "death by Heavenly hands" (*mitah bi-yedei Shamayim*) or excision (*karet*). According to Tosafot (BT *Yevamot* 2a, s.v. *eshet*), "death by Heavenly hands" means that the sinner will die at a younger age than expected. With regard to excision, the maximum life span is fifty according to the Jerusalem Talmud (*Bikkurim* 2:1), which derives this from the fact that *karet* is mentioned in connection with the Levitic family of Kohath (Num. 4:18), who were only active until the age of fifty (Num. 4:3). According to the Babylonian Talmud, the sinner would die between the ages of fifty and sixty. The Talmud proceeds to tell of R. Yosef, who invited his scholarly friends to a party which he made on his sixtieth birthday to celebrate the fact that he had overcome the danger of suffering excision (BT *Mo'ed Katan* 28a). There is also a second aspect of excision, which varies among the commentators as follows:

The Ethics of Numbers

1. Ibn Ezra: There is no additional aspect, so "death by Heavenly hands" and excision are essentially the same (Gen. 17:14).
2. Rashi: He will be childless (*ariri*). Either he will not have children or they will die in his lifetime (Gen. 17:14, BT *Shabbat* 25b, BT *Yevamot* 55a). Abravanel (Num. 15) explains that according to Rashi, "death by Heavenly hands" affects the sinner alone, while *karet* is directed at his children as well.
3. Tosafot (Riva, BT *Yevamot* 2a, s.v. *eshet*): The punishment of dying childless applies only to the two cases where this aspect is mentioned explicitly in the Torah, namely one who has forbidden relations with his aunt or his brother's former wife (Lev. 20:20-21).
4. Rambam: Rambam does not relate the additional punishment to childlessness, but to the destruction of the sinner's soul, so that it does not exist in the world to come. He bases this on the verse concerning a person who willfully worships idols, which states: "For he has shamed the word of the Lord and violated His commandment; this soul will surely be cut off [*hikaret tikaret*], its iniquity remains within it [as long as he has not repented (BT *Sanhedrin* 90b)]" (Num. 15:31), concerning which the Talmud (ibid.) comments: "*hikaret* – in this world, *tikaret* – in the next world." Rambam summarizes his approach in his code of law, where he describes the world to come which awaits the righteous and the absence of that reward for those who have been punished with excision:

> The good that is hidden for the righteous is the life of the world to come. This will be life which is not accompanied by death, and good which is not accompanied by evil.... Whoever does not merit this life is [truly] dead and will

not live forever. Rather, he will be cut off in his wickedness and perish as a beast (*Hilchot Teshuvah* 8:1).[103]

In distinguishing between "death by Heavenly hands" and excision, Rambam states:

This "death by Heavenly hands" is easier than excision, for one who is liable to excision, the punishment remains upon him after death, as stated in the next chapter, but one who is liable to "death by Heavenly hands," when he dies his sins are expiated (*Peirush ha-Mishnayot, Sanhedrin* 9:6).

WHICH SINS ARE NOT PUNISHED BY THE COURTS?

The Mishnah (*Kreitot* 1:1) lists thirty-six sins which are punishable by excision. In connection with each one, the Bible speaks of cutting off the soul from Israel, the community, the nation, or the assembly. Thirty-four of the sins are prohibitions relating to incest (15), desecration of the Sabbath or Yom Kippur (3), idol worship (4), forbidden foods (3), and improper behavior with holy items (9). Two relate to unfulfilled positive commands, namely circumcision and sacrificing the paschal lamb on the eve of Passover.

"Death by Heavenly hands" is for prohibitions concerning which the Torah mentions the death penalty (or in one case simply exacting retribution), but without any reference to the soul or the community, nor to the means of punishment (which would imply humanly-administered chastisement). These laws relate to the suppression or dereliction of prophecy by a prophet (Deut. 18:18-19) and to profanation of the holy (BT *Sanhedrin* 83a).

---

103. See also Rambam's "*Hakdamah le-Perek Chelek*."

Appendix V: Intimate Relations with Gentiles

The Talmud (BT *Avodah Zarah* 36b) discusses the subject of permitted and forbidden relations between Jews and Gentiles, and comes to the following conclusions:

1. It is forbidden by Torah law for a Jewish man or woman to marry a non-Jew from one of the seven Canaanite nations, based on the verse:

   And you may not intermarry with them; you may not give your daughter to his son, nor may you take his daughter for your son. For he will turn your son away from following Me, and they will worship other gods (Deut. 7:3-4).

2. According to R. Shimon b. Yochai, the same is true for other nations as well. Rambam (*Hilchot Issurei Bi'ah* 12:1) and Yosef Karo in the *Shulchan Aruch* (*Even ha-Ezer* 16:1) accept this opinion, since as part of the covenant instituted by Ezra and Nehemiah, the nation promised "not to give our daughters in marriage to the peoples around us, nor take their daughters for our sons" (Neh. 10:31). The assumption is that this was not a new prohibition, but rather one based on Torah

law. *Tur* (*Even ha-Ezer* 16), however, accepts the opposing opinion that the prohibition is only with regard to the seven nations. *Beit Shmuel* (*Even ha-Ezer* 16:1) explains the dispute between Rambam and *Tur*. The former believes that a marital relationship can exist between members of the opposite sex independent of their religions, but the verses prohibit such a relationship between a Jew and a non-Jew. *Tur* holds that such a relationship may exist as a legal entity only between two Jews. The prohibition regarding the seven nations is to have intercourse with one of their members who did not convert, based on the prohibition in the verse to "take," while if the non-Jew converts and marries a Jew, there is a different prohibition based on the word "intermarry."

3. The court of Shem prohibited promiscuous sexual relationships between Jewish women and Gentiles. This is derived from the words of Judah after being told that his widowed daughter-in-law Tamar was pregnant: "Bring her out, and let her be burned" (Gen. 38:24). Tamar is considered to be Jewish either because she was the daughter of Shem (*Gen. Rabbah* 85:10, cited by Rashi *in situ*), or because she would have converted before marrying Judah's son, since the patriarchs are assumed to have lived according to Torah law.

    The Mishnah (*Kiddushin* 4:14) states that Abraham observed the laws of the Torah, based on the verse: "Since Abraham listened to My voice, and kept My charge, My commandments, My statutes, and My Torahs" (Gen. 26:5). The Talmud (BT *Yoma* 28b) states that the word "Torahs" is in the plural form to teach that he kept not only the written law, but the oral law as well. Ramban *in situ* proceeds to show that the patriarchs and leaders after Abraham also continued to observe the laws of the Torah, based on the verse: "For I have chosen him because he commands his sons and his household after him to keep the way of the Lord to perform charitable and just actions" (Gen. 18:19). Apparently, Abraham influenced his descendants throughout the generations to be observant, until the giving of the Torah. The majority of the commentators seem to agree. For example, when Jacob said to Esau "I have sojourned with Laban" (Gen. 32:5), Rashi expands his words as follows: "I lived with the wicked Laban, but I kept the 613 *mitzvot*." Various Midrashim say the same about Joseph (*Gen. Rabbah* 92:4, 94:3) and Judah (BT *Pesachim* 50a). Only Rama (responsum 10) limits the observance of the entire Torah to Abraham, saying that what he transmitted to his children was only the Noahide laws.

4. A Jew who publicly (i.e., before ten or more Jews – BT *Sanhedrin* 74b) has intercourse with a heathen woman may be attacked by zealots. This is one of a very small number of offenses that do not pass through the court system (*Sanhedrin* 9:6, BT *Sanhedrin* 81b), and for which vigilantes are permitted to take the law into their own hands. Other examples are one who steals a holy vessel from the Temple and a priest who performs Divine service in the Temple in a state of impurity. Rambam apparently distinguishes between the case of publicly having relations with a heathen, concerning which he states that the zealot "is considered praiseworthy and ardent" (*Hilchot Issurei Bi'ah* 12:4), and the other cases, where he says that the zealots are "not to be rebuked for this" (*Hilchot B'iat ha-Mikdash* 4:2).

What happens if the event described occurs, but no zealot takes action? The Talmud (BT *Sanhedrin* 82a) refers to the following verse, which it interprets as expressing criticism of the tribe of Judah by the prophet Malachi for being intimate with heathen women: "Judah has dealt treacherously, and an abomination has been committed in Israel and in Jerusalem; for Judah has profaned the holiness of the Lord [in] that he loved and married the daughter [worshipper] of a foreign god" (Mal. 2:11). The Talmudic text continues:

This verse is followed by: "The Lord will excise the men that do this—he who is alert and he who responds, from the tents of Jacob, and he that brings an offering to the Lord of Hosts" (Mal. 2:12). This means: If he is a scholar, he will not have an alert [student or descendant who is] among the Sages, nor [even] a responder [one who is capable of answering scholarly questions] among the disciples; if he is a priest, he will not have a son to offer an offering to the Lord of Hosts.

Combining the two verses, the Talmud understands the metaphor to be implying that one who has intercourse with a heathen woman will be punished with excision (*karet*), and will have no learned offspring if he is a scholar, nor priestly offspring if he is a *kohen*.

5. The Court of the Hasmoneans issued a prohibition for a Jew to have intercourse with a non-Jewish woman even in private, saying that she is forbidden to him on four counts—as a menstrual woman, a non-Jewish slave, a non-Jewess possibly of the seven Canaanite nations, and a married woman according to R. Dimi or a harlot according to Ravin. Although she may be none of these, the fear is that permitting such a relationship will lead one to eventually have relations with women in these categories.

According to Rashi (BT *Sanhedrin* 82a, s.v. *chayav*), the transgressor is punished by lashes for each of these four sins. If lashes are not given, some commentators say that the sinner suffers excision, based on the previously quoted verse from Malachi (*Bach, Even ha-Ezer* 16; *Chiddushei ha-*

Ran, Sanhedrin 82a). However, others say that the verse from Malachi relates only to public fornication (*Chelkat Mechokek, Even ha-Ezer* 16:5; *Nimukei Yosef* on Rif, *Sanhedrin* 18a), and if done privately, the sin is on a rabbinic level.

Rambam (*Hilchot Issurei Bi'ah* 12:2), based on his version of the Talmudic discourse (*Maggid Mishneh in situ*), limits guilt on four counts to the case of a steady non-marital relationship, but regarding one-time occurrences the offender is culpable only on one count—for having relations with a non-Jewish woman which could lead to a marital relationship, punishable by rabbinically ordained lashes for rebellious behavior (*makkot mardut*), as implemented by R. Shila (BT *Berachot* 58a). *Tur* and R. Yosef Karo (*Even ha-Ezer*) adopt Rambam's distinction.

There are two situations where some commentators would say that the prohibition is from the Torah. One is if the non-Jewish person is married. The Bible states: "Therefore, a man will leave his father and his mother, and cleave to his wife, and they will become one flesh" (Gen. 2:24), from which the Talmud derives "to his wife but not to his friend's wife" (BT *Sanhedrin* 58a), and which Tosafot (BT *Kiddushin* 21b s.v. *eshet*) uses as a source for saying that one who violates another person's spouse transgresses a positive commandment-based prohibition (*issur aseh*). This approach conforms with Rambam's view that non-Jewish marriages are formally recognized.

The second case is that of *kohanim* (priests), concerning whom the Torah states: "They may not marry a woman who is a prostitute" (Lev. 21:7). Rambam (*Hilchot Issurei Bi'ah* 12:3) rules according to Rava in the Talmud (BT *Temurah* 29b) that the prohibition includes both Jewish and non-Jewish women. Tosafot (BT *Avodah Zarah* 36b s.v. *mi-shum*) says that this is so only if it is known that the non-Jewish woman was a prostitute, and the Hasmonean decrees expand the prohibition even to the case where that information is not available.

Intimate Relations with Gentiles

6. The prohibition of seclusion in a private place (*yichud*) with a Gentile woman is one of the eighteen decrees made in the upper chamber of the dwelling of Chananiah b. Chizkiah, by a court whose members were from the houses of both Hillel and Shammai (*Shabbat* 1:4, BT *Shabbat* 13b). Some of the other decrees forbade the use of non-Jewish bread, oil, and wine, since the first two might lead to using their wine, and drinking together might lead to having relations with Gentile women. In turn, that might lead to promiscuity with Jewish women as well, and to idol worship. As far as Jewish women are concerned, seclusion with women whom it is forbidden to marry is prohibited by the Torah, for fear that it might lead to an incestuous relationship (BT *Kiddushin* 80a). Seclusion with single Jewish women was prohibited by the court of King David. From the fact that seclusion is prohibited rabbinically, one may understand *a fortiori* that sexual relations are prohibited (*Chelkat Mechokek*, *Even ha-Ezer* 26:1). Rambam (*Hilchot Ishut* 1:4) goes even further, claiming that such relations are even prohibited by the Torah, based on the verse "There may not be a prostitute among the daughters of Israel" (Deut. 23:18), but Ra'avad argues and says that concubinage was permitted on the Torah level, as many such instances are recorded in the Bible, such as those of King Saul (2 Sam. 3:7), King David (2 Sam. 5:13), and King Solomon (1 Kings 11:3). Rambam, however, is of the opinion that they were permitted only to kings. Ramban disagrees with Rambam, and he holds that the verse cited by him refers only to illicit marriages (e.g., to a Canaanite slave) arranged by the father of a young man or woman (*Sefer ha-Mitzvot*, negative command 355).

Appendix VI: Age of Culpability

One is only required to observe the *mitzvot* if he is intellectually mature enough to do so. Therefore, a minor, called a *katan* (male) or *ketanah* (female), is exempt (Rashi, BT *Chagigah* 2a, s.v. *chutz*), because he lacks discretion.[104] However, the Rabbis required minors to observe *mitzvot* for educational purposes preparatory to adulthood (BT *Sukkah* 28b; Rashi, *Avot* 5:21). Ritva (BT *Sukkah* 28b) points out that the suggested age at which a child begins observing *mitzvot* varies with the specific command, and it is different for sitting in a *sukkah*, fasting on Yom Kippur, shaking a *lulav*, and putting on *tefillin*.

When does a minor become an adult? A Mishnah deals with this question:

> If a girl has grown two [pubic] hairs... she is obligated to fulfill all of the *mitzvot* enumerated in the Torah. And similarly a boy, if he has grown two [pubic] hairs, is obligated to fulfill all of the *mitzvot* enumerated in the Torah (*Niddah* 6:11).

---

104. BT *Gittin* 23a; BT *Yoma* 43a; Bartenura, *Menachot* 9:8; Bartenura, *Chulin* 1:1.

AGE OF MATURITY

Note that specific ages are not given. However, in his gloss, Bartenura adds that these physical signs take effect only if the girl is twelve and the boy thirteen, which are the mandatory ages recorded in the Talmud (BT *Niddah* 45b). Although the Mishnah cited from *Niddah* does not specify a given age, a Mishnah in *Avot* (5:21) does mention thirteen as the age at which majority is attained. Rashi suggests two possible sources:

1. In connection with confession for sins one has committed, the verse states: "When a man (*ish*) or woman (*ishah*) commits any sins that a person might commit" (Num. 5:6). From this verse it may be determined that one is only culpable when he is considered to be a man or a woman, as opposed to a child. However, the Midrash (*Gen. Rabbah* 80:10) says that Levi was thirteen years old when he attacked the town of Shechem, and he was called a man in the verse: "Jacob's two sons, Simeon and Levi, Dinah's brothers, each man took his sword, and they came upon the city with confidence, and they slew every male" (Gen. 34:25).

    Maharzo explains how the Midrash derived that Levi was thirteen at the time. Jacob had stated that he spent twenty years in Laban's household (Gen. 31:38). Reuben was born after Jacob had worked for seven years, and according to *Seder Olam Rabbah*, ch. 2, Leah's children were born at intervals of only seven months. Reuben was thus about twelve and a half when they parted from Laban, and according to Rashi (Gen. 28:9, 33:17), the event in Shechem took place two years later, so Reuben was then about fourteen and a half. Subtract fourteen months (Simeon was seven months younger, Levi fourteen months), and it can be seen that Levi had just celebrated his thirteenth birthday.

The Ethics of Numbers

2. Rashi's alternative explanation is that the basis for requiring physical signs to determine culpability is a law transmitted orally at Mt. Sinai (*halachah le-Moshe mi-Sinai*). This fits well with the Talmudic statement:

The laws concerning minimum quantities [of forbidden things], interpositions [the amount of foreign matter which in ritual cleansing constitutes a bar between one's body and the water, thus invalidating the immersion], and [the height of] partitions [with regard to Sabbath, *sukkah*, etc.] are *halachah le-Moshe mi-Sinai* (BT *Sukkah* 5b).

Rashi proceeds to say that the Sages concluded that these physical signs generally appear by the time a boy is thirteen and a girl twelve, so these ages may be substituted for the bodily signs. Even if in fact these signs have not yet appeared, the child is rabbinically required to perform *mitzvot* for educational purposes. If a situation arises in which it is imperative to know whether the child is really obligated, for example if he is deserving of punishment, the child can always be examined.

Prof. Yitzchak Dov Gilat ("*Ben Shlosh Esreh le-Mitzvot*," *Peshita* website) has elucidated Rashi's viewpoint. He points out that the *Mishnayot* which speak of the passage from minority to majority mention only the physical signs (e.g., *Terumot* 1:3, *Yevamot* 10:8, and Rashi's interpretation thereof). As far as the Mishnah which mentions thirteen as the age of culpability, Gilat notes that Me'iri *in situ* points out that this is a later addition which was not part of the original Tannaitic collection. Furthermore, the contents are not meant to be taken in a halachic manner. For example, when it says that a child starts learning Bible at the age of five, it hardly means to fix this as a steadfast rule and to prohibit a precocious child from starting at an earlier age.

Gilat concludes that the predominance of testing for physical signs was cancelled during the Amoraic period because it led to improper discussion of the intimate details of the sexual development of young girls, and to the immodest exposure of young women, especially since according to some opinions the girl was to be examined by men, as women were not to be relied upon for making decisions of halachic import (BT *Niddah* 48b). This situation culminated in the Amora Rava making the following pronouncement: "A minor on attaining the age of majority need not be examined, since it may be assumed that she has developed signs of puberty" (BT *Niddah* 46a, 48b), and in the Rosh's conclusion that determination of majority at the ages of twelve and thirteen, respectively, is in the category of *halachah le-Moshe mi-Sinai* and included in the general statement concerning all halachic measurements found in *Sukkah* 5b (Rosh, responsum 16:1).

Gilat suggests that the Tannaim believed that on the Torah level, children achieved majority at different ages for different commandments, based on various Biblical verses, as cited in the *Mishnayot* in *Chagigah* 1:1 and *Sukkah* 2:8, and summarized in Tosefta *Chagigah* 1:2. Only in the time of the Amoraim was it concluded that Torah-defined majority occurred only at bar and bat mitzvah, while the verses referred to in the *Mishnayot* were only supportive (*asmachtot*) and not definitive, and the earlier ages of requirement were instituted by the rabbis for educational purposes (*chinuch*), as explicated in the Talmud (BT *Chagigah* 4a, *Sukkah* 28b).

Regarding young women, there exists a sub-category of maturity termed *na'arut*, when a young woman is referred to as a damsel (*na'arah*), based on the use of this term in various locations in the Bible (Num. 30:4,17; Deut. 22:23,25). During this period, although basically an adult, she is gradually being weaned away from the protection of her father, who still has limited control over her with regard to certain legal matters. The Talmud states: "The period between the age of damselhood and that of adulthood is only six months" (BT *Ketubot* 39a). Rambam reviews the progression with regard to young women as follows:

> From the day of a girl's birth until she becomes twelve years old, she is called a minor (*ketanah*).... Once a girl manifests the lower sign [of physical maturity], she is referred to as a damsel (*na'arah*) for six months. From the last day of these six months and onward, she is referred to as a mature woman (*bogeret*). The difference between the stages of maidenhood and maturity is only six months (*Hilchot Ishut* 2:1,2).

Regarding men, Rambam summarizes:

> A male, from birth until the age of thirteen, is called a minor (*katan*).... If two hairs grow in the pubic area after he attains the age of thirteen years and one day, he is considered an adult (*gadol*) and a man (*ish*) (*Hilchot Ishut* 2:10).

Rambam has coalesced the two requirements for majority of men and women by requiring both physical (signs) and chronological (age) maturity.

A Gaonic source, on the other hand, bases the period of damselhood on chronological age alone, as follows: "[she is defined as] a damsel from the age of twelve and one day until twelve and six months and one day" (*Sha'arei Tzedek* 3:1:38).

Age of Maturity

Vows and Oaths

The rules regarding maturity with respect to vows and oaths differ from those in general, since the emphasis here is on intellectual, rather than physical, maturity. For a vow or oath to be meaningful, the one who makes it must be aware of the meaning and implication of his words. Obviously, a young child lacks the maturity to responsibly make a vow. The Talmud deals with the minimum age requirements for imposing culpability:

> The vows of a girl who is eleven years and one day old must be examined [to ascertain that she realizes their import]. The vows of a girl who is twelve years and one day old are valid, and throughout the twelfth year they are examined. The vows of a boy who is twelve years and one day old must be examined. The vows of a boy who is thirteen years and one day old are valid, and throughout the thirteenth year they are examined. Before this age [eleven for a girl and twelve for a boy], even though they said: "We know with respect to Whose name we have made our vow, for Whom we have made our dedication [to a holy charity]," their vow is not valid, and their dedication is not valid. After this age [twelve for a girl and thirteen for a boy], even though they said: "We do not know with respect to Whose name we have made our vow, nor for Whom we have made our dedication," their vow is valid, and their dedication is valid (*Niddah* 5:6).

The Mishnah states that although the age of maturity is generally twelve and thirteen for girls and boys, respectively (and according to Prof. Gilat dependent only on physical signs at the Mishnaic level), here their vows are considered valid one year earlier. The Talmud in *Temurah* (2b) bases this law on a verse relating to one who wishes to contribute money to the upkeep of the Temple, which states: "When a man clearly utters a vow, [pledging the] value of lives to the Lord" (Lev. 27:2). Rashi in *Temurah* explains that the verse could have left out the words "clearly utters" and simply said "when a man vows." The extra words teach that even a *mufla samuch le-ish*—one who can clearly utter (comprehend the import of his vow) who is near manhood (thirteen) or womanhood (twelve), but not quite there—can also make valid vows.[105]

Rambam (*Hilchot Nedarim* 11:1-3) apparently posits, on the basis of the Mishnah, that age is the determining factor when validating vows. In *Peirush ha-Mishnayot* (*Niddah* 5:6), he clarifies that although the vow is valid, to suffer lashes (*malkot*), one must have brought the physical signs of maturity, as implied by the Talmud, which states when relating to the designated punishment: "If he did not display two [pubic] hairs, he is considered a minor" (BT *Niddah* 45b). Bartenura (*in situ*), however, says that physical signs are required even for validation, just that as opposed to other cases where majority is demanded, even if he is only in his thirteenth year (but not yet thirteen), if he is sufficiently developed both physically and mentally, his vows are valid. He does not say so explicitly, but the implication is that under these circumstances he would be liable to lashes upon transgression of said vow.

Justifying the Different Ages of Culpability of Men and Women

Although it is ingrained in most Jews that bat mitzvah occurs at the age of twelve and bar mitzvah at thirteen, it is interesting to note that this tradition was not transmitted from the time of revelation

---

105. In BT *Niddah* 46a, the same teaching is learned from an identical formulation in Num. 6:2. Furthermore, BT *Nazir* 62a seems to imply that *mufla samuch le-ish* is learned from the words in Num. 27:2, "when a man," which could have been simplified to "when a person," or even left out entirely.

Age of Maturity

as *halachah le-Moshe mi-Sinai*. On the contrary, regarding the Mishnah-based age for the validation of vows, the Talmud states:

> These [that a girl matures at twelve and a boy at thirteen] are the rulings of Rebbi. [However,] R. Shimon b. Elazar stated: "The age limits that were assigned to the girl apply to the boy [matures at the age of twelve], while those assigned to the boy apply to the girl [matures at the age of thirteen]" (BT *Niddah* 45b).

If Tannaim argue about the rules, then clearly the logic behind those rules must be in dispute as well. Some insights may be obtained by examining their reasoning. The Talmud proceeds:

> What is Rebbi's reason? For it says: "And the Lord God built (*va-yiven*) the rib [which He had taken from the man into a woman]" (Gen. 2:22), which teaches that the Holy One, blessed be He, endowed woman with more understanding (*binah*, of a root that is analogous to that of *va-yiven*) than man.

Maharsha explains that this statement is based on an opinion in the Talmud (BT *Eruvin* 18a) that the first person was created with two faces and two bodies, one male and one female, attached to each other back-to-back. That being the case, when God separated that person into two parts, no new object was constructed, so the Hebrew word *va-yiven*, meaning "build," is not appropriate. Since the Hebrew word for "understanding" (*binah*) is grammatically close to *va-yiven*, the Talmud derives that the woman is endowed with greater intelligence, being that no such word is used in conjunction with the male part of their joint creation.

The Ethics of Numbers

It is understandable that rabbinic commentators, living in the Middle Ages when women had little intellectual, professional, and educational opportunities, found it hard to accept the apparent claim that women are more intelligent than men, especially since other Talmudic sources state the opposite. This divergence of sources led to a variety of interpretations. Specifically, Ritva (BT *Niddah* 45b) notes that the Talmud says in a number of locations (BT *Shabbat* 33b, *Kiddushin* 80b) that women are intellectually inferior (*nashim da'atan kalah*). He reconciles the apparent contradiction by stating that the Talmudic text in *Niddah* did not mean to ascribe greater intelligence to women, but earlier intellectual maturity, and according to Ritva the men eventually surpass them. It should be noted, however, that the Talmudic sources for *nashim da'atan kalah* do not refer to intelligence as much as to temperament, and seem to be saying that (at least in those days) women could be more easily persuaded and even pressured.

Rambam as well must have had difficulty with the positive appraisal of women's intellectual ability. In describing the entrenchment of star worship, he lists the gullible as being "the women, the children, and the common people" (*Hilchot Avodat Kochavim* 1:2). Nor does Rambam display much hope or even interest in changing the situation, as may be inferred from his opinion with respect to women's education: "the Sages commanded that a person should not teach his daughter Torah, because most women cannot concentrate their attention on study, and thus transform the words of Torah into idle matters because of their lack of understanding [literally, the poverty of their mind]" (*Hilchot Talmud Torah* 1:13). It is thus not surprising that in his commentary on the Mishnah, Rambam justifies the earlier age of women's maturity by stating that "the length of their lives is shorter than that of men, in general" (*Peirush ha-Mishnayot*

Niddah 5:6),[106] implying that the entire life-cycle is accelerated accordingly. Presciently, Tosafot explains the shorter life-span as resulting from the high mortality rate formerly associated with giving birth (Tosafot BT *Ketubot* 83b, s.v. *mitah*).

Of course, modern statistics show exactly the opposite to be true, namely that life expectancy for women is greater than that of men,[107] and that women are of equal natural intelligence and greater emotional intelligence than men.[108] Nevertheless, an important insight which may be derived by Rambam's relating the age of maturity to length of life rather than intelligence (as stated in the Talmud) is that although he accepts the Talmudic discussion as the primary determinant of *halachah*, he does not relate to scientific, philosophical, or cultural conjectures voiced by the Sages of the Talmud in the same manner.

R. Tzadok ha-Cohen (*Dover Tzedek*, p. 52) found another way of reconciling the phrase ascribing greater understanding (*binah*) to women. He says that *binah* represents "fear of God," as in the verse "a God-fearing woman is to be praised" (Prov. 31:30), and he proceeds to bring verses showing that women excel in this feature.

---

106. See also Ibn Ezra, Lev. 21:2.
107. According to *The Telegraph* (Sept. 27, 2017), "Gap between Men's and Women's Life Expectancy No Longer Closing, Data Suggests," life expectancy for women at birth is 82.9 years, and for men it is 79.2 years. See also *World Economic Forum* (May 14, 2017), "Why Do Women Live Longer than Men?").
108. "There Really Is No Difference In Intelligence between Men And Women," www.forbes.com (Aug. 1, 2016).

Source Material

Akedat Yitzchak: Classical work of ritual matters and moralizing legends by R. Yitzchak Arama.

Afarkasta de-Anya: Collected responsa of R. David Sperber. The title of the book, which literally means "the handkerchief of a pauper," is taken from the *Zohar* (*Shlach*), which states: "sometimes one finds a precious stone in the handkerchief of a pauper."

Avot de-Rabbi Natan: Tannaitic work by R. Natan, parallels *Ethics of the Fathers* (*Avot*).

Ba'al ha-Turim: Commentary on Torah by the halachist Ya'akov b. Asher, called *Tur*.

Ba'alei ha-Nefesh: Seven-chapter book on the laws of *niddah*, written by R. Avraham ben David (third Ra'avad). Used by decisors: Tosafot, Rashbah, Rosh, Me'iri, *Hagahot Maimoniot*, Yosef Karo. A *ba'al nefesh* is one who controls his own soul in order to treat his wife honorably, as part of his body, since she was taken from his rib, and he is monogamous, unlike animals.

Beit Shmuel: Commentary on *Even ha-Ezer* by R. Shmuel b. Uri Shrageh Feivush. When published together with the earlier commentary *Chelkat Mechokek*, the edition is called *Api Ravrevi* (Great Face).

Chelkat Mechokek: Commentary on *Even ha-Ezer* by R. Moshe b. Yitzchak Yehuda Lima. When published together with *Beit Shmuel*, the edition is called *Api Ravrevi* (Great Face).

The Ethics of Numbers

Covenant and Conversation: Series of essays on the weekly portion by R. Jonathan Sacks. Genesis, Exodus, and Leviticus have been published as books.

Da'at Zekenim mi-Ba'alei Tosafot: Commentary on Torah written by the Tosafists in the 12th and 13th centuries, mostly from the school of Rashi in Germany and France, but some from England and Italy.

Ein Ya'akov: Compilation of all the aggadic material in the Talmud, with commentaries by R. Ya'akov ibn Habib and (after his death) by his son, R. Levi ibn Habib.

Eitz Yosef: Commentary on Midrash, *Ein Ya'akov*, *Seder Olam Rabbah*, and the Siddur, by Chanoch Zundel b. Yosef.

God, Man, and History: Basic Jewish philosophy by Dr. Eliezer Berkovits.

Guide for the Perplexed: Basic Jewish philosophy by Rambam.

Haggadah: Manual with prayers and customs for conducting the Passover Seder.

Ha'amek Davar: Commentary on the Torah by the Netziv, Naftali Zvi Yehuda Berlin.

Harchev Davar: Commentary on the author's Ha'amek Davar, both written by Naftali Zvi Yehuda Berlin.

Igrot Moshe: Seven-volume responsa of R. Moshe Feinstein.

Kli Yakar: Commentary on the Torah by R. Shlomo Ephraim Luntschitz.

Kuzari: Basic Jewish philosophy by Yehuda Halevi.

Likutei Torah: Commentary on the Torah by the *Ba'al ha-Tanya*, collected and edited by his grandson, the *Tzemach Tzedek*.

Mechilta de-Rabbi Yishmael: Halachic Midrash on Exodus. Based on the teachings of R. Yishmael b. Elisha, R. Akiva's contemporary, and redacted by Rav.

Mechilta de-Rashbi (R. Shimon b. Yochai): Halachic Midrash on Exodus. Based on the teachings of R. Akiva. Compiled in the 5th century.

Mei ha-Shiloach: Magnum opus of the Izhbitzer Rebbe, in which he teaches that depression is the ultimate denial of God. Burned by some who thought his ideas heretical. Influenced R. Hutner, R. Shlomo Carlebach.

The Ethics of Numbers

Midrash ha-Gadol: Comprehensive Midrash on the Torah, based on Talmudic, Geonic, and classical Midrashim. Edited by the Yemenite leader, R. David b. Amram Adani, in the 14th century and considered the magnum opus of Yemenite Jewry.

Midrash Lekach Tov: See Pesikta Zutrata.

Midrash Rabbah: Name given to ten sets of Midrashim on Torah and the five Megillot. Compiled and edited between 6th–10th centuries.

Midrash Sechel Tov: Compiled by the European Jew Tuviah b. Eliezer, during the time of Rashi and the Rif. Collection of Midrashim gathered from the Talmud and Midrash.

Mishneh Torah: See Yad ha-Chazakah.

Mul Etgarei ha-Tekufah: Essays on the Jewish approach to modern issues by Professor Yehuda Levi.

Netzach Yisrael: Book by Maharal on Tisha B'Av and the final deliverance.

Or ha-Chaim: Commentary on the Torah written by R. Chaim ben Attar.

Orot ha-Kodesh: Philosophical (*Chochmat ha-Kodesh*) and ethical (*Musar ha-Kodesh*) writings of R. Kook.

Pesikta Zutrata: Also called *Lekach Tov*. Each homily starts with "*tov*." Written by Tuvia b. Eliezer, Rashi's contemporary. Explains weekly portions and Megillot.

Pirkei de-Rabbi Eliezer: 54-chapter Midrash aggadah. Retells Biblical stories. Traditionally ascribed to R. Eliezer b. Hyrcanus, but Zunz claims it was written in the 8th century in an Islamic country.

Pitchei Teshuvah: Concise collection of rulings by halachic decisors on three of the four sections of the *Shulchan Aruch* (patterned after *Sha'arei Teshuvah* by R. Chaim Mordechai Margolis on *Orach Chaim*), gathered by R. Avraham Tzvi Hirsch Eisenstadt.

Rif: Hebrew acronym for R. Yitzchak Alfasi, and also for R. Yoshiyahu Pinto, the author of the eponymous commentary on *Ein Ya'akov*.

Seder Olam Rabbah: Chronological record from Adam to Bar Kochba, attributed to the Tanna Yosi b. Chalafta (ca. 160). Quoted in Talmud, Mishnah, *Mechilta, Sifra, Sifrei*.

Sefer ha-Chinuch (Book of Education): Systematic discussion of the 613 *mitzvot*, published anonymously in 13th-century Spain, variously attributed to Aaron ha-Levi or his brother Pinchas. Based on Rambam's count, ordered according to the weekly portion. Gives Biblical sources, philosophical underpinnings, basic laws. *Minchat Chinuch*, by Yosef b. Moshe Babad (1800–1874), provides legal commentary.

Sefer ha-Ikkarim: Written by Yosef Albo. Proposes three principles of faith: existence of God, revelation, and Divine justice (i.e,. reward and punishment).

Shitah Mekubetzet: Anthology of commentaries on various Talmudic tractates, prepared by R. Bezalel Ashkenazi.

Sifra (Torat Kohanim): Midrash Halachah (legal Biblical exegesis) on Leviticus. Rambam attributes it to Rav, and Malbim to R. Chiya. From school of R. Akiva. Quoted frequently in Talmud

Sifrei: Midrash Halachah (legal Biblical exegesis) on the books of Numbers and Deuteronomy, preceded and followed by aggadic sections. Final redaction in the time of the Amora'im.

Siftei Chachamim: Supercommentary on Rashi's commentary on the Pentateuch, gathered from earlier exegeses on Rashi. Written by Shabtai ben Yosef Bass. Considered so essential that there exists a concise summary, *Ikkar Siftei Chachamim*, which appears with Rashi.

Siftei Kohen: Allegoric-kabbalistic commentary on Torah, by renowned kabbalist R. Mordechai ha-Kohen of Safed, with kabbalistic explanations and *gematriot*.

Siftei Kohen: Commentary on *Yoreh De'ah* by Shabtai ben Meir ha-Kohen (*Shach*).

Tanna de-Vei Eliyahu: Midrash taught to third-century Amora, Anan, by Elijah (BT *Ketubot* 106a). Consists of *Seder Eliyahu Rabbah* (larger) and *Seder Eliyahu Zuta* (smaller). Final redaction in late 10th century. Describes evolution of the world and Jewish history.

Tanchuma: Aggadic interpretations of the weekly portions, attributed to R. Tanchuma. Edited in 5th century, before Midrash Rabbah and Talmud, which quote it.

Targum Onkelos: Official translation when reading the Torah in Talmudic times (and today for Yemenites). Tradition states that it was conveyed to Moses at Sinai, and mostly forgotten until it was recorded by Onkelos the convert. "Reading the weekly portion twice and targum once" refers to Targum Onkelos.

Targum Yonatan: Official translation of prophets, ascribed to Yonatan b. Uziel. Targum Yonatan on the Torah (pseudo-Yonatan) composed in 7th or 8th century.

Torah Temimah: Collection of Talmudic and Midrashic teachings related to the verses of the Torah, with commentary. Prepared by R. Baruch ha-Levi Epstein.

Tosafot Yom Tov: Mishnah commentary by R. Yom Tov Lipmann Heller. Comparable to Tosafot on the Talmud, just as Bartenura's Mishnah commentary is comparable to Rashi.

Yad ha-Chazakah: Code of law containing 14 books (the Hebrew numerical value of *yad* is 14), written by Rambam. Also called *Mishneh Torah*, the repetition of the Torah. Compiled ca. 1170-80, while Rambam was living in Egypt. Lithuanian yeshiva rabbis used it as a guide to Talmudic interpretation and methodology.

Yad Rama: Commentary on *Bava Batra* and *Sanhedrin* by R. Meir b. Tudrus ha-Levi.

Yalkut Shimoni: Collection of Midrashim arranged according to the books of the Bible, compiled by Menachem ha-Kohen Rapoport.

Zohar: Literally, "splendor." Foundational work of Jewish mystical thought known as Kabbalah. Discusses the nature of God, structure of the universe, nature of the soul.

Commentators

Abravanel, Yitzchak (1437-1508): Born to a wealthy family in Lisbon, Portugal. Wrote three types of works: exegesis of Bible and Haggadah, philosophy, and apologetics.

Abulafia, Meir b. Tudrus ha-Levi (1170-1244): Born in Spain. Kabbalist, poet, Talmudist and halachic decisor. Was *rosh yeshiva* and *dayan* in Toledo, together with grandson of Ri Migash and Avraham b. Natan ha-Yarchi (author of *Sefer ha-Manhig*). Author of *Yad Rama* on *Bava Batra* and *Sanhedrin*, responsa, as well as commentaries on other tractates, which have been lost.

Albo, Yosef (1380-1444): Born in Monreal, Aragon. Student of Hasdai Crescas. Had medical knowledge, was versed in Aristotle. Wrote *Sefer ha-Ikkarim*.

Alfasi, Yitzchak (Rif, 1013-1103**):** Born in Algeria. Studied in Kairouan, Tunisia, under Rabbeinu Nissim b. Ya'akov and Rabbeinu Chananel b. Chushiel. Compiled summary of halachic conclusions in each tractate (*Sefer ha-Halachot*), on which Ran wrote a commentary. Headed yeshiva in Fez. Famous students include Yosef ibn Migash (Ri Migash) and Yehuda Halevi. Left responsa in Arabic, translated as *She'elot u-Teshuvot ha-Rif.*

Arama, Yitzchak (1420-1494): Born in Spain. Talmudist, philosopher. Wrote *Akedat Yitzchak* ("Binding of Isaac"), a philosophical, homilctic commentary on Torah.

The Ethics of Numbers

Asevilli, Yom Tov b. Avraham (1250-1330): Born in Seville, Spain (Asevilli means "from Seville"). Student of Ra'ah and Rashbah. Became rabbi of Saragossa. Famous for his commentary on the Talmud. Known by the acronym Ritva.

Asher b. Yechiel (Rosh, Rabbeinu Asher, 1250-1328): Born in Germany. Great-grandson of Ra'avan (Tosafist). Student of Meir of Rothenburg. Worked in money-lending, wealthy. Fled to Toledo, became rabbi after being recommended by Rashbah. Wrote abstracts of Talmudic law that are printed at the end of each tractate. Father of *Tur*.

Ashkenazi, Bezalel (1520-1592): Student of Radbaz and teacher of the Ari in Egypt. Wrote *Shitah Mekubetzet* on numerous tractates. Moved to Eretz Yisrael and became rabbi of Jerusalem.

Avraham ben David (Third Ra'avad, 1120-1199): Became rabbi and *rosh yeshiva* in Posquières. Wrote critiques on Rif and Rambam, as well as *Ba'alei ha-Nefesh*, and studied Kabbalah.

Ba'al ha-Tanya: - See Borukhovich, Shneur Zalman.

Barfat, Yitzchak b. Sheshet (Rivash, 1326-1408): Born in Barcelona. Student of R. Peretz ha-Kohen, Chasdai Crescas, and especially the Ran. Initially engaged in business, but eventually became rabbi in Saragossa. As a result of Christian persecution, he may have been forcefully baptized, but escaped to Algiers, where he served as rabbi, and was followed by Rashbatz. Wrote 517 responsa. Opposed Kabbalah.

Bass, Shabtai ben Yosef (1641–1718): Born in Kalisz, Poland. Wrote *Siftei Chachamim*. Studied Talmud, singing. Appointed bass singer at Prague Altneuschule, where he got his name.

Ben Attar, Chaim (1696-1743): Born in Meknes, Morocco. Talmudist, Kabbalist. Wrote *Or ha-Chaim* commentary on Torah. One of four called holy (*kadosh*), in addition to Ari, Alshich, *Shlah*. Teacher of Chidah. Buried on Mount of Olives.

Berkovits, Eliezer (1908-1992): Born in Hungary. Ordination from R. Akiva Glasner (*Dor Revi'i*) and R. Yechiel Weinberg at Hildesheimer. Ph.D. in Philosophy, U. of Berlin. Wrote *Tnai be-Nissu'im u-ve-Get*; *God, Man, and History*.

The Ethics of Numbers

Berlin, Naftali Zvi (Netziv, 1816-1893): Born and learned in Mir, Belarus. First wife was daughter of R. Yitzchak of Volozhin; second wife was his niece, daughter of R. Y.M. Epstein (*Aruch ha-Shulchan*). *Rosh yeshiva* of Volozhin, 1854-92. Wrote *Ha'amek She'eilah* (on *She'iltot*), *Ha'amek Davar* (on Torah).

Borukhovich, Shneur Zalman (Shneur Zalman of Liadi, the Alter Rebbe, 1745-1812): Born in Poland, great-grandson of Maharal. Wrote *Shulchan Aruch ha-Rav*, *Tanya* (exposition of Chassidic philosophy), *Torah Or*, and *Likkutei Torah* on weekly portion. Founder of Chabad dynasty in Liadi.

Chanoch Zundel b. Yosef (1780?-1859): Lived in Bialystok, where he taught Midrash, and composed commentaries on Midrash (*Tanchuma*, *Midrash Rabbah*, *Pesikta de-Rav Kehana*), *Ein Ya'akov*, *Seder Olam Rabbah*, the Siddur, and the Haggadah (*Meishiv Nefesh*). Commentaries are in two parts and named after his father: *Eitz Yosef* (short explanations), *Anaf Yosef* (longer explanations).

Chizkiya b. Mano'ach (*Chizkuni*, 1250-1310): Born in France. Wrote *Chizkuni*, based on Rashi, but used twenty other commentaries. Wandered the world to find proper explanations. Quotes by name only Rashi, Dunash b. Labrat, *Yosippon*, and *Physica*.

Duran, Shimon b. Tzemach (Rashbatz, 1361-1444): Born in Majorca, relative of Ralbag. Student of philosophy, astronomy, mathematics, and medicine, which he practiced. After persecution of 1391, escaped to Algiers, replaced Yitzchak b. Sheshet (Rivash) as rabbi in 1407. Wrote *Magen Avot* (polemic against Christians, Muslims), and commentaries on Bible, Ethics of the Fathers, Mishnah, Talmud, Rif, and the Haggadah. Major 15th-century decisor, wrote *Tashbetz* (*Teshuvot Shimon b. Tzemach*). His son, Rashbash (Shlomo b. Shimon), also authored many responsa.

Eidels, Shmuel Eliezer ha-Levi (Maharsha, 1555-1631): Born in Poland to Maharal and Klonymus families. Mother-in-law, Eidel, supported him. Wrote commentary on Tosafot and aggadic parts of Talmud. Knew Kabbalah, believed in reincarnation.

The Ethics of Numbers

Einhorn, Ze'ev Wolf (Maharzo, 1790?-1862): Born in Grodno, Lithuania. Wrote commentary on *Midrash Rabbah*, which he extended in *Netiv Chadash*. Showed that the Midrashic interpretation follows from a detailed analysis of the Hebrew text of Biblical verses.

Eisenstadt, Avraham Tzvi Hirsch (1813-1868): Lithuanian communal rabbi, who wrote *Pitchei Teshuvah* on *Shulchan Aruch*.

Emden, Ya'akov (Yavetz, 1697-1776): Born in Germany. Involved in business, except when rabbi of Emden. Accused Yonatan Eybeshitz of being Sabbatean. Friendly with Moses Mendelsohn. Believed Christianity and Islam have important roles to play in God's plan. Wrote commentary on Jewish prayer book (*Siddur Beit Ya'akov*), the Mishnah (*Lechem Shamayim*), and responsa (*She'eilat Yavetz*).

Epstein, Baruch Halevi (*Torah Temimah*, 1860-1941): Lithuanian rabbi, son of author of *Aruch ha-Shulchan*. Learned in Volozhin under his uncle the Netziv. Wrote *Torah Temimah*, a commentary on Torah and Megillot, citing Talmud and Midrash on each verse, with explanations.

Feinstein, Moshe (1895-1986): Born in Uzda, Belarus, on 7 Adar; was great-great-grandson of brother of Vilna Gaon. Studied under R. Isser Zalman Meltzer. Moved to New York in 1936, headed Mesivta Tiferet Yerushalayim and Moetzet Gedolai ha-Torah. Considered foremost *posek* in the United States. Wrote *Igrot Moshe* (responsa), *Dibrot Moshe* (Talmudic novella), *Darash Moshe* (weekly portions). Died in 5746, and 5746th verse in the Torah states: "Moshe had finished writing down the words of this Torah" (Deut. 31:24).

Gerondi, Yonah b. Avraham (Rabbeinu Yonah, 1180-1263): Born in Gerona, Spain (birthplace of R. Zerachiah ha-Levi, Ran, and Ramban). Student of R. Shlomo Min Hahar, and teacher of Rashbah. Talmudic works: commentary on Rif (only *Berachot* preserved) and *Aliyot de-Rabbeinu Yonah* (novella on *Bava Batra*). Ethical works: *Sha'arei Teshuvah*, and commentary on Ethics of the Fathers.

Gershom b. Yehudah (Rabbeinu Gershom Me'or ha-Golah, 960-1040): Born in Metz, established yeshiva in Mainz. Primary student was

Ya'akov b. Yakar, Rashi's teacher. Famous for synod he called, which decided to (a) prohibit polygamy, (b) require the consent of both parties to a divorce, (c) modify the rules concerning those who became apostates under compulsion, and (d) prohibit opening others' correspondence. Wrote Talmudic commentary, responsa, *selichot*.

Gilat, Yisrael Zvi (b. 1954): Associate Professor of Law at Netanya Academic College, formerly in Dept. of Social Work at Bar Ilan. Ordained rabbi.

Greenblatt, Ephraim (1932- 2014): Born in Jerusalem. Studied in Rechovot under R. Menachem Shach, and at Mesivta Tiferet Yerushalayim under R. Moshe Feinstein, who sent him to Memphis, Tenn., where he served as rabbi, head of the *beit din* and *kollel*, *shochet*, and *mohel*. Wrote responsa (*Rivevot Ephraim*), Torah commentary (*Rivevot Ephraim al ha-Torah*), and work on ethics (*Revavot ve-Yovlot*).

Ha-Kohen, Mordechai (1523-1598): Born in Safed. Student of Moshe di Trani (Mabit) and Yosef Karo, contemporary of R. Yosef di Trani (Maharit, son of Mabit). Wrote *Siftei Kohen* on Torah. Left Safed for financial reasons, became rabbi in Aleppo (1570).

Ha-Kohen, Shabtai ben Meir (1621-1662): Born in Vilna, married the daughter of the wealthy Shimon Wolf, a great-grandson of the Rama. His magnum opus is *Siftei Kohen* (*Shach*), a commentary on *Yoreh De'ah*. In *Nekudot ha-Kessef*, he responded to the criticisms of the Taz.

Hame'iri, Menachem (1249-1306): Born in Provence, France. Magnum opus is *Beit ha-Bechirah* on the Talmud, which provides background and conclusions on each topic based on Rashi, Rambam, Ra'avad, Rif, and Ri Migash. Not universally available until 1920, and accordingly not utilized in halachic development. Wrote *Kiryat Sefer* for scribes. Held that discriminatory laws against Gentiles only related to idol worshippers.

Halevi, Yehuda (1075-1141): Born in Spain. Student of Moses Ibn Ezra and Rif. Educated in Jewish scholarship, philosophy, medicine. Knew Avraham Ibn Ezra. Wrote poetry, *Kuzari*. According to legend, he was killed by an Arab horseman on arrival in Jerusalem.

Heller, Yom Tov Lipmann ha-Levi (1579-1664): Born in Bavaria. Studied under Maharal. Wrote *Tosafot Yom Tov* on Mishnah, *Ma'adanei Yom Tov* on the Rosh. Rabbi in Krakow. Ancestor of Arye Leib Heller (*Ketzot ha-Choshen*) and his brother, Yehuda Heller Kahana (*Kuntras ha-Sfeikot*).

Hertz, Joseph (1872-1946): Born in Hungary, left for New York in 1884. Ordained at JTS in 1894, was a rabbi in the US and South Africa before becoming chief rabbi of England in 1914. Wrote commentary on Torah and the Siddur.

Hirsch, Samson Raphael (1808-1888): Born in Hamburg. Student of R. Ya'akov Ettlinger. Rabbi in Frankfurt. Father of Torah with *derech eretz* movement. Wrote *Nineteen Letters of Ben Uziel* in defense of tradition; *Chorev* as an explanation of *mitzvot*; and commentary on the Torah.

Horovitz, Yeshayahu (1565-1630): - Born in Prague. Magnum opus is *Shnei Luchot ha-Brit* (basis of the acronym, *Shlah ha-Kadosh*), an encyclopedic compilation of ritual, ethics, and mysticism. Moved to Eretz Israel in 1621.

Ibn Ezra, Avraham (1089-1167): Born in Tudela. Excelled in philosophy, astronomy/astrology, mathematics, poetry, linguistics, and Biblical exegesis. In Granada, met his friend (and perhaps father-in-law) Yehuda Halevi. Wrote Biblical commentary.

Ibn Habib, Ya'akov (1460 –1516): Born in Spain. After expulsion, settled in Salonika. Collected all *aggadot* from Babylonian Talmud and many from Jerusalem Talmud in *Ein Ya'akov*. Died after two of six orders printed. Son, Levi, completed it, without *aggadot* of Jerusalem Talmud.

Izhbitzer Rebbe: see Leiner, Mordechai Yosef.

The Ethics of Numbers

Isserles, Moshe (**Rama**, 1520-1572): Received questions from Yosef Karo. Wrote *Ha-Mappah* on Karo's Code, and *Darkei Moshe* on the Tur. Inscribed on his tombstone is: "From Moshe [ben Maimon] until Moshe [Isserles] there was none like Moshe."

Karo, Joseph (*Mechaber*, 1488-1575): Born in Toledo. After Spanish expulsion, spent time in Turkey prior to his arrival in Safed in 1535, were he was ordained by R. Ya'akov Beirav, and taught R. Moshe Alshich and R. Moshe Cordovero. For 32 years, wrote and proofread his *Beit Yosef* commentary on the *Tur*, which he then summarized in his classic Code of Law (the *Shulchan Aruch*), based on majority decisions of Rambam, Rosh, and Rif.

Kimchi, David (**Radak**, 1160-1235): Born in Provence. Wrote commentaries on Prophets, Genesis (seeks historical, ethical underpinnings), Psalms, Chronicles. Influenced by Ibn Ezra, Rambam; favored the latter in the controversy regarding his works. Delved into philosophy, science.

Kook, Avraham Yitzchak (1865-1935): Born in Latvia, student of Netziv, son-in-law of Aderet. Became rabbi of Yafo (1904); first Israeli chief rabbi (1921); founded Mercaz Harav (1924). Close with secular, religious, Zionist, and *charedi* communities. Wrote on Talmud, Jewish thought.

Kotler, Aharon (1891-1962): Born in Russia, studied in Slabodka yeshiva under the Alter of Slabodka (R. Nosson Tzvi Finkel) and R. Moshe Mordechai Epstein, then joined his father-in-law, R. Isser Zalman Meltzer, in Slutsk. Saved from World War II in 1941 by Va'ad ha-Hatzalah. In US, founded Lakewood Yeshiva in 1943. Headed Moetzet Gedolai ha-Torah. Wrote responsa, Talmudic commentary.

Leiner, Mordechai Yosef (**Izhbitzer**, 1801-1854): Born in Tomashov, Poland, descendant of Meir Katzenellenbogen (Maharam Padua), Saul Wahl, the Tosafists, Rashi, and King David. Disciple of Simcha Bunim of Peshischa and R. Menachem Mendel of Kotzk. In 1839, became rebbe in Tomashov, then Izhbitz. Disciples include R. Yehuda Leib Eiger (grandson of R. Akiva Eiger), R. Tzadok ha-

Kohen, his own son R. Ya'akov and grandson Gershon Henoch of Radzin, who reintroduced *techelet* and compiled the magnum opus of the Izhbitzer, the *Mei ha-Shiloach*.

Lima, R. Moshe b. Yitzchak Yehuda (1604-1657): Born in Lithuania. Friendly with R. Heschel of Krakow (teacher of *Beit Shmuel*, *Shach*, and *Taz*). In 1650 was appointed rabbi of Vilna (in whose *beit din* the *Shach* sat) and later of Brisk. Author of *Chelkat Mechokek* on *Even ha-Ezer*.

Loew, Yehuda b. Betzalel (**Maharal mi-Prague**, 1520-1609): Born in Poznan, Poland. According to tradition, of Davidic descent. Served as rabbi in Nikolsberg, Moravia and Prague. Important Talmudic scholar, mystic, philosopher. Wrote *Gur Aryeh*, supercommentary on Rashi, *Gevurot Hashem* on Passover, *Netivot Olam* on ethics, and numerous philosophical works. Teacher of Yom Tov Lipman Heller (Tosfot Yom Tov) and David Ganz (Tzemach David). Influenced R. Dessler, R. Kook, and R. Hutner. Ancestor of Alter Rebbe and R. Nachman of Breslav.

Luntschitz, Shlomo Ephraim (1550-1619): Born in Luntschitz, Poland. Student of Maharshal. *Rosh yeshiva* in Lvov. Rabbi of Prague after Maharal. Primary student was Sheftel Horowitz, son of *Shlah*. Wrote *Kli Yakar* (magnum opus) and *Olelot Ephraim* (sermons).

Luria, David (**Radal**, 1798-1855): Born in Belarus. Child prodigy, scion of wealthy family (Maharshal). Knew science, medicine, foreign languages. Wrote responsa and commentaries on Mishnah, Talmud, *Midrash Rabbah* (*Chidushei ha-Radal*), *Zohar*.

Luzzatto, Shmuel David (**Shadal**, 1800-1865): Born in Trieste. Wrote popular Torah commentary. Blames Rambam for accepting Aristotelian philosophy. Maintained whole book of Isaiah was written by him; believed that the book of Kohelet was written after King Solomon.

Maharal mi-Prague: see Loew, Yehuda b. Betzalel.

Maharsha: see Eidels, Shmuel Eliezer.

Maimonides: see Rambam.

The Ethics of Numbers

Meir Leibush b. Yechiel Michel (Malbim, 1809-1879): Born in Ukraine. In 1859 became chief rabbi of Bucharest. Argued with upper class, who wanted changes. Imprisoned, then liberated by Montefiore on condition that he leave Romania. Magnum opus is his commentary on Bible.

Me'iri: see Hame'iri, Menachem.

Nachmanides: see Ramban.

Netziv: see Berlin, Naftali Zvi.

Nissim b. Reuven of Gerona (Ran, 1320-1376): Born in Barcelona. Teacher was R. Peretz ha-Kohen. Physician, astronomer, and scribe. Received queries from entire diaspora. Wrote sermons and commentary on Rif, Talmud, Bible. Students include Rivash, Hasdai Crescas, Yosef Chaviva (*Nimukei Yosef*).

Onkelos (first century): Nephew of Hadrian, who converted and translated Torah into Aramaic. Contemporary of R. Akiva, R. Yishmael.

Ovadiah mi-Bartenura (1445-1515): Student of Maharik (Yosef Colon). Born in Bertinoro, where he became rabbi. In 1486 he moved to Eretz Yisrael. Best known for his popular commentary on the Mishnah, based mainly on Rashi and Rambam.

Pinto, R. Yoshiyahu (1565-1648): Born in Damascus. Father was a Spanish refugee who attained wealth, married sister of Chaim Vital. Ordained by R. Ya'akov Abulafia, who was ordained by R. Ya'akov Beirav II. Wrote *Ma'or Einayim* (Rif) on *Ein Ya'akov*, *Kesef Mezukak* on Torah.

Ra'avad: see R. Avraham ben David.

Rabinowitz, Tzadok ha-Kohen (1823-1900): Born in Lithuania. Great-grandson of Chacham Zvi. Child prodigy: at 1, blessed mother's milk; at 3, learned Talmud, Tosafot. Met Izhbitzer, became his *chassid*, and later (against his will) rebbe of Lublin. Wrote *Pri Tzadik, Tzidkat ha-Tzadik, Dover Tzedek*.

Radak: see Kimchi, David.

Radal: see Luria, David.

The Ethics of Numbers

Ralbag (1288-1344): R. Levi ben Gershon, or Gersonides. Born in Provence, France; philosopher, Talmudist, mathematician, and astronomer/astrologer. Never had a rabbinical post, maybe because of the uniqueness of his opinions. Wrote commentary on Tanach. Served as a doctor for the courts of the nobility in Southern France. Invented an instrument to observe the stars and planets. Produced a camera that anticipated features of the modern camera. Wrote *Milchamot Hashem* to reconcile religion and Aristotle, but that work was opposed by many. Wrote *Ma'aseh Choshev* on square and cube roots, and combinatorics (using mathematical induction), as well as other mathematical works.

Rama: see Isserles, Moshe.

Rambam (Maimonides, 1138-1205): Born in Cordoba. Wrote commentary on Mishnah, *Sefer ha-Mitzvot, Yad ha-Chazakah, The Guide for the Perplexed*. Court physician. Buried in Tiberias. Epitaph: From Moshe (Rabbeinu) to Moshe (Maimonides) there was none like Moshe.

Ramban (Nachmanides, 1194-1270): Born and became rabbi in Gerona. Medical doctor. Wrote *Chidushei ha-Ramban* on Talmud, *Igeret ha-Kodesh* on marriage, Torah commentary. Students: Rashbah, Ra'ah (*Chinuch*). 1263 - won debate with Pablo Christiani, but had to relocate to Israel.

Ran: see Nissim b. Reuven of Gerona.

Rapoport, Menachem ha-Kohen (1520-1596): Born in Porto. Descendant of Rapa family. Changed name to Rapoport (Rapa of Porto). Learned Talmud, medicine. Witnessed burning of Talmud in Venice. Rabbi in Verona and Cologne. Wrote *Mincha Belula,* edited *Yalkut Shimoni.*

Rashbah: see Shlomo b. Avraham Ibn Aderet.

Rashbam: see Shmuel b. Meir.

Rashi: see Shlomo Yitzchaki.

Ritva: see Asevilli, Yom Tov b. Avraham.

Rosh: see Asher b. Yechiel.

The Ethics of Numbers

Saadiah b. Yosef Gaon (882-942): Prominent rabbi, Jewish philosopher, and exegete of the Gaonic period. Active in opposition to Karaism and defense of rabbinic Judaism. Founder of Judeo-Arabic literature. Magnum opus is *Emunot ve-De'ot* (Jewish philosophy).

Sacks, Jonathan (b. 1948): Born in London. Received degrees from Cambridge (MA), Kings' College (PhD). Ordination from Jews' College and Eitz Chaim. Appointed chief rabbi after R. Jacobovits, in 1991. Wrote *Dignity of Difference* and *Covenant and Conversation* on the Torah, and commentaries on the Siddur, Machzor, and Haggadah.

Segal, David ha-Levi (1586-1667): Student and son-in-law of *Bach* (Yoel Sirkus). Wrote a commentary on *Shulchan Aruch*, called *Turei Zahav* ("Golden Columns"), known by the acronym *Taz*. Fled to Moravia from the pogroms of 1648. In 1654 became rabbi of Lvov.

Sforno, Ovadia b. Ya'akov (1475-1550): Born in Cesena, Italy. Studied math, philosophy, medicine. Contacts included Reuchlin, Meir Katzenellenbogen, Maharik. Wrote commentary on Torah and Megillot, selecting from Rashi, Ibn Ezra, Rashbam, Ramban, and adding his own interpretations.

Shach: see ha-Kohen, Shabtai ben Meir.

Shadal: see Luzzatto, Shmuel David.

Shlah: see Horovitz, Yeshayahu.

Shlomo b. Avraham Ibn Aderet (Rashba, 1235-1310): Born in Barcelona. Medieval halachist, rabbi of main synagogue in Barcelona, leader of community, and successful banker. Student of Rabbeinu Yonah and Ramban, teacher of Ritva and Rabbeinu Bachya. Wrote Talmudic commentary, *Torat ha-Bayit* on *kashrut*, *Avodat ha-Kodesh* on the laws of Shabbat and Holidays, and responsa.

Shlomo Yitzchaki (Rashi, 1040-1105): Born in Troyes. Student of Ya'akov b. Yakar (Worms), who was student of Rabbeinu Gershom. Wrote commentary on Talmud, Tanach (supercommentaries: *Gur Aryeh* by Maharal, *Ha-Mizrachi* by Re'em, *Yeri'ot Shlomo* by Maharshal).

The Ethics of Numbers

Shmuel b. Meir (Rashbam, 1085-1158): Born in Ramerupt, Northern France. Son of Yocheved, Rashi's daughter. Shepherd, vintner. Rashi's student, elder brother of Rabbeinu Tam. Earliest Tosafist. Wrote basic commentary on Bible. Completed Rashi on *Bava Batra*, *Pesachim*.

Shmuel b. Uri Shrageh Feivush (1640-1698): Born in Poland, studied under R. Heschel of Krakow (teacher of *Shach* and *Taz*). Rabbi in Poland and Germany. Author of *Beit Shmuel* on *Even ha-Ezer*.

Shmuel David Luzzatto (1800-1865): Born in Trieste; studied Talmud, languages, science, and Hebrew. A warm defender of Biblical and Talmudic Judaism, strongly opposed to philosophical Judaism. Praises Rambam's *Mishneh Torah*, but blames him for accepting Aristotelian philosophy which, he says, brought no good to the Rambam himself while causing much evil to other Jews. Also attacked Ibn Ezra and Spinoza. Wrote many works in Hebrew, Italian, German, and French. Best known for his commentary on the Pentateuch.

Shneur Zalman of Liadi: see Borukhovich, Shneur Zalman.

Soloveitchik, Joseph B. [Yosef Dov ha-Levi] (1903-1993): Born in Russia. Descendant of R. Chaim of Volozhin and Tosfot Yom Tov. Mother was a cousin of R. Moshe Feinstein. Wrote *Lonely Man of Faith*, *Halachic Man*. Advocated compatibility of Torah and academic scholarship. After his demise, a large literature was developed encompassing his philosophic, hashkafic, and halachic lectures throughout his years as *rosh yeshiva* of Yeshiva University.

Sperber, David (1877-1962): Born in Galicia. In 1922 was appointed head of *beit din* in Breshov, Romania. Worked with Va'ad ha-Hatzalah to save Jews during World War II. Moved to Israel in 1950. Member of Moetzet Gedolai ha-Torah and one of the founders of Chinuch Atzmai. Collected his responsa in *Afarkasta de-Anya*.

Strashun, Shmuel (Rashash, 1793-1872): Born in Lithuania. Studied under R. Avraham Danzig (*Chayei Adam*). When Napoleon invaded Russia, moved to Vilna, where he became a leader of the Jewish community. Wrote extensive annotations on Talmud, *Midrash*

Rabbah. Like Vilna Gaon, eschewed *pilpul*, sought correct text and interpretation. Had wide knowledge of Hebrew grammar, history, geography, and foreign languages.

Taz: see Segal, David ha-Levi.

Tur: see Ya'akov b. Asher.

Tzadok ha-Kohen: see Rabinowitz, Tzadok ha-Kohen.

Ya'akov b. Asher (Tur, Ba'al ha-Turim, 1269-1343): Son of Rosh, born in Cologne. Moved to Castile with his father. Wrote *Arba'ah Turim* (code of law); *Rimzei Ba'al ha-Turim* (concise Torah commentary); and *Perush al ha-Torah*, which quotes Ramban, Saadiah Gaon, Rashi, and Ibn Ezra.

Ya'akov b. Meir (Rabbeinu Tam, 1100-1171): Born in Ramerupt, son of Yocheved, Rashi's daughter, brother of Rashbam and Rivam (Yitzchak). Most important Tosafist and halachic authority. Student of father (Meir b. Shmuel) and brother (Rashbam). Known for communal enactments improving Jewish family life, education, and women's status. Legend states that when Rashi was holding his infant grandson, the baby touched the *tefillin* that were on Rashi's head, and Rashi predicted that this grandson would later disagree with him about the order of the scripts that are put in the head *tefillin*. Held *mezuzah* should be affixed horizontally (Rashi held vertically). Wrote *Sefer ha-Yashar* (novella and responsa, poetry, *piyutim*, and *selichot*).

www.ingramcontent.com/pod-product-compliance
Lightning Source LLC
Chambersburg PA
CBHW031603110426
42742CB00037B/820